THE
EVERYTHING®
FAMILY TREE
BOOK

The Everything Series:

The Everything® After College Book
The Everything® Baby Names Book
The Everything® Bartender's Book
The Everything® Beer Book
The Everything® Bicycle Book
The Everything® Casino Gambling Book
The Everything® Cat Book
The Everything® Christmas Book
The Everything® College Survival Book
The Everything® Dreams Book
The Everything® Etiquette Book
The Everything® Games Book
The Everything® Get Ready for Baby Book
The Everything® Golf Book
The Everything® Home Improvement Book
The Everything® Jewish Wedding Book
The Everything® Low-Fat High-Flavor Cookbook
The Everything® Pasta Cookbook
The Everything® Study Book
The Everything® Wedding Book
The Everything® Wedding Checklist
The Everything® Wedding Etiquette Book
The Everything® Wedding Organizer
The Everything® Wedding Vows Book
The Everything® Wine Book
The Everything® Family Tree Book

THE
EVERYTHING®
FAMILY TREE
BOOK

Finding, Charting, and Preserving Your Family History

William G. Hartley

Adams Media Corporation
HOLBROOK, MASSACHUSETTS

An Everything® Series Book. The Everything® Series is
a registered trademark of Adams Media Corporation.

Published by Adams Media Corporation
260 Center Street, Holbrook, MA 02343

ISBN: 1-55850-763-9

Printed in the United States of America.

J   I   H   G   F   E   D   C   B   A

Library of Congress Cataloging-in-Publication Data
Hartley, William G.
The everything family tree / by WIlliam G. Hartley.
p.   cm.
ISBN 1-55850-763-9
1. Genealogy. 2. United States—Genealogy—Handbooks, manuals, etc. I. Title.
CS16.H35   1998
929'.1—dc21   97-39087
CIP

This publication is designed to provide accurate and authoritative information with regard to the subject matter covered. It is sold with the understanding that the publisher is not engaged in rendering professional advice. If legal advice or other expert assistance is required, the services of a competent professional person should be sought.
— From a *Declaration of Principles* jointly adopted by a Committee of the American Bar Association and a Committee of Publishers and Associations

Illustrations by Barry Littmann

This book is available at quantity discounts for bulk purchases.
For information, call 1-800-872-5627 (in Massachusetts, call 781-767-8100).

Visit our home page at http://www.adamsmedia.com

Contents

5. Tape-Recording Personal and Family Oral Histories

Part 3: Sharing Your Family History

Appendix 1: A Full-Life Story: Topics and Questions

Introduction: Finding Your Family's Heritage: Adventure and Fulfillment

A fact of life today, from California to Maine and from Alaska to Florida, is that doing genealogy, or tracing your family tree, is one of America's most popular pastimes. Genealogy is the activity whereby we identify family descent—who descends from whom—generation after generation. Once upon a time it was the preserve of upper-crust folks wanting to prove they descended from royalty or bluebloods. But today it is an activity widely engaged in by people from every walk of life.

Why is this so? Why is there such intense interest in family trees? One big reason is that genealogy is a great adventure that is challenging, exciting, and fun. Another key reason is that seeking and identifying one's ancestors is a very fulfilling experience.

People like adventures. Adventure implies doing something new, usually something exciting and more expansive than normal day-to-day experiences. Some enjoy taking a long-anticipated vacation to a fabled place like England or Hawaii. Others get a rush from going into the mountains to try their hand at catching fish in lakes or streams, or to hunt for deer. Prospectors and treasure hunters are thrilled when they make a worthy find. Many delight in reading detective novels and trying to solve the crime before the author tells the solution. Movies that take us back in time to earlier historical periods are popular, such as the Old South in *Gone with the Wind* or Old England in *Robin Hood* or *Ivanhoe*. Millions feel great pleasure when solving crossword puzzles or trying to answer quiz show questions on *Jeopardy* or *Wheel of Fortune* before the contestants do. More than a few people enjoy meeting new people on travel tours, at conventions, or in clubs or organizations.

Genealogy is an activity that combines most if not all of these elements: hunting; curiosity; challenges; puzzle solving; doing detective work; experiencing new people, places, and periods; and feeling delight and joy when finding something you've been searching for. Ask any genealogist and he or she will tell you that people feel excitement and enthusiasm during the search to identify ancestors.

The adventure of the search is one big part of genealogy's appeal, but even more attractive is its ability to satisfy us with

The Definition

The word "genealogy" is derived from the Greek, meaning the tracing of the descent of family and individuals. Genealogies are often referred to as family trees and sometimes pedigrees.

The word pedigree is derived from the French meaning crane's foot. In early British genealogies, a three-line mark resembling a crane's foot was used to show lines of descent—thus the word pedigree.

Regardless of what term is used to describe genealogies, they have existed since very ancient times, and all cultures have some form of genealogy.

knowledge of who we are and who our family is and has been through time. Along with discovering names, dates, and people from the past, we discover parts of ourselves. Genealogy helps us answer the question, "Who am I?"

The more we find out about our family backgrounds, the more sense we have of who we are.

Genealogy provides other benefits and worthwhile results. Locating distant and unknown relatives, for example, often creates new friendships and builds brand-new family ties. Also, some people are able to find needed genetic and hereditary information that can be life-saving.

Families: Where Names Matter

In the "Folsum Prison Blues" song, a prisoner complains that in the prison "they call me by a number not a name." To the motor vehicle department and the Social Security administration, we are numbers more than names. Yet, even to be a name instead of a number is not that much of an improvement—that is, if your name is merely one of thousands in a federal census or a city directory. Other than for celebrities, the main place where people are more than mere names on a list, where they are real persons and individual identities, is in their families. In a family, no one goes by a number. In a family, names matter.

Names matter in families because the families give the names in the first place. Who we are in terms of names and as human beings comes primarily from our family. The last name, or surname, is vitally important. By law, so far, a person usually receives the father's last name as his or her own last name. Or perhaps the mother's last name is given. But very few last names are invented out of thin air. Last names are key links in a family chain.

Parents often give babies a first name chosen just because it sounds good, because it is "in" at the time, or because it is the name of a relative the parents like. Middle names frequently are

picked because they flow nicely with the first name or to honor a close relative, such as an aunt or uncle.

So, to search out our family roots is to search out our family members by name. Simply put, genealogy is a detective name game.

Seeing Where We Fit In

Across America there is a great longing to belong. Widespread interest in genealogy shows that people have a hunger and thirst to know who their parents' parents and grandparents and the generations before them were. To visit the grave of the immigrant ancestor from five generations ago satisfies like a sweet roll when you are hungry. To read a letter written by a great-grandmother to her daughter quenches the thirst like drinking fresh spring water. To find out that one of your relatives fought in a particular Civil War battle produces a sense of pride and belonging.

Genealogy Is Everywhere

Thousands upon thousands of people are doing genealogy—tracking down information about parents, grandparents, and ancestors. Researchers constantly use the family records sections of public libraries. Libraries contain hundreds of thousands of books about particular families or genealogy lines. Computer nets buzz between genealogy Web sites. Magazines and television programs focus attention on genealogy activity. Among thousands of genealogy organizations in America's counties, many meet regularly and publish local guides to old cemetery, court, and church records. Boy Scouts can earn a Family History merit badge. Thousands of family organizations operate at national and local levels. Most large libraries have family history reference sections, genealogy reference specialists, and guidebooks for the beginning genealogist.

Some high school and college history classes ask students to do simple genealogy exercises designed to let students see their families' situations as immigrants coming to America or during major events like the Great Depression, the influenza epidemic of 1918, or the Civil War.

A Warning

There is no Surgeon General's warning about starting to trace your family tree, but there should be. There needs to be a warning that says something like: "Danger. Those who venture to find their family's genealogy run great risk of becoming addicted to the search."

Because of widespread interest in family history, scores of professional genealogists make their livings by searching for genealogy information for clients who hire them. Because of genealogy interest, publishers have produced scores of important handbooks and guidebooks designed for beginners and specialists, for genealogy research in general, and for very specific genealogy research problems such as Jewish genealogy, adoptions, immigrants to Canada, and Native American research.

Several large urban and university libraries are recognized as being important genealogy research centers, serving a very interested public, including:

National Archives in Washington, D.C.
Latter-Day Saints (Mormons) Church Family History Library in
      Salt Lake City (with 2,500 branch libraries around the world)
New England Genealogical and Historical Society in Boston
Newberry Library in Chicago
New York Public Library
Sutro Library in San Francisco

Introductory genealogy classes are available in every state. Many libraries, local genealogy societies, and community education programs offer these. Or, you can visit one of the LDS Church's 2,500 family history centers and receive beginning instructions there. On TV or at a library you might want to view segments of the 1997 PBS special, "Ancestors." Each of the ten half-hour episodes gives how-to advice.

Why Do People Get Started?

Curiosity, often fed by the urge to know one's identity but sometimes acting on its own, causes people to think about their past family members. A woman visits Ellis Island and wonders who in her own families were the immigrant ancestors, where they came from, and when they arrived in America. A man walks by the Gettysburg battlefield monument and wonders if one of his ancestors fought in the Civil War. Or, a person inherits a faded photograph of a great-grandparent and, looking into that person's eyes, wonders where and when that person lived and what life was like for that ancestor.

Interest in genealogy strikes people in every walk of life, every social class, every ethnic group, young and old, male and female:

- Among those of western European descent, some take pride in discovering that their family way-back-when had a family crest or shield or coat of arms.
- Descendants who find they had a Scottish family with its own tartan like to have a blanket or tie or goblets featuring that tartan design.
- Descendants of *Mayflower* passengers join a *Mayflower* organization.
- Many white people brag about Native American ancestry they might have.
- Famous African-American author Alex Haley, who wrote *Roots*, enjoyed telling audiences about his Irish ancestry as much as about his African forebears. His *Roots* labors sharpened African-Americans' interests in seeking their genealogies, including generations trapped in slavery.
- Many families of Asian background inherit a reverence for ancestors that requires that they know and tap into genealogies extending back centuries.

1620

Plymouth Rock

Putting a Foot Inside the Genealogy Door

All it takes to start "doing genealogy" is to write down your full name, and then your father's and mother's full names. That's the start. That's how anyone begins to list and figure out the names that link together to form the family tree. That puts the foot inside the genealogy door.

This book is designed to help you put more than your foot inside the door. Chapters 1 and 2 open the genealogy door conveniently and generously wide for you.

Shaking and Shaping the Family Tree

"Family tree" is a term applied to one's genealogical past. A tree has a main trunk with branches that extend out indefinitely. The family tree image is a nice one, implying a branch, and then branches from that branch, and then new branches and twigs as the family grows and spreads. But the family tree image provides a limited view of the family. Three other descriptions seem more useful to show what the genealogy patterns are.

1. *An upside-down triangle or pyramid with the point at the bottom and base at the top.* This is the most popular approach people use when doing genealogy. Not counting remarriages, a person typically has two parents, four grandparents (two couples), eight great-grandparents (four couples), sixteen great-great-grandparents (eight couples), and so on backward in time. From you (at the bottom point) working upward, this forms the upside-down triangle. This upside-down pyramid describes an *ancestral family*—your ancestors back four generations from you.

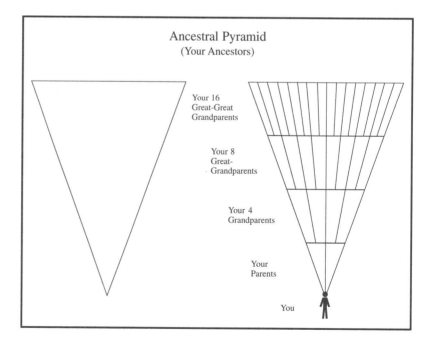

Ancestral Pyramid
(Your Ancestors)

Your 16
Great-Great
Grandparents

Your 8
Great-
Grandparents

Your 4
Grandparents

Your
Parents

You

2. *A rightside-up triangle or pyramid with the point at the top and the base at the bottom.* This describes a family coming down through time from one common set of ancestors. Its point is one set of great-great-grandparents, and then as the pyramid widens it includes all their children, then widens to include all of their children's children, and so on down to the big base at the bottom—all the living descendants of that couple. This rightside-up pyramid describes a descendant family, or all the descendants from one common ancestor.

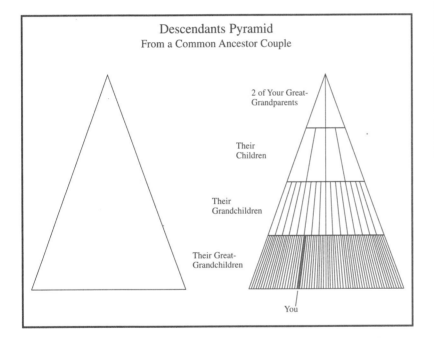

Descendants Pyramid
From a Common Ancestor Couple

2 of Your Great-Grandparents

Their Children

Their Grandchildren

Their Great-Grandchildren

You

Oral Histories

Most tribes, clans, families, groups had an oral tradition of reciting who begot whom. Even in modern-day United States, families pass down stories about who married whom, when individual family members died, when grandchildren and great grandchildren were born.

In most societies, however, the oral tradition was eventually written down or some other device was designed to assist genealogy memory. Among the Incas of Peru, a system of recording by means of ropes and knots was used. The Maoies of New Zealand used a complex bead system to keep track of genealogy. A system of early writing known as "ogham" was used in Ireland and runes were used in Scandinavian countries.

3. *The Christmas tree with one triangle sitting on top of another triangle just like it.* This is the direct-line family. It starts with a couple at the top and branches out to show their children, one of whom is the direct line to the present, but—to keep it from becoming too big and wide—it continues down to only the children of the child who is the direct-line ancestor. Then, that child is dealt with as a married person with children—like the tip of the next pyramid down—so

another set of branches flares out from the trunk. But that next generation, again, shows only the direct-line child, his or her spouse, and their children.

Genealogy and Literature

Often a record of a genealogy can be found in the literature of a country. In India, students of the literary epics *Ramayana* and *Mahabharata* have found the genealogies of Hindu royal lines.

The national book of Ethiopia, the *Kebra Nagast* or *The Glory of the Kings* was most likely composed in the 14th century, but it was based on oral tradition and written records that go back in Ethiopia to the fourth century A.D. According to this book, the royal line that ruled Ethiopia until 1975 was descended from Solomon and the Queen of Sheba.

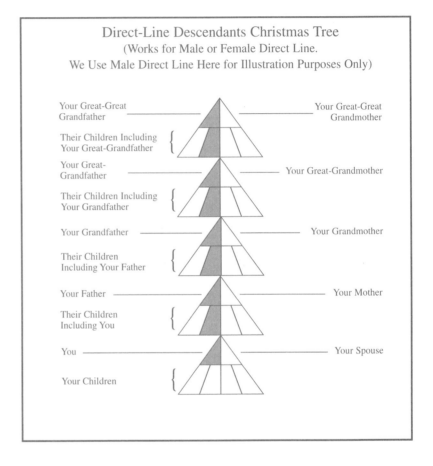

Direct-Line Descendants Christmas Tree
(Works for Male or Female Direct Line.
We Use Male Direct Line Here for Illustration Purposes Only)

Your Great-Great Grandfather — Your Great-Great Grandmother

Their Children Including Your Great-Grandfather

Your Great-Grandfather — Your Great-Grandmother

Their Children Including Your Grandfather

Your Grandfather — Your Grandmother

Their Children Including Your Father

Your Father — Your Mother

Their Children Including You

You — Your Spouse

Your Children

In real life, most of us can only "handle" in our minds the Christmas-tree version of the family. That is, as children we know our brothers and sisters and parents—our own little triangle or pyramid. And we know our uncles and aunts and first cousins. So, we tend to be able to account for two generations. But, even though we know a third generation, our grandparents, we usually

do not know all of their brothers and sisters, and their children and grandchildren. That is, it's great if we know our uncles and aunts and first cousins, but please do not expect us to know all of our great-aunts and great-uncles, and those second and more distant cousins. Those become too distant in relationship, if not in location, for us to care about.

When we marry, our children will "inherit" two of these Christmas-tree versions of the family, one for the father's family and one for the mother's. When we become parents and then grandparents, we keep track of our children's children and probably of all our grandchildren. But very likely, our grandchildren will not know all of our own brothers and sisters, or those who are our own nieces and nephews.

Upside-down and rightside-up triangles and Christmas trees? Where all these diagrams lead is here:

> The direct-line family becomes the trunk of the family tree that we try to identify first, when doing genealogy research.

Each ancestor or descendant, no matter which way you want to research, is a blank. So, to "do" your genealogy, you try to fill in the blanks. For each person, the basic information to find is what we call *vital information*. That is, we need to unearth key vital or life facts—birth, marriage, and death information—about each person in the family:

full proper name
day, month, year, and place of birth
day, month, year, and place of marriage
full information about spouse(s)
day, month, year, and place of death
full information about every child from each marriage

Chapter 1 provides samples of the basic genealogy charts: the pedigree chart with places to list direct-line ancestors and the family group chart on which a couple and all their children can be listed.

Family History Is Genealogy—and Much, Much More

Genealogy is one way to find, preserve, and share a family heritage. But, the family's heritage is furthered through doing other projects in a range of other non-genealogy activities. Many families do several of these other activities automatically, just because they seem to be good things to do. Among the common activities are:

writing the life story of a relative
tape-recording the life story of a relative
writing one's own life story, or parts of it
sending and receiving family letters
keeping a personal diary or journal
making scrapbooks for oneself or for a family member
taking, storing, displaying, and sharing photographs, slides,
    and videos
taking proper care of old family letters, documents, and objects
holding family reunions
    taking trips to sites important to their ancestors' lives

Chapters 3 through 8 explain and explore each of these non-genealogy activities.

This book, then, provides a supermarket of ideas so that you, the reader can view the "products" and then choose those that appeal or matter the most to you.

Part 1
RESEARCHING YOUR FAMILY HISTORY

CHAPTER ONE

Climbing the Family Tree: Easy Beginning Steps at Home

Genealogy in Biblical Times

One of humankind's oldest records, the Bible, contains detailed genealogies through the male line, showing descendants of Noah, Shem, Ham, Abraham's children, Ishmael, Esau, Jacob, and others. The New Testament provides two genealogies for Jesus Christ, showing his father Joseph's descent, one from Abraham (in Matthew 1) and one from Adam (in Luke 3).

Genealogy seeks to discover and chart vital information about each direct-line family member.

Parents, grandparents, great-grandparents . . . how far back does it go? Great-great-grandparents and then back, back, back in time . . . How many generations back can you name or find the names of your ancestors? In the spaces below, without looking anything up, try to record two generations from memory:

(FATHER'S FATHER'S FULL NAME)

(FATHER'S FULL NAME)

(FATHER'S MOTHER'S FULL NAME)

(YOUR FULL NAME)

(MOTHER'S FATHER'S FULL NAME)

(MOTHER'S FULL MAIDEN NAME)

(MOTHER'S MOTHER'S FULL MAIDEN NAME)

Now, can you do the next generation, too—your eight great-grandparents? How far back do you think you can name the names, without doing any serious research?

By official count, thousands of people descend from the Pilgrims' *Mayflower* company. To belong to the Society of Mayflower Descendants, they have to show on genealogy charts their direct-line

ancestors back to a passenger or crewman on that famous ship—a dozen generations or more.

Now and then you will run into people who have genealogy charts showing their descent from English royalty who lived long before Shakespeare did. Those charts show more than twenty generations or progenitors.

How do these people know their genealogy? Where do their charts of their ancestors come from? How does anyone find out what their own genealogy is? Is genealogy something everyday people can do, or must they hire professional genealogists to do the research?

Almost anyone can "do" genealogy and find names and dates for their family tree dating back several generations. By following a few simple, basic steps, you can start compiling a worthwhile genealogy of your own family.

By dictionary definition, *genealogy* is "a recorded history of the descent of a person or family from an ancestor or ancestors," or "the science or study of family descent." Genealogy is a research activity wherein a person seeks to learn and chart vital information about someone's ancestry, generation by generation. To discover direct-line progenitors, genealogy-seekers try to find the full names and birth, marriage, and death information of each ancestor, if possible. A person who produces a family's genealogy is a researcher and a fact gatherer, but need not be a writer or a historian.

Those with long genealogies going back to the 1600s or earlier are exceptions. Most people who do genealogy feel lucky to trace the family tree even five generations back. To track ancestors back to anyone living before 1800 is a real, and satisfying, accomplishment. Many Americans try to trace their genealogies back to an ancestor who first came to this country, the immigrant ancestor, and feel content if they can discover that much of their genealogy.

Two Basic Genealogy Charts

To map genealogy, you need two types of simple charts: the pedigree chart and the family group chart. The object with each is to "fill in the blanks" by recording accurate birth, marriage, and death details. Here are samples of both of these charts:

"Only the 'Vital' Facts, Ma'am"

Genealogy does not seek full life details or even full chronologies on a person. Instead, it concentrates on only the "vital" facts of that person's life: birth, marriage, and death. Genealogy requires the full name of the person and then the dates and locations of that person's birth, marriage, and death. To be exact, for each ancestor one needs his or her:

- Full name
- Date of birth (day, month, year)
- Place of birth (city, county, state)
- Date of marriage (day, month, year)
- Place of marriage (city, county, state)
- Date of death (day, month, year)
- Place of death (city, county, state)

Governments call birth, marriage, and death records "vital records" which are kept by each state.

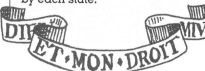

Pedigree Chart

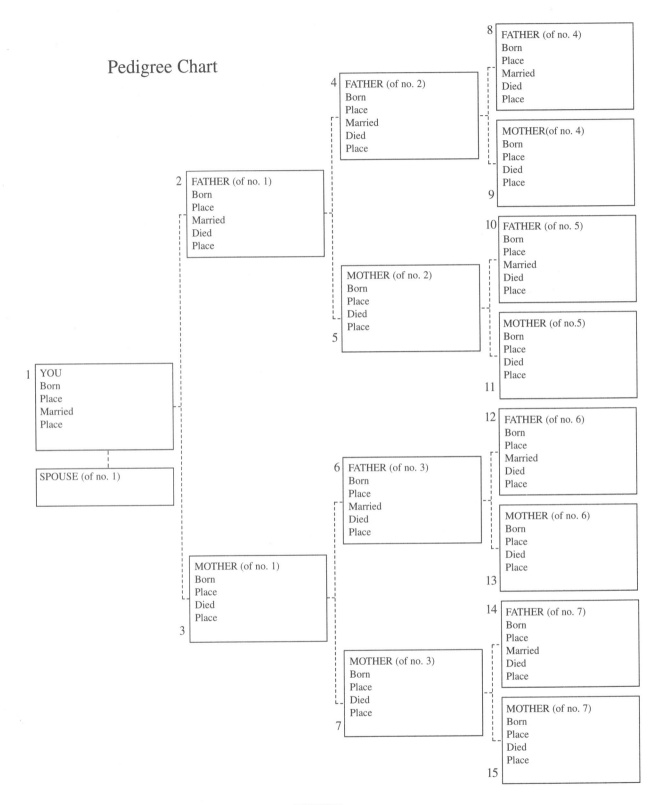

8 | FATHER (of no. 4)
Born
Place
Married
Died
Place

9 | MOTHER (of no. 4)
Born
Place
Died
Place

4 | FATHER (of no. 2)
Born
Place
Married
Died
Place

10 | FATHER (of no. 5)
Born
Place
Married
Died
Place

11 | MOTHER (of no.5)
Born
Place
Died
Place

2 | FATHER (of no. 1)
Born
Place
Married
Died
Place

5 | MOTHER (of no. 2)
Born
Place
Died
Place

1 | YOU
Born
Place
Married
Place

SPOUSE (of no. 1)

12 | FATHER (of no. 6)
Born
Place
Married
Died
Place

13 | MOTHER (of no. 6)
Born
Place
Died
Place

6 | FATHER (of no. 3)
Born
Place
Married
Died
Place

3 | MOTHER (of no. 1)
Born
Place
Died
Place

14 | FATHER (of no. 7)
Born
Place
Married
Died
Place

7 | MOTHER (of no. 3)
Born
Place
Died
Place

15 | MOTHER (of no. 7)
Born
Place
Died
Place

Family Group Record

Husband's name

Born	Place
Chr.	Place
Mar.	Place
Died	Place
Bur.	Place

Father	Mother

Husband's other wives

Wife's name

Born	Place
Chr.	Place
Died	Place
Bur.	

Father	Mother

Wife's other husbands

Children

1 Sex	Name		Spouse	
	B/Chr	Place	Mar.	Place
	Died	Place	Bur	Place

2 Sex	Name		Spouse	
	B/Chr	Place	Mar.	Place
	Died	Place	Bur	Place

3 Sex	Name		Spouse	
	B/Chr	Place	Mar.	Place
	Died	Place	Bur	Place

4 Sex	Name		Spouse	
	B/Chr	Place	Mar.	Place
	Died	Place	Bur	Place

5 Sex	Name		Spouse	
	B/Chr	Place	Mar.	Place
	Died	Place	Bur	Place

6 Sex	Name		Spouse	
	B/Chr	Place	Mar.	Place
	Died	Place	Bur	Place

7 Sex	Name		Spouse	
	B/Chr	Place	Mar.	Place
	Died	Place	Bur	Place

8 Sex	Name		Spouse	
	B/Chr	Place	Mar.	Place
	Died	Place	Bur	Place

Other Marriages

Geneology Charts

Blank charts you can use are provided in this chapter and in the appendices. You can obtain printed blank charts from most larger libraries, local genealogical societies, and the LDS Church Family History Center nearest you. Or, you can use one of several computer programs for recording and saving genealogy, which will produce pedigree charts and family group charts for you.

Step 1: Write Down What You Already Know

Most people grow up knowing who their parents and grandparents are. (Adoption situations are discussed in Chapter 2.) They know relatives who were alive during their lifetimes and with whom they have had some contact. And, usually, they have heard about a few relatives who lived before they were born.

So, start your genealogy adventure by buying or making yourself a blank pedigree chart and a couple of blank family group charts. Then, on the pedigree chart, start with yourself and write down your own vital information on the first line at the left. Then, write down what vital information you know about your parents. Next, fill in all you can about your grandparents, and then for any direct-line relatives behind them in time.

Pedigree or family group charts have blanks for the vital facts for each name, so try to fill in these blanks. For example:

2.
Name: Charles Alton HARTLEY
Born: 17 June 1881
Where: Koscuisko Co., Indiana
Married: 28 Oct. 1903
Married Place: _____
Died: 4 June 1937
Where: Portland, Multnomah, Oregon

1.
Name: Charles Alton HARTLEY, Jr.
Born: 17 Sept. 1909
Where: Amarillo, Potter, Texas
Married: 16 Dec. 1935
Married Place: _____
Died: _____
Where: _____

3.
Name: Elizabeth Catherine MARTIN
Born: 17 Feb. 1882
Where: Fort Wayne, Allen, Indiana
Died: 1 Mar. 1958
Where: Portland, Multnomah, Oregon

Pedigree Chart

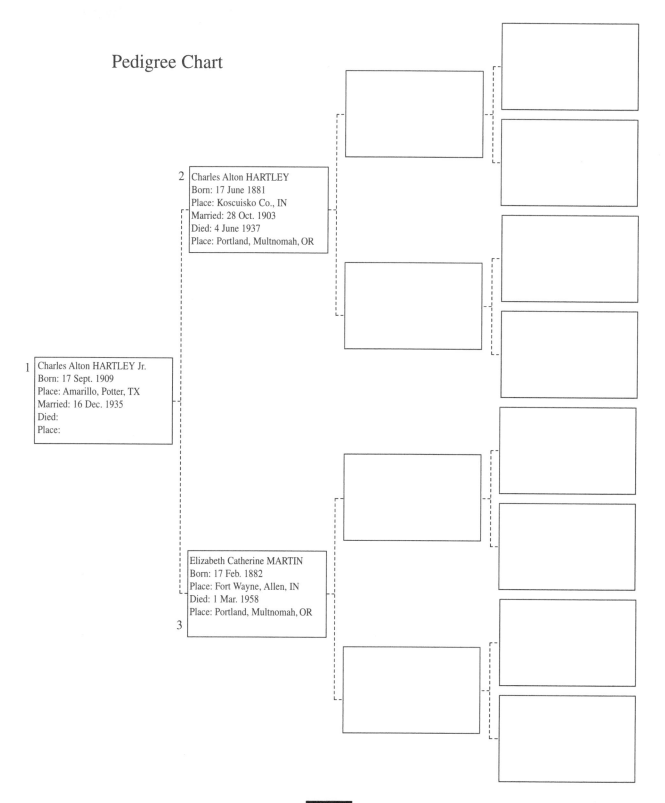

1 Charles Alton HARTLEY Jr.
Born: 17 Sept. 1909
Place: Amarillo, Potter, TX
Married: 16 Dec. 1935
Died:
Place:

2 Charles Alton HARTLEY
Born: 17 June 1881
Place: Koscuisko Co., IN
Married: 28 Oct. 1903
Died: 4 June 1937
Place: Portland, Multnomah, OR

3 Elizabeth Catherine MARTIN
Born: 17 Feb. 1882
Place: Fort Wayne, Allen, IN
Died: 1 Mar. 1958
Place: Portland, Multnomah, OR

After you have filled in as many blanks as you can on your pedigree chart, see what you can do with the other chart, the family group chart. A family group chart has spaces provided for you to list vital information for an entire family unit—father, mother, and each child in birth order from first to last. So, for your own immediate family, record what you know. If you are married and have children, do a chart listing everybody in your own family unit and their birth, marriage, and death dates and places (including county). Or, if you are single, fill out a family group chart for your parents. On that chart you will be listed as their child, along with any brothers and sisters you have.

Once you have filled in some blanks on your pedigree chart or your family group chart, you will have started to map your genealogy. Congratulations!

You will often see gaps in the information you have. That's OK. Everybody who starts doing genealogy faces gaps. Those gaps are what you try to fill—they are what drive your searches for information.

Step 2: Draw Information from Records in Your Home

Few of us can recall details of date and place very well. So, you will need to find some records that contain the information you can't remember or were never told. After you write on the charts what you know, the next thing to do is to rummage through the house for more information. Look through scrapbooks and photo albums, closets and drawers, attics and basements, to find any records that contain genealogy information about your immediate family.

Some families record birth, marriage, and death information in the family Bible. Often, a family has saved a marriage, birth, or death certificate; a will; or some obituary notice. Scrapbooks can be good sources of vital information, especially birth and wedding announcements, citizenship certificates, and copies of obituaries. Family pictures can be helpful, too. A wedding photograph of the grandparents, for example, might have the wedding date and place written on the back of it.

When you find new information in the records in your home—names, dates, and places—add it to your pedigree and family group charts. Your goal is to find out full names and dates.

Family Group Record

Husband's name

Born	Place
Chr.	Place
Mar.	Place
Died	Place
Bur.	Place

Father	Mother

Husband's other wives

Wife's name

Born	Place
Chr.	Place
Died	Place

Bur.

Father	Mother

Wife's other husbands

Children

1 Sex	Name		Spouse	
	B/Chr	Place	Mar.	Place
	Died	Place	Bur	Place
2 Sex	Name		Spouse	
	B/Chr	Place	Mar.	Place
	Died	Place	Bur	Place
3 Sex	Name		Spouse	
	B/Chr	Place	Mar.	Place
	Died	Place	Bur	Place
4 Sex	Name		Spouse	
	B/Chr	Place	Mar.	Place
	Died	Place	Bur	Place
5 Sex	Name		Spouse	
	B/Chr	Place	Mar.	Place
	Died	Place	Bur	Place
6 Sex	Name		Spouse	
	B/Chr	Place	Mar.	Place
	Died	Place	Bur	Place
7 Sex	Name		Spouse	
	B/Chr	Place	Mar.	Place
	Died	Place	Bur	Place
8 Sex	Name		Spouse	
	B/Chr	Place	Mar.	Place
	Died	Place	Bur	Place

Other Marriages

Names and Nicknames

Many people go through life being called by their nickname rather than their full, proper name. You know him as Bill, but his real name is William. He goes by Chuck, but his real name is Charles. She is "Grandma Betsy," but her real name is Elizabeth.

Many proper names have fairly standard nickname counterparts. Here are some of the more typical ones:

Henry	Hank or Harry
Richard	Dick, Rick, Rich
John	Johnny, Jack
James	Jimmy, Jim
Elizabeth	Beth, Eliza, Liz, Betsy, Bessie, Libby
Margaret	Maggie, Peggy, Meg, Madge

Step 3: Ask Relatives for Information

After you have recorded what you know and scoured the records in your home for information, it is time to look beyond the walls of your own house—but not beyond your own family. The next step is to contact relatives and ask them for genealogy details you need. In many families there is one person who seems to be the family historian, the one who everyone believes has the most information about the family's genealogy and records. If your family has such a knowledgeable person, contact him or her and obtain genealogy information he or she has already collected.

Contact others, too—parents, brothers and sisters, uncles and aunts, grandparents, and other relatives—and ask them for details needed to fill in the blanks on the genealogy charts. This can be done by visiting them in their homes, talking to them on the telephone, or writing/e-mailing them.

Sometimes a genealogy interview in their home works well. If you have a relative who knows a lot of the family's genealogy facts, visit and record what he or she remembers. Take a tape-recorder with you and interview him or her, recording the oral genealogy information on tape. (Don't videotape, at least during your first visit; videotaping can be too intimidating.) Ask specific questions. If your relative can't be precise about dates, you can help him or her approximate the time setting by asking questions like, "Was that before or after Frank went into the army?" or "Did they marry before her mother died?" or "Do you remember who else was at their wedding?" Answers can help you narrow down the needed date, to help you when you search government marriage records. Also ask them who else they think you should contact about genealogy details.

For best results when contacting any relatives, ask for specific details: "Aunt Rosa, I need to find out when and where your and Dad's parents died." "Grandpa, do you know the full names of your grandparents?" "John, do you remember in what town Mom and Dad were married?"

Likewise, when writing to a relative, be specific. Tell them what information you need. To make it easy, send them a pedigree or family group chart filled in with what you already know but with

spaces marked with a highlighter where you need information. Be sure to include a large, self-addressed, stamped envelope with extra postage. You need to make it as easy as possible for them to mail items to you. It is typically useful to follow up your mailing with a phone call to be sure they received your letter and to encourage them to respond.

What kinds of records should you ask about? Find out if they have any genealogy lists, a family Bible with genealogy items recorded in it, certificates, scrapbooks, clippings, photographs, diaries, letters, and written biographical sketches about family members.

Ask them to send you copies of what you need. If you must borrow these items, be sure you give the relatives a list of what they are loaning you, and you keep a copy of the list, too. (Then, be sure to return everything as soon as possible.)

While tracking down details about people in your grandparents' generation or before them, you need to find relatives who descend from those same people—distant cousins you do not yet know. Your older relatives usually can identify a person or two in these distant families whom you can contact.

Ask relatives if they know where family members in previous generations are buried. Then, try to visit the cemeteries and record information from the family headstones or from the sexton's record books.

You can make your genealogy search more fruitful and more enjoyable if you involve another relative or two in the project. If others seem interested in what you are doing, invite them to help you on the project.

(continued)

Katherine	Kathy, Kate, Kit
Mary	Mamie, Molly, Polly, Minnie
Eleanor	Ella, Nell, Nora
Edward	Eddie, Ted, Teddy
Amelia	Millie, Mildred
Dorothy	Dora, Dottie

Your genealogy should include proper names. Some people put the nickname of the person on the chart in parentheses, however: Richard (Dick) Allen Southwick.

Step 4: Create a Notetaking and File System

No file system is easier than using manila folders. When you find more information about various relatives, create a folder for your mother's side of the family and another one for your father's side. In time you will have a file folder for each family unit or married couple on your family tree. (If a man was married three times, you

might have three folders for him, and the same for a woman who married more than once.) Into the folders place such items as your family group chart; notes you copy from a family record; notes you write down from telephone inquiries; photocopies of obituaries, certificates, letters, and family information written on pages of the family Bible; and photographs.

In addition to file folders you can use a 3-ring binder. Divide it into sections and identify each section with a little plastic tab on the outside edge of its first page. Each section can be devoted to one family unit or families with the same last name. Because this is your notetaking binder, it's a good idea to write in it your full name and address—in case it gets lost. Then, insert in the front of the binder or at the front of each section a fact sheet and/or a copy of your pedigree or family group charts. In the appropriate sections of the binder, write down your research findings on 3-hole lined paper. Take this binder with you when you go out to interview relatives or to do research.

When you take notes, enter information about only one family on the same sheet of paper. That way, you can easily file the notes in the folder or binder section assigned to the right family. Also, when you receive letters that contain genealogy information, file those in the appropriate binder section or, better yet, the appropriate file folder.

Genealogy Software Packages

Increasingly, genealogists are putting their findings into computer files. Computerized genealogy programs are generally affordable, and they are useful—but not necessary. Genealogy software packages do require a computer with a lot of memory—at least 16 megabytes of RAM—and a fast speed. If you already have access to such a computer, you probably will want to buy a genealogy software program and use it for storing the genealogy information you find.

Genealogy software packages currently on the market provide very useful systems for entering and charting genealogy information. Scores of computer genealogy programs are displayed at the larger bookstores. Family Tree-Maker has been the most popular one

recently. Among others widely used are Personal Ancestral File, Ancestral Quest, Reunion, Family Origins, Family Matters, Family Treasures, Family Fathering, Brother's Keeper for Windows, Cumberland Family Tree, The Master Genealogist for DOS and Windows, Roots IV, and Visual Roots. New ones continually come onto the market.

These systems basically let you do two types of operations: data entry, or entering your genealogy information, and printing out your information. For example, Personal Ancestral File (PAF) is software produced by the Church of Jesus Christ of Latter-day Saints (LDS). It lets you input vital information by names that are linked by family relationship. With names so linked in the database, you can print out pedigrees or family group sheets whenever you want. PAF also lets LDS members record LDS religious ordinances for each person in the database, but this feature can be turned off for non-LDS genealogists. On the down side, PAF printouts of charts are not very attractive, while Ancestral Quest lets you produce nice-looking charts.

By computerizing your genealogy information, you eliminate the hard work of hand-printing or typing onto blank charts. With the correct software, you can input, store, retrieve, and study information quickly and without searching through boxes and drawers of genealogy charts and file materials. And, you can make your computer quickly create charts tailored to include whatever information you want shown.

How to Write Information on the Charts

Dark and Neat Print or Type

Do your working draft of your pedigree and family group charts in pencil. For the finished charts or ones to be photocopied, however, you should type, word-process, or hand-print the information in black ink.

Full Names

In spaces calling for a person's name, write in the full name in its normal order, not last name first. For women, use their full maiden names. Experienced genealogists capitalize each person's

Can You Trust the Information?

"Is what you know accurate? Most people would accept your testimony about your parents and brothers and sisters because you were an eyewitness to much of what has happened in their lives. But it is not so clear that your recollection would be good enough to document the vital events in your grandparents' lives. This brings us to an obvious but important rule in genealogy: although all statements must be documented, the greater the separation in time and place between a researcher and an ancestor, the more necessary it is to corroborate personal testimony with information from other sources," from *Shaking Your Family Tree* by Ralph Crandall, published by Yankee Books.

entire surname on their charts—making surnames easy to spot and preventing any confusion about which name is the first name and which is the surname.

Numbered Names

Each blank space for someone's name on a printed pedigree chart has a number. The first person on the chart's left side is number one and his/her father is number two, mother is number three, paternal grandfather is number four, paternal grandmother is number five, the other two grandparents are numbers six and seven, the paternal great-grandfather is number eight, and so on. These numbers are useful when you run out of space on the right-hand side of the chart and need to use one of those people in the far-right column as the starting person on a new pedigree chart that takes that lineage farther back than the first chart has space for.

Children's names on a family group chart are also numbered, but not those of their spouses. Because each name is numbered, you can add details about any person on your chart—putting it in information spaces or on the back of the chart—simply by writing that person's number next to the information. For example, if the husband had another wife later in life, you could put at the bottom or back of the chart something like this:

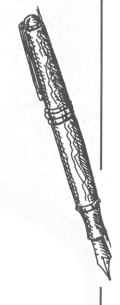

(1) second wife Mary Terwilliger

On a family group chart, if anyone had more than one spouse, the additional spouses' names are indicated on the same line after the original spouse's name on the chart, and each is identified by which number spouse they were:

Wife: (1) Carry Engstrom, (2) Tamson Light

Copy Numbers Carefully

When handwriting or printing your notes taken from others' sources, be very careful to record numbers clearly. When in a rush, people often write a 1 that looks like a 7, a 3 that looks like an 8, a 4 that looks like a 9, or a 6 or 9 that looks like a 0.

Abbreviations

Some printed genealogy charts include the abbreviations b., m., and d. beside certain lines to be filled in. These abbreviations' meanings are:

b. = birth
m. = marriage
d. = death

Some charts also add these abbreviations:

bp. = birthplace
mp. = marriage place
dp. = death place

When writing the day, month, and year on the charts, abbreviate the month to its first three letters, with no period after them, except spell out June (so it isn't confused with Jan.):

4 Apr 1943   31 Dec 1887   20 June 1911

Use the full names of cities or towns and of counties, but abbreviate the names of states and foreign countries. For states, use the U.S. Postal Service's two-letter abbreviations (see Appendix 2).

Abbreviate foreign countries using three letters. See standard abbreviations for many of the modern countries and for some that existed in the nineteenth century in Appendix 2.

Documenting Your Sources of Information

It is vital that you keep a research log. This is a listing of whom you contact, where you look for information, and what you find from each source. Include in it addresses and phone numbers. Also include full names of books or published items from which you take notes, and list where you found those items. This research log is a record of what you've tried to do, where you've looked, and whom you've contacted. This helps you find those items or people again,

Can You Trust the Information?

"At some point you will have to evaluate the genealogical information you have found. If you are lucky, all your sources will provide the same data, but that just doesn't happen. Inconsistencies, discrepancies, and impossibilities in your sources will raise red flags signaling problems for you," from *How to Trace Your Family History* by Bill R. Linder, published by Fawcett.

and if you forget what you've examined already, you can check your list to be sure you didn't already look at that source.

"Trust me" genealogy data is not good enough. You need to know where you found your information. Others need to know where it came from, too. Genealogists document their sources right on the pedigree or family group chart. You can do that by using the numbers on the charts to make notes on the bottom or back of your page:

(1) marriage date from marriage certificate in Helen Wilson's scrapbook, Tacoma, Washington
(2) Jane Doe interview with Anthony Catale, June 3, 1995, copy in Jane Doe's possession, Worcester, MA
(3) genealogy data in Wilson family Bible, in possession of Clarissa Williams, Norfolk, VA

Most computer genealogy programs provide places for you to list notes and documentation for any information you enter into your genealogy database.

Step 5: Decide What Missing Details You Want to Find

After filling in blanks on your pedigree and family group charts, you can easily spot any gaps in your information. You might be missing, for example, the day and month of someone's birth, a grandfather's middle name, or the date and place of your great-grandmother's death.

Pick out one or more of these missing facts, and then try to find them. Let these gaps guide your next genealogy labors.

Here is an example of a short pedigree chart that is mostly complete:

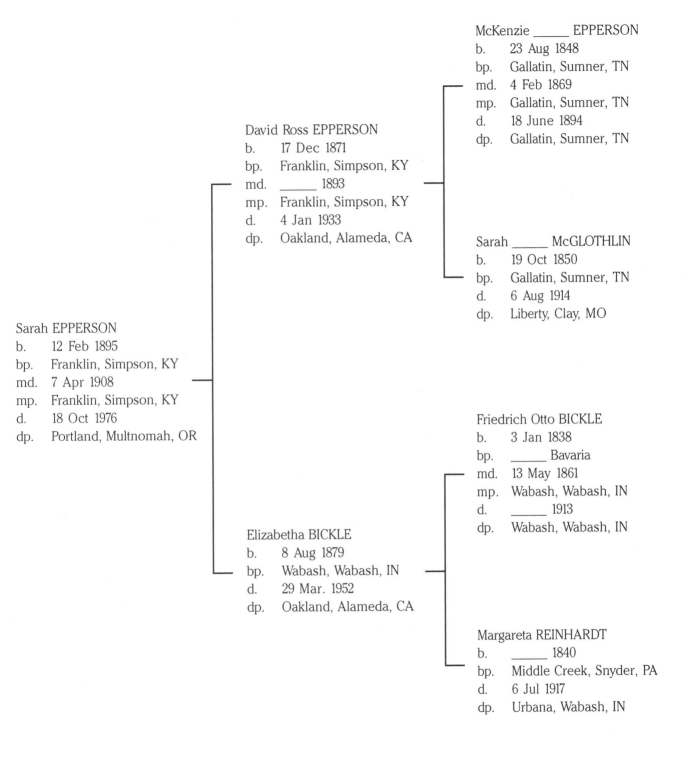

McKenzie _____ EPPERSON
b.   23 Aug 1848
bp.   Gallatin, Sumner, TN
md.   4 Feb 1869
mp.   Gallatin, Sumner, TN
d.   18 June 1894
dp.   Gallatin, Sumner, TN

David Ross EPPERSON
b.   17 Dec 1871
bp.   Franklin, Simpson, KY
md.   _____ 1893
mp.   Franklin, Simpson, KY
d.   4 Jan 1933
dp.   Oakland, Alameda, CA

Sarah _____ McGLOTHLIN
b.   19 Oct 1850
bp.   Gallatin, Sumner, TN
d.   6 Aug 1914
dp.   Liberty, Clay, MO

Sarah EPPERSON
b.   12 Feb 1895
bp.   Franklin, Simpson, KY
md. 7 Apr 1908
mp. Franklin, Simpson, KY
d.   18 Oct 1976
dp.   Portland, Multnomah, OR

Friedrich Otto BICKLE
b.   3 Jan 1838
bp.   _____ Bavaria
md.   13 May 1861
mp.   Wabash, Wabash, IN
d.   _____ 1913
dp.   Wabash, Wabash, IN

Elizabetha BICKLE
b.   8 Aug 1879
bp.   Wabash, Wabash, IN
d.   29 Mar. 1952
dp.   Oakland, Alameda, CA

Margareta REINHARDT
b.   _____ 1840
bp.   Middle Creek, Snyder, PA
d.   6 Jul 1917
dp.   Urbana, Wabash, IN

Pedigree Chart

1 Sarah EPPERSON
Born: 12 Feb. 1895
Place: Franklin, Simpson, KY
Married: 7 Apr. 1908
M. Place: Franklin, Simpson, KY
Died: 18 Oct. 1976
Place: Portland, Multnomah, OR

2 David Ross EPPERSON
Born: 17 Dec. 1871
Place: Franklin, Simpson, KY
Married: 1893
M. Place: Franklin, Simpson, KY
Died: 4 Jan. 1933
Place: Oakland, Alameda, CA

3 Elizabeth BICKLE
Born: 8 Aug. 1879
Place: Wabash, Wabash, IN
Died: 29 Mar. 1952
Place: Oakland, Alameda, CA

4 McKenzie ? EPPERSON
Born: 23 Aug. 1848
Place: Gallatin, Sumner, TN
Married: 4 Feb. 1869
M. Place: Gallatin, Sumner, TN
Died: 18 June 1894
Place: Gallatin, Sumner, TN

5 Sarah Ann McGLOTHLIN
Born: 19 Oct. 1850
Place: Gallatin, Sumner, TN
Died: 6 Aug. 1914
Place: Liberty, Clay, MO

6 Friedrich Otto BICKLE
Born: 3 Jan. 1838
Place: Bavaria
Married: 13 May 1861
M. Place: Wabash, Wabash, IN
Died: 1913
Place: Wabash, Wabash, IN

7 Margareta REINHARDT
Born: 1840
Place: Middle Creek, Snyder, PA
Died: 6 July 1917
Place: Urbana, Wabash, IN

8

9

10

11

12

13

14

15

Notice the information gaps that need to be filled in on this pedigree chart:

McKenzie Epperson's middle name or initial
The women's middle names, if they had any
Sarah Epperson's married name
David Ross Epperson's marriage day and month
Friedrich Otto Bickle's birthplace in Bavaria and the day and
    month of his death
Margareta Rheinhardt's day and month of birth

As another example, here is a family group chart compiled before the children's deaths. This chart is almost complete, but notice what genealogy details are missing:

Charles Alton HARTLEY
b.   1881
bp.   Kosciusko, IN
md.   28 Oct 1903
mp.   Portland, Multnomah, OR
d.   4 June 1937
dp.   Medford, Jackson, OR

Elizabeth Catherine MARTIN
b.   17 Feb 1882
bp.   Fort Wayne, Allen, IN
md.   28 Oct 1903
d.   6 Mar 1958
dp.   Medford, Jackson, OR

Children:

Helen Marie HARTLEY
b.   22 June 1904
bp.   Wabash, Wabash, IN
d.   23 Jul 1904 (infant)

Edna Mae HARTLEY
b.   8 Feb 1907
bp.   Wabash, Wabash, IN
md. 3 Jan 1925, Almon George BALCH

Charles Alton HARTLEY, Jr.
b.   17 Sep 1909, Amarillo, Potter, TX
md. 16 Dec 1935, Norma MINER

John (Jack) Martin HARTLEY
b.   6 Jul 1911
bp.   Portland, Multnomah, OR,
md. (1) June DAVIS (2) Louise Pitts CLARK

Missing are Charles Sr.'s birth month and day, Charles Jr.'s marriage place, and Jack's marriage dates. (Kosciusko is the county name, so the father was born out in the country and not in a town.)

Genealogy collecting is somewhat like fishing in various ponds. The first ponds you try are your own memory and records at home. The next ponds you go to are your relatives'. After you have written down your genealogy information from your memory, your home records, and your relatives, examine your charts and see what information is missing. Pick out some missing facts you really want to find. If you and your relatives do not have the details you need, though, how do you find them? Obviously, you have to look someplace else—you need to fish in other ponds. In Chapter 2 you will read about the next genealogy steps, which will take you fishing for information in the stocked ponds called libraries and archives.

Family Group Record

Husband's name	Charles Alton HARTLEY	
Born	1881	Place Kosciusko, IN
Chr.		Place
Mar.	28 Oct 1903	Place
Died	4 Jun 1937	Place Medford, Jackson, OR
Bur.		Place

Father		Mother	
Husband's other wives			

Wife's name	Elizabeth Catherine MARTIN	
Born	17 Feb.1882	Place Fort Wayne, Allen, IN
Chr.		Place Portland, Multnomah, OR
Died	6 Mar. 1958	Place Medford, Jackson, OR
Bur.		

Father		Mother	
Wife's other husbands			

Children

	Sex	Name			Spouse		
1	F	**Helen Marie HARTLEY**			Spouse		
		B/Chr 22 Jun. 1904	Place Wabash, Wabash, IN		Mar.	Place	
		Died 23 Jul. 1904 (infant)	Place		Bur	Place	
2	F	**Edna Mae HARTLEY**			Spouse Almon George BALCH		
		B/Chr 8 Feb. 1907	Place Wabash, Wabash, IN		Mar. 3 Jan. 1925	Place	
		Died	Place		Bur	Place	
3	M	**Charles Alton HARTLEY**			Spouse Norma MINER		
		B/Chr 17 Sep. 1909	Place Amarillo, Potter, TX		Mar. 16 Dec. 1935	Place	
		Died	Place		Bur	Place	
4	M	**John (Jack) Martin HARTLEY**			Spouse June DAVIS		
		B/Chr 6 July 1911	Place Portland, Multnomah, OR		Mar.	Place	
		Died	Place		Bur	Place	
5		Name			Spouse		
		B/Chr	Place		Mar.	Place	
		Died	Place		Bur	Place	
6		Name			Spouse		
		B/Chr	Place		Mar.	Place	
		Died	Place		Bur	Place	
7		Name			Spouse		
		B/Chr	Place		Mar.	Place	
		Died	Place		Bur	Place	
8		Name			Spouse		
		B/Chr	Place		Mar.	Place	
		Died	Place		Bur	Place	

Other Marriages

Child # 4: Louise Pitts CLARK

CHAPTER TWO

Finding Information Beyond the Family's Walls

After scouring your mind, your home, and your living relatives for genealogy information, you need to start searching for information elsewhere. "Decide what missing details you want to find"—Step 5 in the last chapter—and change roles from collector to researcher. You are ready to take Step 6 and become a genealogy researcher in library, archival, and community records. Once again comparing genealogy work to fishing, there are a number of good ponds in which you need to fish that are beyond your family's own pools of records and recollections.

Genealogists search in censuses; birth, marriage, and death records; newspaper obituaries; military records; immigrant records; county tax ledgers; church and cemetery records; wills; and property deeds. In other words, researchers study an array of records. It sounds overwhelming, but it's not. There is a progressive, logical way in which to conduct the search, and this chapter's purpose is to show you how best to do that searching.

No matter where you look for genealogy details, genealogy research always focuses on location. Where your ancestors once lived is the engine that guides your research. It helps to think about records in terms of their closeness to the person. So, you look close at hand at your own family records, and then you look for local records where the person lived, then state records, and finally federal records. The closer to the person being researched, the better the records.

Genealogists before you have paved the research paths to the good fishing ponds for you. Because of the increasing interest of the past twenty-five years in genealogy and family history research, libraries and archives frequently have a staff member who is expert in those areas. Many librarians go the extra mile to be helpful, particularly to new researchers. Librarians with good genealogy sections frequently offer introductory genealogy classes. Some 2,500 LDS Family History Centers worldwide provide introductory classes and training, and sometimes free hands-on tutoring.

Many handbooks provide basic and specialized genealogy research instructions. Your local library can locate for you published guides to records in any of the states. These guidebooks are very helpful and save the researcher much time, much money, and many

1692

Salem Village

wasted phone calls. They identify which state, county, local agency, or library has what kinds of records.

The LDS Family History Library in Salt Lake City publishes a series of terrific *Research Outlines* for each state in the United States, and for Canada and many other countries. Although low-cost, these booklets are as useful as expensive hardbound guidebooks. The *United States Research Outline*, fifty-two pages long, gives instructions about where to find and how to use two dozen types of records, including:

biography	history
cemeteries	land/property
census	maps
church records	military
court records	newspapers
directories	obituaries
emigration	probate records
immigration	taxation
gazetteers	vital records
genealogy	

National and Local Genealogical Societies

In many towns and counties across America there are local genealogical societies. These volunteer groups hold meetings and share information. They compile genealogical data about families who have lived in the area since settlement began there. They create registers, indexes, and other finding aids of the local records containing genealogy information. Some publish newsletters that provide lists of names extracted from such local records as wills and probates, cemetery headstones, property tax ledgers, and church christening entries. For example, the Indiana Genealogical Society publishes a quarterly magazine called *Indiana Genealogist*, produces six newsletters a year, and holds an annual genealogy conference. A guide to these organizations is Mary K. Meyer's *Directory of Genealogical Societies in the U.S.A. and Canada* (Pasadena, MD).

The National Genealogical Society

Founded in 1903 in the District of Columbia, The National Genealogical Society (NGS) has been located at Glebe House in Arlington, Virginia since 1985.

The NGS if a nonprofit organization with a national membership of over 17 thousand members. Most of its members are individuals, but its institutional members include genealogical and historical societies, family organizations, libraries, and other organizations.

You may reach the National Genealogical Society at:

Electronic Addresses:
NGS Library:
  ngslibe@wizard.net
All other inquiries:
  76702.2417@compuserve.com.

America's leading organization is the National Genealogical Society, or NGS. Among the better-known specialized genealogical societies are the Mayflower Society and the Daughters of the American Revolution (DAR). The NGS publishes the *National Genealogical Society Quarterly*, aimed more at the serious, experienced genealogist. More helpful to beginners is the magazine *The Genealogical Helper* (published by Everton Publishers in Logan, UT), which provides how-to instructions and discusses queries received from readers.

The National Archives

The National Archives is the official repository for all federal government records. Its main center is in Washington, D.C., but it has branches, or regional archives, located in:

Atlanta	Los Angeles
Boston	New York
Chicago	Philadelphia
Denver	San Francisco
Fort Worth	Seattle
Kansas City	

The National Archives publishes guides and finding aids to help the beginning genealogist find information in its vast record collections.

Step 6: Check Already Collected Genealogies and Biographies

Begin actual research by looking first for records already compiled and prepared for research use. Because genealogists are fact collectors, many have contributed collections of their family's genealogy facts to libraries and genealogy databases. It is possible that someone else has already pulled together some of the genealogy for one or more of your family lines back a few generations. It's fun to discover such a coincidence, and it's a waste of time digging for information others have already found. So, it's best to check what has already been collected before starting brand-new research.

How do you find out what has already been collected and compiled? You (1) check libraries that specialize in genealogy books and records, and (2) scan through the ever-growing computer databases of genealogy information. Library shelves, and now computer disks and the Internet, are loaded with genealogies already pulled together.

Thousands of families have collected detailed genealogies and published them in book form, so that others who link into those families can benefit from their research. Genealogy organizations and private companies are compiling sets of records and indexing them in order to make them available to genealogy-seekers.

It makes little sense, therefore, to go looking for information someone else has already found and made available to researchers. You need to find out what other genealogy information useful to you has been pulled together. That way, you can copy into your notes and charts what has already been done.

Look for biographies or biographical sketches in local libraries. Many towns and counties have books containing biographical sketches, particularly of founding settlers of an area. And, they have published histories that contain biographical parts that tell about many of the local citizens. Check also at larger libraries that have good genealogy sections and in your nearest LDS Family History Center's catalog of holdings.

Collected Genealogies and Biographies in Libraries

America has several libraries devoted entirely to genealogical research books and records. These include the New England Historic Genealogical Society in Boston, the Daughters of the American Revolution Society Headquarters in Washington, D.C., the Newberry Library in Chicago, and the New York Biographical and Genealogical Society.

The LDS Family History Library is recognized as the premier genealogy library in the world. It is located in Salt Lake City, Utah, and, although operated by the Church of Jesus Christ of Latter-day Saints, it is open to the public. The massive main library operates branch Family History Centers in hundreds of communities

(continued)

Address:
National Genealogical
    Society
4527 17th Street, North
Arlington, VA 22207-2399

Telephone:
(703)525-0050—Office
(800)473-0060—Toll Free
(703)841-9065—Library
(703)525-0052—Fax

Office Hours:
Monday-Friday
    9 a.m. to 5 p.m.

Library Hours:
Monday & Wednesday
    10 a.m. to 9 p.m.
Friday & Saturday
    10 a.m. to 4 p.m.

Archives and Libraries with Important Genealogical Collections

Allen County Public Library, Fort Wayne, IN

American Antiquarian Society, Worcester, MA

Dallas Public Library, TX

Detroit Public Library, MI

Historical Society of Pennsylvania, Philadelphia, PA

Lee Library, Brigham Young University, Provo, UT

Los Angeles Public Library, CA

New York Public Library, New York City, NY

State Historical Society of Wisconsin, Madison, WI

Sutro Library, San Francisco State University, CA

Western Reserve Historical Society, Cleveland, OH

(*Note*: For a listing of libraries with genealogical collections, see P. William Filby, *Directory of American Libraries with Genealogy or Local History Collections*, Wilmington, DE: Scholarly Resources, Inc., 1988.)

around the world, each usually located in an LDS Church building. For decades the LDS Church has been microfilming millions of records from around the globe and collecting books of published genealogies and biographies. In the LDS Family History Centers, the public has access to computerized records and can order books and microfilm to be sent to a branch center from the main Family History Library in Salt Lake City. To find a center close to you, look for a listing in your telephone book for the nearest congregation of the Church of Jesus Christ of Latter-day Saints, and call and ask where the nearest LDS Family History Center is located. Or, contact a public library and ask them where the nearest one is.

The flagship of America's great general libraries is the Library of Congress. In order to be an outstanding reference center to service the A-to-Z demands for information from federal government agencies, the Library of Congress seeks to obtain and provide copies of nearly every book published in the United States. The U.S. copyright office, where all publishers must obtain copyrights for their books, operates in connection with it. To obtain a copyright, the publisher must give the Library of Congress copies of the book.

In the subject areas of history, biography, and genealogy, the Library of Congress contains an incredible collection of books and even typescript materials. Their card catalog of holdings is computerized and can be accessed throughout the United States. You can search the Library of Congress's holdings for genealogy books with your families' surnames. To do that, visit a nearby university library or large public library, which can connect with the Library of Congress's computerized card catalog.

Every state sponsors a major library devoted to historical materials related to that state. These state history libraries are located in each capital city, but some have branch libraries elsewhere. Every state has its own historical society or division of state history, whose operations revolve around the state's history library. Such state historical libraries contain large collections of published books and local sources useful to genealogists.

Even most university libraries and several major public libraries have sections and librarians just for genealogy and family history. If you live near one of these specialized libraries, take time to go there

and find out what genealogy holdings they have, if any, about each of your family lines.

Your best library work is local, in the area where your relatives that you are researching lived. Libraries and archives exist not only to warehouse records, but also to make those records available to researchers. Librarians and archivists, therefore, work hard to help the user find materials, so they create registers, inventories, finding aids, and guides to their records. The National Archives, for example, publishes a booklet called *Using Records in the National Archives for Genealogical Research.* It explains to researchers how they can find and use these federal records:

<table>
<tr><td>censuses</td><td>Washington, D.C., records</td></tr>
<tr><td>naturalization records</td><td>land and homestead records</td></tr>
<tr><td>personnel records</td><td>passenger lists</td></tr>
<tr><td>military service records</td><td>Native American records</td></tr>
</table>

Most archives, and several libraries, have tight security requirements. In some cases you have to show photo identification; leave coats, purses, and briefcases in lockers on the premises; and take notes only in pencil rather than ink. Most archives and libraries provide typewriters or electrical outlets for computers or typewriters.

Collected Genealogies on Computer Databases

Genealogy databases for use on computers are mushrooming in number and in coverage of genealogy sources. Private firms and public agencies are inputting records and indexing them to be accessed from personal computers. These computerized genealogical records are of two kinds: (1) compiled genealogies that link people together, or that at least provide the vital birth, marriage, and death information about individuals; and (2) computerized records that are indexed so that you can do research with them more readily than going to county courthouses or church parishes to find the information yourself. Before looking at the second type of computerized records, which is something you do as part of genealogy research (see "Genealogy, Computers, and the Internet" later in this chapter), examine the first type to find vital information already pulled together about your relatives.

The National Archives

The dates of records in the National Archives include the Federal population censuses from 1790-1920; military records from the American Revolution to 1900 and ship passenger arrival lists from 1820 through 1957.

Database and Index

Ancestral File is a database of linked individuals whose genealogy records have been submitted to the file by LDS members and nonmembers.

International Genealogical Index, or IGI, is an incredible index of millions of names in a database that provides birth and marriage details.

Private genealogy businesses are constantly creating new databases and making them available by subscription, on the Internet, or on disks that you can purchase. These include collections of pedigree and family group charts. You can look at compiled chart information, as well as names of individuals accompanied by their vital details. The LDS Church Family History Library is a main producer of such computerized data, as are several private firms marketing genealogy products.

A primary starting point is a massive database called *FamilySearch*, available for research in LDS Family History Centers and larger libraries that have genealogy sections. *FamilySearch* includes six record sets, and is adding more sets all the time. *FamilySearch* contains two files of compiled genealogical information, listed by name, that genealogy researchers have found and submitted to the master file. Using your ancestors' names, look them up in both the Ancestral File and the IGI (International Genealogical Index), and copy whatever information is there.

Similarly, private companies have generated and made available to the public large files of family group and pedigree charts. United Ancestry developed a CD-ROM package containing nearly one million pedigree-linked names. Everton, a leading genealogy company, produced a CD-ROM called *Family Pedigrees: Everton Publishers, 1500–1990*, containing some 100,000 family groups, or about one million names. Also, individual genealogists with their own Web sites have put thousands of pedigree and family group charts on the Internet (see the Internet discussion later in this chapter).

Step 6, then, is to look for books and databases of genealogy materials already collected and made accessible for research. In Step 7, you become the researcher who searches in the original records themselves.

Step 7: Research in Local Records

In many towns and counties there are local genealogical societies whose members compile genealogies of residents who have lived there since the founding of the community. They also produce finding aids to the area's birth, marriage, and death records. Some

publish newsletters containing lists of names extracted from such local records as wills and probates, cemetery headstones, property tax records, and church christening records.

Libraries are primarily repositories for books, printed materials, typescripts, and some handwritten records. Every state has an official archive where state government records, including those for counties and cities, are stored and made accessible. State archives are located in the state's capital city. Official government records, housed, cataloged, and indexed in the federal and state archives, contain great treasures of genealogical information. Therefore, the serious genealogy-seeker needs to do research in records found not only in libraries but also in government archives.

What follows is a discussion of the major types of records genealogy researchers find most useful.

State Vital Records of Birth, Marriage, Death, and Divorce

Because your goal is to find vital information about a relative, a good starting point for your research is with the official vital records—the birth, marriage, and death information recorded in the locality where your relative lived, or where you think he or she lived.

Each state has the equivalent of a bureau of vital records. Sometimes it is called "Bureau of Vital Statistics," "Division of Records and Statistics," "Division of Public Health," "Vital Records Division," or some similar title. No matter the name, the state agency is where you go to obtain birth, marriage, and death certificates. States require a fee for each certificate, from $5 to $20. Sometimes you pay first and then wait one to two months for the state agency to mail the record to you.

Birth records are confidential in most states, and are available only to the person whose certificate it is and to that person's descendants. Birth records typically contain the person's name, the date and place of birth of the individual, his or her parents' names (and sometimes their ages, residences, places of birth, and occupations), and the name of the person who delivered the baby.

Two Great Finding Aids

Two comprehensive books of finding aids for genealogy records, which many consider to be the bible reference books of the trade, are both published by the genealogy company Ancestry, Inc., in Salt Lake City, Utah:

Alice Eichholz, ed., *Ancestry's Red Book: American State, County, and Town Sources* (rev. ed. 1992).

Loretto D. Szucs and Sandra Hargreaves Luebking, *The Source: A Guidebook of American Genealogy*, rev. ed. 1997 (Salt Lake City, UT: Ancestry, Inc., 1997).

Death records contain information similar to that found on birth certificates, as well as the residence of the deceased person, cause of death, information about the undertaker, and the doctor's signature. A married woman's death record usually is filed under her married name, not her maiden name.

Until the mid-1800s, divorces were granted by courts and through specific acts of state legislatures. In 1866, the federal government declared that a legislative divorce was illegal. Since then, and in many states well before then, divorce has been a civil action determined in local courts. Divorce records, therefore, are found in court volumes containing normal court cases, in separate records books designated just for divorce cases, or in specialized records books. Court docket books list the plaintiff and defendant and the date the divorce case started. Divorce records contain the court's judgment. Files in the divorce case include vital facts about the parties to the divorce and about their children. Marriage data is also included. Rights to privacy cause divorce records to be closed for a period of years, so they can be accessed only with the permission of the divorced party. You should consult published guides to vital records and to the courts in the state where the divorce took place.

Table 2-1 shows that most states did not assume legal responsibility for vital records until the turn of the last century. The first to start keeping vital records was Massachusetts in 1841, and the last was New Mexico in 1920. You can find vital records at the state records agency for people who were born, married, or died during the twentieth century, and in a few states for earlier years.

Contact a state agency to find out if it has birth, marriage, or death information you are seeking for a particular relative. To do that you need the agency's name and address. A valuable, inexpensive guide to states and the departments in which their vital records are kept is *Where to Write for Vital Records: Births, Deaths, Marriages, and Divorces*. It is published by the U.S. Department of Health and Human Services. It lists each state, then shows where each type of vital record is kept, gives addresses for obtaining the documents, and provides a near-current list of the price for each certificate. The booklet is obtainable for a small fee by writing to the U.S. Government Printing Office, Washington, D.C. 20402. Find the right address and then send an inquiry letter to that agency, stating what specific birth, marriage, or death information you are seeking, and ask them how much they charge for the certificates. Include in your letter a self-addressed, stamped envelope to make it easy for them to reply to you.

Local Vital Records

Your search for birth, marriage, and death data before 1900 will take you beyond official state records and into other kinds of records at the local level. In terms of marriages, local civil governments have been in charge of recording marriage information in marriage registers since the beginnings of the county or town. You can find marriage records from the early 1600s in New England towns, and from the early 1700s in counties in the South. For a small fee, town and county officials will provide you with copies of requested marriage entries.

The U.S. Census Bureau

The Census Bureau doesn't provide genealogical information. The Bureau *collects* the data. You can get access to census records through the National Archives Microfilm Rental Program, which many public libraries and historical societies participate in.

Census information collected from individuals is made available to the public after 72 years. Information on businesses becomes available after 30 years.

Prior to the states taking legal responsibility for vital records, a small proportion of the nation's counties and towns registered the local vital information. New England states have more complete vital records from before 1900 than most other regions because local officials recorded the life events in their area. Nearly two-thirds of Massachusetts towns, for example, have published their early vital records. Rhode Island has published vital records annually since 1847.

TABLE 2-1					
STATE	DEATH	BIRTH	STATE	DEATH	BIRTH
Alabama	1908	1908	Montana	1907	1907
Alaska	1913	1913	Nebraska	1905	1905
Arizona	1909	1909	Nevada	1911	1911
Arkansas	1914	1914	New Hampshire	1905	1905
California	1905	1905	New Jersey	1848	1848
Colorado	1907	1907	New Mexico	1919	1919
Connecticut	1897	1897	New York	1880	1880
Delaware	1881	1881	North Carolina	1913	1913
D.C.	1855	1871	North Dakota	1908	1908
Florida	1899	1899	Ohio	1909	1909
Georgia	1919	1919	Oklahoma	1908	1908
Hawaii	1896	1896	Oregon	1903	1903
Idaho	1911	1911	Pennsylvania	1906	1906
Illinois	1916	1916	Puerto Rico	1931	1931
Indiana	1900	1907	Rhode Island	1852	1852
Iowa	1880	1880	South Carolina	1915	1915
Kansas	1911	1911	South Dakota	1905	1905
Kentucky	1911	1911	Tennessee	1914	1914
Louisiana	1914	1914	Texas	1903	1903
Maine	1892	1892	Utah	1905	1905
Maryland	1898	1898	Vermont	1857	1857
Massachusetts	1841	1841	Virginia	1912	1912
Michigan	1867	1867	Washington	1907	1907
Minnesota	1900	1900	West Virginia	1917	1917
Mississippi	1912	1912	Wisconsin	1907	1907
Missouri	1910	1910	Wyoming	1909	1909

Federal Ten-Year Censuses

Starting in 1790 and every ten years thereafter, federal government census takers have gone through cities, towns, and countrysides counting and listing residents. These census records now are on microfilm, and most have name indexes. (The 1890 census is an exception: An accidental fire destroyed these records.)

Even though the census officially is a federal government record, it really is a local record that identifies the populace place by place. Many states have name indexes to the federal censuses of their state. A seventy-year restriction on access to censuses means that the 1920 census is the latest one you can consult, and that the 1930 census will be open to research in the year 2000.

Copies of the federal censuses are widely available. National Archives branches (see list earlier in this chapter) have microfilm copies for you to use, as do major universities. State historical societies and archives have at least that state's complete censuses. The LDS Family History Library makes copies of particular parts of the censuses available to patrons at its branch libraries.

When you find your ancestor on a census, you find a lot of other valuable information, too. You find your ancestor's location. You find how many others were living in the household, and, starting with the 1850 census, the names of those in the household. By tracing your relative through several censuses, you find out where they lived when, the ages of the occupants of each household, and places of birth. However, census information is only as good as the person who gave the census taker the information, and sometimes guesses or even false information was provided. And, census takers missed people and so did not count or list everybody.

You need to look for an index to the censuses before you go to the census pages themselves. Most but not all of the censuses are well indexed. Every census from 1790 to 1850 has statewide indexes, as do most of the 1860 and 1870 censuses. The indexes are printed or on microfilm or microfiche. You can even find some county indexes to federal censuses, prepared by local genealogists or librarians.

Indexers of the 1880, 1900, 1910, and 1920 censuses used a "Soundex" system, which is a phonetic index. That is, it indexes together those names that sound the same or similar rather than in

Census Facts

Since a congressional mandate in 1790, censuses have polled different kinds of information. More recent censuses contain more information than earlier ones.

Between 1790 and 1850, the ten-year censuses only obtained the name of the head of the household and listed others in the household according to sex and age categories.

In 1850, the census began to list the names, ages, occupations, and birthplaces of each person.

The 1880 census was the first to list the state or country of birth of each person's parents. The census also began to indicate what the relationship is among those in the same household.

The 1910 census was the first to give the month and year of birth. It also includes each person's age, the number of years the person had been married, his or her immigration year, and citizenship status.

Archives for Major U.S. Religious Denominations

Adventists, Washington, D.C.
American Baptists,
   Rochester, NY
Southern Baptists,
   Nashville, TN
Brethren in Christ Church,
   Grantham, PA
Church of Christ, Scientist,
   Boston, MA
Church of Jesus Christ of
   Latter-day Saints
   (Mormons),
   Salt Lake City, UT
Churches of Christ,
   Memphis, TN
Congregational, Boston, MA
Disciples of Christ,
   Nashville, TN
Greek Orthodox,
   New York, NY
Jewish, Cincinnati, OH;
   Waltham, MA
Evangelical Lutherans,
   Chicago, IL

alphabetical order. Thus, Smith, Smythe, and Schmidt are listed together. Instructions in the front of the published state indexes show you how to code the consonants in the last names you are looking up, and then how to find the right microfilm index that contains those names. That index in turn shows you what microfilm reel of the federal census to view.

Federal ten-year censuses are not the only censuses taken in this country. There have been special federal censuses, including the 1840 List of Pensioners, which lists pensioners of the Revolutionary War or other military service, and the 1890 List of Union Veterans, including their widows. American colonies took censuses. U.S. territories seeking statehood administered censuses. Cities and states have conducted their own censuses. Among special state censuses are those conducted prior to 1925 in Illinois, Iowa, Kansas, Massachusetts, Minnesota, Mississippi, New Jersey, New York, and Wisconsin. State censuses can be found by looking in library catalogs under the name of the state and then under the "census records" listings.

Most libraries with censuses have finding aids that explain how to use each census. Some have specially printed forms designed for particular censuses, making it easy for you to take notes.

When you find a relative in a census, take notes, but also make a photocopy from the microfilm. Be sure you list on the photocopy the name of the census, the location, the microfilm number, and the census book and page number.

Local Church and Religious Records

In addition to state and local records, local churches have maintained registries of births, marriages, and deaths.

America has a diverse religious background. Over the centuries, its residents have belonged to hundreds of different churches, synagogues, and religious organizations. Religious bodies have kept records of their members and of ordinances and special ceremonies, including baptisms, weddings, and funerals. Very often, religious records are the only source you can find for marriage information in early American communities.

You can consult records of religious groups in the communities where your relatives lived. Contact today's churches or religious groups in that locality and ask where the old records are. Some churches have centralized their old records, but others retain them within the community. J. Gordon Melton's *The Encyclopedia of American Religions* 2nd ed., *published by Gale Research Co., Detroit, 1987,* provides addresses for more than 1,000 denominations.

(continued)

Missouri Synod Lutherans, St. Louis, MO

United Methodists, Madison, NJ

Pentecostal, Tulsa, OK

Presbyterians, Philadelphia, PA; Montreat, NC

Episcopalian, Check local parishes

Reformed Church, New Brunswick, NJ

Roman Catholic, Notre Dame University, South Bend, IN; Catholic University, Washington, D.C.

Quakers (Society of Friends), Swarthmore, PA for Hicksite records; Haverford, PA for Orthodox records

United Church of Christ, Boston, MA; Lancaster, PA

Unitarian and Universalist, Harvard Divinity School, Cambridge, MA

Cemetery Records

Cemetery records include tombstones, sextons' lists of burials, and plot ownership and maintenance information. Cemeteries have been created by towns, cities, churches, and even by families on their own farm properties. In thousands of counties, local volunteers have located public and private cemeteries and hand-copied headstone inscription information. This information has been typed up and made available at local libraries and state historical societies. Published guides to a given state's records can tell you where to find cemeteries and their records.

Court Records

Court records can provide you with birth, marriage, and death details; immigration and citizenship information; names of others in the family; dates and places of residency; and career and religion details. Probate records, dealing with wills and estates and inheritances, contain valuable genealogical information. Citizenship records, too, can be extremely informative about an immigrant ancestor.

America's judicial system includes state courts that handle civil and criminal matters relating to state laws, and federal courts that deal with matters of federal law. Courts have existed to deal with particular areas and jurisdictions, such as county, circuit, district, superior, and supreme courts; and with specific legal matters, such as orphans courts, probate courts, and common pleas courts. (Regarding adoptions, see Chapter 3.)

Court records are harder to access than other types of records. They are neither indexed well nor filed together in one book. Court records are in sequential record books related to how the case pro-

Records in Great Britain

When the Normans conquered England in 1066 they set about to compile a land register as a basis of regular taxation. The information was finally put together and published in what was called the Domesday Book of 1086. Copies of the Domesday Book of 1086 and be found in most research libraries.

Unfortunately the next edition of the Domesday Book was not published until 1146, however records of taxation or litigation can be helpful in tracing your family's genealogy in Great Britain.

gressed—from scheduling in docket books, to actual court minutes, to judgments rendered, to case files containing documents relating to the finished case. They contain legal terminology sometimes hard to understand. And, while federal court records before 1950 usually can be located in a National Archives branch, many state and local court records have not been collected into the state archive but remain in the courthouse, where you have to go to research them. Despite their complexities, though, court records are sources to explore, especially after other records have been searched.

Probate Records and Wills

Probably less than 25 percent of Americans draw up wills, which are legal documents specifying how the person wants his or her estate—belongings and assets—bequeathed to relatives and others. When a person who has left a will dies, a probate court carries out the will's instructions. The judge makes the final decision regarding how the estate is to be distributed, taking into account the validity of the will and the legal demands of creditors.

For those ancestors who left a will that went through probate, you can find court records of those proceedings. These probate records (alternatively called a probate packet, case file, estate file, or probate estate papers) contain a copy of the will, the individual's death date, the names and relationships of family members and their current residences, and an inventory of the person's property and its value. Records can identify adoption and guardianship details, too.

When looking for a relative's probate records, start by referring to a published guide to probate records, which your library has on the shelves or can obtain for you. You need to check for probate records in each locality where the person owned property. For example, if James Butler owned land on both sides of the Kentucky-Tennessee border when he died in the 1840s, two counties, each in a different state, might have probate files on him.

Contact the county courthouse. Address your inquiry to the probate court, and request a search of their indexes for the time period and surnames you are interested in. You can request photocopies of probate packets.

Newspapers

For many decades, local newspapers have published obituaries and lists of births in the area. Many small-town newspapers have published announcements of engagements, reports of weddings, and notices of divorces. You need to know the approximate date and place in order to search successfully for newspaper notices about your relatives.

Libraries contain guides to newspapers in the various states. These guides are organized by location. They list what newspapers were published during which period of time, and then they show where surviving copies of those newspapers can be seen. Many states have microfilm collections of their communities' newspapers, and you can see these microfilms at the state's historical society or in your own library through inter-library loans.

Some researchers obtain information by putting an ad or article in a newspaper in the place where their family had ties, asking for information or for the names of people to contact about the family.

Obituaries

Newspaper obituaries were commonplace during the twentieth century, less so in the late nineteenth century, and rare before that. When you know the death date, or approximate death date, for one of your ancestors, and know where he or she lived at the time, check a local newspaper for an obituary. Obituaries, while not always accurate, sometimes provide the date and place of birth of the deceased, the parents' names, and the names of siblings and other kin and where the deceased lived. Descendants of these relatives (hence your distant cousins) sometimes can be tracked down and asked for information relating to that common ancestor.

City Directories

Annual city and county directories, which contain alphabetical lists of names and addresses of residents, have been published since the early days of our republic. These directories have no relationship to telephone books.

City directories provide a wealth of historical and personal information such as lists of city residents and their occupations and addresses; civic information; names and addresses of churches, schools, and city and county officers; and sometimes maps. Directories not only list the residents alphabetically by surname of the head of the household, but they also give a summary of the city's situation that year (population, description of the place, main economic factors, thumbnail histories of the community, etc.); lists of businesses, churches, and government agencies; and advertisements for local businesses.

City directories are found in libraries by looking under the city name and under "directories" or "gazetteers." In situations where the cities and towns are very small, the directories are county directories, with listings for each town and for rural residents, but without street addresses.

For a particular town's directory, contact the local public library or the state historical society. Better yet, major public and university libraries have a massive microfiche collection of city directories dating back from before 1881 called *City Directories of the United States*. A register accompanies the collection, listing all the cities for which directories are available. The Library of Congress provides the largest collection of city directories.

Immigration and Naturalization Records

If our immigrant ancestors generated any records by coming to America, the records would be of two kinds: ship arrival passenger lists and naturalization records from seeking citizenship.

Ship Passenger Arrival Lists

By now, experts have pulled together indexes of early passenger arrival records of immigrants who came to America prior to 1820. One such standard reference index is P. William Filby's ten-volume *Passenger and Immigration Lists Index*, Gale Research Co., Detroit, 1981. Other passenger arrival list indexes are available from the National Archives and through major genealogy centers, such as the LDS Family History Library in Salt Lake City, Utah.

Between 1820 and 1902, when ships carrying immigrants docked in America their officers were required to turn in passenger lists to U.S. Customs agents. These handwritten lists in large ledger books contain each immigrant's name, age, sex, occupation, country of origin, and place of intended residence. Starting in 1883 ships' masters had to turn in a ship manifest of passengers to the U.S. immigration authorities—later the Immigration and Naturalization Service. These lists included the exact birthplace or last residence, marital status, previous U.S. residence, and names of relatives in the home country and the United States for each immigrant.

Immigrants arrived through various ports on the east, west, and south coasts of the United States. Not all passenger lists for all ports have survived, but thousands have. Not all of those passenger arrival lists have been indexed yet, though. New York City was the main arrival port between 1820 and 1920, processing some 24 million immigrants. The National Archives has New York passenger arrival lists for the years 1820 to 1919. However, indexes only cover the years 1820 to 1846 and then resume for the years 1902 to 1920. There are passenger arrival lists for Boston for the years 1820 to 1874 and from 1883 to 1935, but not all of those lists are indexed. For other port cities, the same kinds of patterns for lists and indexes hold true.

Among the main departure ports in Europe for emigrants going to America was Hamburg, Germany. Between 1850 and 1934, Hamburg recorded the names of emigrants leaving from its port. Those departure lists are indexed, and both the lists and indexes can be seen on microfilm in major U.S. libraries.

Naturalization and Citizenship Records

Millions of immigrants to the United States filed for or became naturalized citizens. In the process, they created a paper trail of records, which contain useful genealogy information, that you can seek.

Up until 1952, the immigrant seeking citizenship appeared before a federal or district court judge and declared his intent to become a citizen. The court required him to file papers of intent, or First Papers. (After 1952, a verbal commitment replaced the filing of intent

Immigration Records

Immigration records for major US ports, Boston, New York, Philadelphia, Baltimore and New Orleans, have been kept since 1820. Other ports such as Mobile and Galveston began keeping records later in the 1800's. Western ports such as the San Francisco and Seattle ports began keeping records in the last decade of the 1800's.

The immigrations records, are microfilmed and available at the National Archives. The information includes: name of ever passenger on ship, including those born or died on board; full name; age, sex; place of origin and destination.

papers.) The immigrant then had to file Final Papers verifying that he had met the requirements for citizenship. Over the years, our country's requirements for citizenship have changed, but basically the person had to prove residency in America for a certain period of time, usually five years, and good moral character. So, the immigrant provided supporting information, such as affidavits and statements by witnesses, which went into his citizenship application file. After 1906, he had to bring to court a certificate of arrival, showing when, where, and how he entered America. He then had to take an oath of allegiance to the United States and sign it. After that, the court issued an order of citizenship and gave the applicant a certificate of his citizenship.

A naturalization file contains reliable information about the immigrant's date and place of birth; place of origin; date of arrival in America and sometimes the name of the ship; the Americanization of his name (from an Old Country name to a less foreign-sounding name); and his places of residence in America.

When researching for older naturalization records, start by looking in court records for the county or city where you know, or think, your immigrant ancestor lived. Since 1929 most naturalization processes have taken place in federal courts. When seeking these more recent naturalization files, you should visit your library and consult a guidebook to the state's records. This guidebook will tell you what court records to check and where they are located. Also, you can consult guidebooks designed to help you find your immigrant ancestor.

The Immigration and Naturalization Service in Washington, D.C., has an index and copies of naturalization records for 1906 to 1956. The Service's district offices hold the records for the years after 1956. You can send inquiries to the INS, 425 Eye Street, NW, Washington, D.C. 20536.

Military Records

Among the biggest sets of records in the National Archives is those of our country's military units and personnel. America has fought in many wars. Millions of our citizens have served in the armed forces. Chances are good that one or more of your relatives served at some time or another in the military. If they did, the military offices kept records about them and their service.

Families do a pretty good job of passing down the generations the names of relatives who served in the Revolutionary War, the Civil War, or the two World Wars. But, even if your family has no tradition of military service, it's still worth checking to see if male ancestors who lived during the war periods did in fact serve. It's possible, too, that an ancestor enlisted in the military during peacetime.

Four kinds of military records contain personal information about the serviceperson. First, there is a service record of his or her actual participation in a branch of the armed forces. The service record includes a muster roll of his or her enlistment; personal details such as physical descriptions, marital status, residence, occupation, and birth information; and the muster-out roll and discharge details. And, for those who served voluntarily during wartime between 1775 and 1903, the federal government created a compiled service record. Also in the service record are miscellaneous records that include payroll information, hospital registers, prison and court martial documents, and promotion facts.

A second military record deals with veteran's benefits. Federal and state governments granted certain veterans pensions or free bounty lands as rewards and compensation for their service, or as payments for disabilities caused by war. A veteran's pension file is in the National Archives. In the file is his application for a pension and documentation of his disability, if any. Likewise, a veteran's widow's pension file contains useful life and family history details. Indexes to pension records are available for the Revolutionary War, War of 1812, Mexican War, Civil War, Spanish-American War, the Philippines Insurrection, and for various Indian Wars.

Between 1776 and 1855, the federal government also provided bounty lands for those who served in the nation's wars. Veterans or their heirs could claim this bounty land by filing an application at a nearby courthouse. Approved applicants received a land warrant, which most veterans either sold or exchanged rather than to take possession of the land itself.

1861

Civil War

The third set of military records, draft records, were begun in 1863 when the government initiated the draft. The government has maintained draft records since then. During World War I, all men eligible for military service had to register for the draft, and those registration cards are available to researchers. The file, called the "World War I Selective Service Draft Registration Cards, 1917–1918," includes cards on about 24 million men. You can see the cards or send an inquiry about a particular serviceman to:

Archives Branch
Federal Center
557 St. Joseph Avenue,
East Point, GA 3004

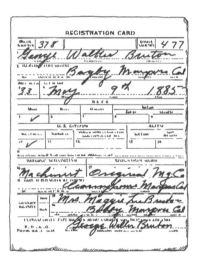 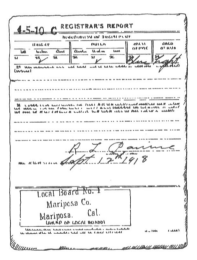

Then there are the records of the regular military forces. The National Archives has seventy-one reels of microfilm that contain the *Registers of Enlistments in the U.S. Army, 1798–1914*. These registers contain personal information about each enlistee's birthplace, age, occupation, and physical description.

The Veterans Administration in Washington, D.C., maintains an index record of all servicemen and women buried in national or federal cemeteries.

Land Records

Since the first decade that Europeans came to the United States, settlers have claimed ownership of land and have bought and sold it. Land transactions involved paperwork—deeds of ownership, a government record of sales and purchases, and maps and written descriptions of the land. Land records, then, can provide names of people and show when they lived and exactly where they owned property. Much of the present United States started out as federal land, which the government sold to land owners. Therefore, the National Archives and its branches have federal lands records showing transactions wherein private individuals obtained public lands, putting those lands forever in the private domain.

Several types of federal land grants produced the transfers of public-domain lands to private ownership. The best-known grant is the homestead, which, after 1862, private persons obtained at minimal cost by living on a parcel of land for five years and making improvements on it. The federal government granted lands to states, to railroads, and to military veterans (bounty lands). The government opened a case file on each person who obtained land, filing therein applications, affidavits, and correspondence relating to the transaction.

For information about federal land grants, contact the National Archives in Washington, D.C., or obtain one of their guide booklets about federal land records. Also check with large libraries to view published volumes of transcripts and indexes for portions of the federal land records, by state or by county.

For land transactions involving private properties, contact the local county recorder's office in the courthouse in the county where the property is located. Ask to see the deed and mortgage books; these have indexes. To inquire, you need to identify the land's location in terms of the grid system of land surveys—what range, township, and section number the property is in.

Maps

Good map collections are found in libraries, county recorder's offices, state historical societies, and National Archives branch offices.

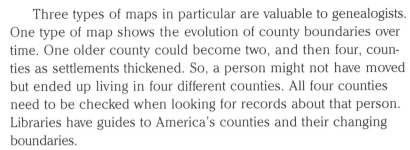

The Oral Tradition

To read a genealogy from the oral tradition that was written down, look to the Old Testament or the Koran. Most historians agree, that the genealogies found in the Book of Genesis probably originated in oral tradition and may have existed for many generations before being written down. Behind all early genealogies, such as the lists of the kings of Sumer in Ancient Mesopotamia, lies oral tradition.

Three types of maps in particular are valuable to genealogists. One type of map shows the evolution of county boundaries over time. One older county could become two, and then four, counties as settlements thickened. So, a person might not have moved but ended up living in four different counties. All four counties need to be checked when looking for records about that person. Libraries have guides to America's counties and their changing boundaries.

The second type of map that is very helpful to researchers is a period map, which shows the place decades or centuries ago when your ancestors lived there. Also of great value to genealogists is the third type of map: land ownership maps, produced by local governments and by commercial companies.

Railroad Records

Railroad employees often were not property owners and did not stay in one location for long periods of time. Therefore, they sometimes do not show up in conventional records. Two types of railroad records that contain useful genealogical information are the Railroad Retirement Board Records and the Railroad Company Employment Records.

The Railroad Retirement Board Records are a product of acts of Congress in the mid-1930s that created a federal railroad-retirement organization. To qualify for the retirement program, employees had to work for the railroad for at least ten years. Thus, files for short-term employees are not found in those records. More than one million railroad employees and nearly as many spouses, along with two million survivors, have benefitted from the retirement program. In order to receive benefits, applicants had to file forms, and these forms comprise a valuable genealogical source. Also filed are employment histories and death certificates. To inquire about the files, write to:

United States Railroad Retirement Board
884 Rush Street
Chicago, IL 60611

The Railroad Company Employment Records, some going back to the nineteenth century, belong to the scores of major and minor railroads. So, you must look for the records either at the railroad company's archives or in museums and historical societies. Southern Pacific employment records, for example, are in the California State Railroad Museum Library in Sacramento. Records for the Burlington Northern, the Northern Pacific, and the Great Northern Railroads are in the Minnesota Historical Society in St. Paul.

To find a particular railroad's records, consult one of several catalogs and directories. Very helpful is a section of the genealogy reference book *The Source: A Guidebook of American Genealogy,* (published by Ancestry, Inc., Utah) called "Fifty Largest Transportation Companies." It provides addresses of various railroad companies.

Fraternal Societies

Because America historically has been a nation of joiners, your ancestors might have belonged to an association, fraternal order, lodge, or secret society. Millions of Americans have belonged to such societies as:

Ancient Free and Accepted Masons (Freemasonry)
Order of Eastern Star
International Order of Odd Fellows (IOOF)
Benevolent and Protective Order of Elks (BPOE)
Lithuanian Alliance of America
Ancient Order of Hibernians of America
Knights of the Maccabees
Modern Woodmen of America

In order to join, the person had to file an application, and the organization also kept records of members' participation. Possibly you will discover that a relative you are researching belonged to one of these organizations—from evidence found in local histories, in obituaries, on headstones, in family sources, or among the ancestor's artifacts. If so, consider contacting the organization and asking about records of your ancestor. Addresses for these organizations are

Genealogies with a Purpose

Many of the genealogies from the oral tradition were influenced by cultural or religious groups. In some cultures, such as in ancient Greece and Rome, the purpose of the genealogy was an attempt to show descent from an eponym—a person, probably mythical, from whom a people, tribe, clan, or a country got its name.

obtainable in Alvin J. Schmidt's, *Fraternal Organizations* (Westport, CT: Greenwood Press, 1980).

Genealogy, Computers, and the Internet

The Internet, or information highway as it is called, is an invisible telecommunication spider-web of electronic lines and connections that link together many Web sites of information. Even if you haven't had hands-on experience with the Internet, you probably know people who use it. Millions of Americans with computers are linked to the Internet.

The Internet is able to bring the world, it seems, to the desktop computer. This ability is revolutionizing how we do genealogy—making some genealogy research faster, less costly, and easier than the old, standard methods of research. The Internet is linking together libraries and genealogists, databases and home computers. For those with access to computers, the Internet is making genealogy know-how and source materials available to more people than was happening before the information highway age. If you don't own a computer, you probably can use one at a public library that is already connected to an Internet server.

Lots of genealogy-related material is "on the Net." However, don't plan on finding your genealogy already done for you, that all you have to do is push a "print" button to get it. Rather, expect the Internet to show you where and how to research particular kinds of records, and to allow you to look at some records that are computerized.

To look, scan, or "surf" the Internet, you need a computer. Then you need to subscribe to an online Internet service. America Online, CompuServe, and Prodigy are perhaps the best known right now, but there are dozens of national and local services you can join for a monthly fee. To connect your computer to their service, you need a modem, which transforms electronic signals for your computer, and a telephone line that plugs into your computer.

Once connected, your start-up menu on your opening screen will let you choose the Internet option and then connect you with your

server. When your server's page comes on your screen, you can then access a number of network sites and programs. The Internet is much like a phone system for your computer screen—you type in an address or Web site number and your Internet service connects you to that Web site. Once there, the site has a homepage that tells you what to do and how to view information files available for you at that site.

You can look for subjects on the Internet by going to a search engine site. Some of the search engines now popular are Yahoo!, Excite, AltaVista, and Infoseek. By going to the search command they give you and following its instructions, you can enter the word *genealogy* and the search engine will display on your screen a vast number of genealogy sites. You can go to any of those sites by moving your cursor (pointer) to that underlined site and clicking the mouse. One genealogy site was developed to work with a PBS TV ten-part genealogy how-to-do-it series called *Ancestors*. You can access this Web site at:

http://www.kbyu.byu.edu/ancestors.html

When you call up and go onto the World Wide Web or other gateways to the Internet, each spot on the Net will offer you connections to a dozen other sites that contain information. You can go to site after site, and no two sites will suggest the same list of next sites for you to check. Even though you go to one site, learn from it, and then go to another one it recommends—and then do the same thing again from that next site—your screen menu has a wonderful "go back to" command, like a backspace on a typewriter. This command lets you instantly go back to the previous file, and back to the one before that if you want, so that you can go backward through the same Web connections you came forward on.

Many Internet sites have a FAQ—Frequently Asked Questions—file that provides valuable help to beginners. Also, the Internet will let you "chat" with others who have similar interests or are doing the same surname searches as you are. You can visit with others on any number of "bulletin boards" and in "chat rooms." Also, hundreds of Computer Interest Groups, or CIGs, have formed. A magazine called

An Archivists' Tip: The World Wide Web

Here are the on-line addresses for popular Internet search engines:

Yahoo!	http://www.yahoo.com
Alta Vista	http://altavista.digital.com
Web Crawler	http://www.query.webcrawler.com
Excite	http://www.excite.com
InfoSeek	http://www.guide.infoseek.com

Here's a list of the major on-line services to contact about rates and memberships.

America On-line	(800) 827-6364
Compuserve	(800) 848-8990
The Microsoft Network	(800) 386-5550

The Web is extremely helpful in finding where to look for genealogical information.

But do not expect that you will be able to do your genealogical research on the World Wide Web. Old records are handwritten on paper and now exist either on paper or on microfilm and only a very few are in a electronic format. It is extremely expensive to convert old records to an electronic format.

Genealogical Computing features a directory of CIGs in its first issue each year. Or, librarians can help you find such directories.

To journey into the world of the Internet and become involved in remote accessing of information from your home computer is an exciting experience of discovery. A few genealogy Web sites are becoming known as the best ones at which to begin a genealogy search. They have menus of the best Web sites to be consulted, and they group these by category and/or location, such as adoption records, county records, vital records, Jewish records, libraries, surname files, census indexes, etc. Among the most widely used Web sites that people check first when seeking genealogy information on the Net are:

National Archives	http://www.nara.gov
Library of Congress	http://lcweb.loc.gov
Everton Publishers' homepage	http://www.everton.com
Genealogy Online	http://genealogy.org
Genealogy homepage	http://www.genhomepage.com/world.html
Infobases Family History Division	http://www.familyhistory.com
Genserv-World Wide Gedcom Data	http://soback.kornet.nm.kr/~cmanius/
Family Tree Maker Online	http://www.familytreemaker.com
Ancestry	http://www.ancestry.com
Cyndi's List of Genealogical Sites	http://www.oz.net/-cyndihow/sites.htm.
RootsWeb Genealogical Data Cooperative Page	http//www.rootsweb.com

Ancestry, perhaps America's leading commercial genealogy company, boasts on its Web site that it adds a new database every working day. Cyndi Howell's homepage (see "Cyndi's List" above) includes more than 20,000 links to information. It includes good links for those doing ethnic searches, and a continually updated list of family surname sites being posted by individual genealogists.

But because the network is so vast and is changing almost daily, much of what you read here will be outdated even before the printer's ink dries on this page.

A Web site that promises to become a *Yellow Pages* type of reference tool is the USGenWeb project. It is producing a Web page for most if not all counties in the United States, state by state. These sites offer the Net user an array of information about each county—lists of online databases; registration spots, where you can enter your own research interests and post your particular genealogical questions; lists of holdings in local libraries; addresses and phone numbers for local archives, genealogical societies, and libraries; information on how to find local church, cemetery, court, and land records; and contact persons who are willing to do genealogical research for a fee. The project's goal, as stated to Web users, is to make genealogy research, arranged by geographical location, available to everyone at no cost. The access address is:

http://www.usgenweb.com/XX

(In place of XX you type in the two-letter abbreviation of the state in which you want to do county research.)

Individual families also are creating their own Web pages, which you can find through some of the providers listed above, particularly Cyndi's List.

Records Available on Computer

Only a small proportion of computerized records are on the Internet that you can bring up on your screen and search. Thousands of valuable records, or databases, are computerized but available only on the palm-sized CD-ROM disks. Personal computers can have drives that let you look at 3.5" disks, perhaps the old 5¼" floppy disks, and CD-ROMs—like the music CDs you buy in a record store. With a CD drive in the computer, you can look at incredibly huge collections of records valuable to genealogy research. We are just at the beginning stage of this information revolution. Month by month the amount of files available for research mushrooms.

As noted, Ancestry, a leading genealogy firm, has as a slogan that it produces a new genealogy database for computer users every day. Examples of the types of records being input and then published on CD-ROMs are these recent databases from Ancestry:

Early Quaker Records of Virginia
Massachusetts Town Vital Records
Boston Births, Baptisms, Marriages, and Deaths, 1630–1699
Boston Births from 1700 to 1800
Virginia 1790 Census

Among the pioneering databases available on CD-ROMs through commercial firms, the LDS Church Family History Centers, or local libraries are:

Social Security Death Index. This file contains vital information for about 50 million deceased persons who had Social Security numbers and whose deaths were reported to the Social Security Administration. Most of the information is from 1962–1988, although the files include some data from as early as 1937. The file lists the person's name, Social Security number, birth date, state of residence where the Social Security number was issued, month and year of death, and place of residence at the time of death. The index is updated periodically.

Military Death Index. This file lists almost 100,000 U.S. servicemen and servicewomen who died in the Korea and Vietnam conflicts, including dates of birth and death, residence, place of death, and rank and service number.

Scottish Church Records Index. This is an index of nearly 10 million names, listed primarily in the Church of Scotland (Presbyterian) parish records and similar annals. A few other denominations' records are included. Entries date from the 1500s through 1854, with a few later entries. These are an excellent source for names, dates, places of birth, and marriages.

LDS Family History Library Catalog. This is a massive catalog of books and records housed in the Family History Library in Salt Lake City. Searches can be made by entering names, subjects, and places. Many of the sources in this central library can be sent by inter-center loan to the hundreds of LDS Family History Centers throughout the world.

Civil War Soldiers. A massive resource now being created is an index of some 5 million names of soldiers who served in the Civil War, on both sides of the conflict. The National Archives and National Park Service want the public to be able to enter a soldier's name in the computers at Civil War battlesites and other resource centers, and have the computer reveal life details and military service information about that soldier, along with information about his unit and its battles. Hopes are that libraries and the public can buy a CD-ROM set that contains this massive database.

General Land Office Records. The Bureau of Land Management is making available its General Land Office (GLO) records at their Springfield, Virginia, research room. Records for a dozen states are ready, and more are being prepared all the time. On a computer terminal, you can type in a name and find out if that person bought or homesteaded on federal lands. If they did, you can read and copy descriptions of the land and dates when it changed hands.

Early Massachusetts Records. A firm called Search & Research, in Wheat Ridge, Colorado, offers a *Mayflower Legacy* CD-ROM that contains vital records of Pilgrim-founded towns, and a fourteen CD-ROM set called *Early Vital Records of the Commonwealth of Massachusetts to 1850.*

Other major new databases are the 1851 English census; the 1871 Canadian census; various state censuses; increasing numbers of indexes for selected tax, marriage, and death records; various military records; and the Ellis Island immigration records.

E-mail

In addition to the Internet connections, your online service provider makes it possible for you to have e-mail, or electronic mail. You establish an e-mail address, and it allows you to send information to other people's e-mail addresses, and vice versa. People can communicate back and forth via their computer screens, even sometimes without delays. You can develop new friendships and establish

Computer Genealogy Programs

Two computer programs on the market that offer various help in putting together your family tree are: Mindscape Ultimate Family Tree and Borderbund® Family Tree Maker.

Mindscape Ultimate Family Tree is priced at $19.99 and for searching names, has access to one million names from completed genealogies and offer free professional genealogy searches of over 315 million names. It creates a complete family journal and includes a large selection of genealogy charts and reports.

Borderbund® Family TreeMaker ranges in price from $19.99 to $89.99, depending on how complex a program you buy. It offers multiple resources, including extensive federal records and a large genealogy database. In addition the program can print out family trees, books or reports as well as make family Web pages.

relationships with distant cousins through e-mail and over the Internet. (Many relatives now use e-mail as the way they keep in touch with each other, instead of phone calls or letters sent via the postal service.)

There is a danger, however, in totally trusting information you obtain via the Internet or even from CD-ROMs. Misinformation gets posted as well as facts. Errors, once put on the Net and copied, can spread quickly. What's circulated in written form seems to carry the ring of authority. But, like people who spray graffiti on buildings or the computer villains who take delight in creating viruses to cause computer users hardship, a few in genealogy circles maliciously post false genealogy information on the Net to harm genealogists.

Newsgroups and Bulletin Boards

Via computer you can access newsgroups, which are subject-specific electronic bulletin boards. Ask your Internet provider or a computer-savvy librarian how to access these. Among the leading genealogical newsgroups are:

alt.genealogy	soc.genealogy.methods
soc.genealogy.surnames	soc.genealogy.german
soc.genealogy.misc	soc.genealogy.marketplace
soc.genealogy.computing	soc.genealogy.jewish

CHAPTER THREE
Adoptions, Ethnic Research, and Specialized Genealogy Concerns

D ecades of genealogy research by America's European-rooted, white population have discovered the basics of how to track down their ancestors. But, to move beyond the western European, Christian, mainstream, bloodline family is to encounter different kinds of genealogy problems requiring special, tailored approaches.

Adoptees, for example, face unique and difficult challenges in tracing their family tree. For African-Americans in the United States, slavery created naming and record-keeping circumstances that make it impossible in too many cases to find out who a particular slave's parents were. Jewish people have unique cultural and political/geographic backgrounds that require specialized kinds of research. For families newly arrived in America, their genealogy efforts must concentrate on homeland records more than American sources.

For many of these special situations, genealogists are still in the pioneering stages of finding sources and figuring out research directions. Nevertheless, several good beginning guidebooks and places to find help are available.

Adoption

Adoptions make genealogy research difficult, even though legal adoptions generate a good amount of records and documentation. Court records for adoptions include such legal documents as consents to adopt, consents for adoption, and decrees of adoption. But adoption records in this century are sealed by court order and inaccessible to the public.

Adoptees who are legally blocked from knowing the identity of their birth parents face two choices, one easy and one hard. Many accept their adoptive parents as their only parents. Law makes the adoptee belong to this new family—it grafts them into the family tree. So, they take their adoptive parents' family lines and research genealogy along those. But others pursue an abiding curiosity about their biological parents and the generations before them. And, it is not uncommon for adoptees to seek and collect the genealogy of both their adoptive parents and their birth parents.

Women, usually single mothers, give up their children for adoption for many reasons. Courts and child welfare agencies have a legal say in how adoptions are arranged and carried out. The well-being of the mother giving up the child and the well-being of the child who becomes adopted are both best preserved when the adoptive parents can become the child's full parents in reality. Many adopted children never discover they were adopted. The state, the courts, and the adoption system must guarantee to the mother giving up the child and to the parents adopting the child that the birth mother's identity can be kept secret. Therefore, children who learn they are adopted face sturdy legal blockades when trying to find out who their birth parents are or were.

In most cases the birth parent or adopted child can be found, and most searchers ultimately find "a measure of completion." ("Search Shouldn't Be Taken Lightly," *Deseret News*, Nov. 23, 1995.) But the search often is very difficult, and it sometimes uncovers death, prison, or other problem situations. When something intended to be kept unknown becomes known, great risks emerge, risks both to psychological well-being and to family relationships. Not everyone welcomes a reunion. Some birth parents absolutely do not want to be found. Some biological parents never tell their subsequent spouses or children that they have another child out there somewhere. A generation ago, most adoptions were entered into with the understanding that everyone's privacy would be protected. Fears of rejection haunt both the parent who seeks the child she gave up and the child seeking his or her biological parent.

Today, great debate and public interest swirl around the legal right of the adopted child to know who the birth parents were. Increasingly, states are opening adoption records by passing laws that say an adoptee has the right to a copy of the original birth certificate listing the biological parents' names. Those with medical problems linked to their heredity are gaining sympathy from the courts and becoming exceptions to the guaranteed secrecy. If you fit that category, you should talk with an attorney who can explore with you your state's laws regarding an adoptee's right to be provided with needed hereditary and health-related information about his or her birth parents.

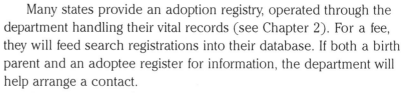

Adoptive Support Groups

Currently, several registries and support groups exist to help adoptees and birth parents find each other. Among national organizations you can contact are:

The American Adoption Congress
  1000 Connecticut Avenue, N.W., Suite 9
  Washington, D.C. 20036
  (800) 274-6736

Council of Equal Rights in Adoption
  401 E. 74th Street, Suite 17D
  New York, NY 10021-3919

Many states provide an adoption registry, operated through the department handling their vital records (see Chapter 2). For a fee, they will feed search registrations into their database. If both a birth parent and an adoptee register for information, the department will help arrange a contact.

The International Soundex Reunion Registry accepts registrations from parent and child reunion-seekers. The registry is committed to keeping the identities of the birth parents and the adopted child undisclosed unless all parties are agreeable to the reunion. Children must be of legal age in order to register. If both parties are registered and want to find each other, a match is made. The address is:

International Soundex Reunion Registry
P.O. Box 2312
Carson City, NV 89702

The Internet has become a new medium where adoptees and birth parents can look for each other. Use a search engine (Webcrawler, Yahoo!, Excite, AltaVista, or Infoseek—see Chapter 2) and enter "adoption" as the subject you want to search. You will be shown several adoption forum Web sites that provide current information and guidance.

Relevant books about adoption include Judith Geidman and Linda Brown's *The Birth Bond*, Arthur Sorsky's *The Adoption Triangle*, and Carol Shafer's *The Other Mother*.

But what about adoptions back a few generations? Genealogy research often strikes a dead-end when the adoptee involved is long deceased. How to find his or her birth parents becomes a big-league research challenge.

In times past, but less so today, society was cruel to unmarried women who gave birth and also to the child involved. The child was considered illegitimate, which carried a strong negative social and legal stigma. To avoid public humiliation, mothers facing such births, and often their family members, tried to take care of "the problem" as quietly and secretly as possible. One common solution was for the expectant mother to go away from the community for an extended visit somewhere, deliver the baby, give it up for adoption, and return home without her community and even close family knowing about it.

If genealogy answers about parenthood are to be found for long-ago adoptees, they will come from pursuing clues regarding date and place of birth or of adoption. You must search for birth records for that time period to find out which mothers delivered around the birth date of the adoptee. Church baptism or christening records might be helpful.

Also, you can make educated guesses about the adoptive parents' distant relatives—often a family arranged for a very distant relative to adopt the child, especially if that family was having trouble bearing children of their own. Sometimes the adopted child's name includes a name linked to the birth parents.

In some families, one of the older relatives might remember hearing some family rumors about where the adopted child came from. So, those older relatives should be asked. Old letters and life sketches relating to the place and the time period of the adoption also might contain useful information or hints regarding the parentage question.

When collecting genealogy "down" the family to the present—tracking the children, grandchildren, and other descendants of an ancestor—any child adopted into the family should be treated like a birth child. His or her descendants ought to be treated as bloodline family.

Researching African-American "Roots"

During the late 1960s, in reaction to student protests and pressures, universities across America began to offer Black History and Black Studies classes. Fairly quickly, research into black history became a vital part of the historian's work. Serious studies soon appeared in historical journals and books, providing new information and identifying new records and source materials about African-Americans in U.S. history: slavery, the abolition movement, the Underground Railroad, the Civil War, Reconstruction, the Freedman's Bureau, black cowboys and soldiers on the American frontier, black migrations north, black music and literature, black soldiers in America's wars, and black men and women who made major contributions to the nation's development.

Alex Haley's book and TV series *Roots* appeared during that explosion of interest in black history. *Roots* excited the nation about genealogy and sparked much genealogy research by African-Americans. Since then, our understandings of how to pursue black genealogy research has passed through an infancy stage and is now nearing maturity.

Follow the Basic First Genealogy Steps

Even when ethnic backgrounds are involved, you must begin your genealogy quest by following the same steps outlined in Chapter 1:

- write down what you already know, using pedigree and family group charts
- draw information from records in your home
- ask relatives for information and tape-record interviews with them
- create a notetaking and file system
- decide what missing details you want to find

When those steps are taken, you begin the actual research work, as explained in Chapter 1. Thus, for generations from the present back to 1870, you look for vital records, do census research, check for wills, seek church records, check newspaper and city directories, and pursue many of the same research approaches outlined earlier.

Few African-Americans are fully black; almost all have complexions ranging from near-black to near-white. During slavery, white males partnered with black slaves, producing generations of mixed-race offspring. In addition, African-Americans paired with members of several Native American tribes. Several tribes lived in slave states, and runaway slaves sometimes escaped to tribal preserves and took up homes there. Intermarriage between African-Americans and Native Americans has not been uncommon.

In addition to checking the usual genealogy sources, African-American genealogy research requires some unique approaches. For example, in terms of the federal censuses, blacks appear by name starting with the 1870 census. Censuses from 1870 to the present

have listed the race of the person being enumerated. The censuses for 1790, 1800, and 1810 count only free persons, not slaves. The 1820 census lists slaves by category but not by name. Both the 1850 and 1860 censuses include slave schedules that list slaves by sex and age, but not by name. To conduct census research for black ancestors, use your families' surnames and look for slave owners with that same name or one spelled somewhat like it (Wight, White, Waite). By checking the age and sex of the owners' slaves, perhaps you can find circumstantial evidence that your ancestor was in that group.

Blacks were being included in vital records compiled by the states by the turn of the twentieth century. However, through the first quarter of this century, midwives rather than doctors delivered many African-American children, so no birth certificates were issued. For birth records, then, you must look for family records such as family Bibles and for church records.

African-Americans who served in the U.S. military and in state militias can be found in military records, including military pension records (see Chapter 2). Slaves fought in the Revolutionary War and in the War of 1812. Many were granted their freedom in return for their service. Blacks also fought in the Civil War. The North had several all-black units. Since then, African-Americans have served their country in all of America's major wars. So, military records are a source to be searched.

Slave narratives are another source. More than 8,000 slave narratives have been located. During the New Deal, Work Projects Administration workers interviewed ex-slaves still living, and transcripts of nearly 4,000 of those interviews are available.

Black genealogy also depends heavily on oral tradition. Much is to be learned from Alex Haley's celebration of the stories of the family being passed to the next generation orally. You need to interview the oldest relatives and pick their memories about their parents and grandparents, and about traditions regarding the family's distant past. Names and dates are required, certainly, but also capture the stories of the family. (See the discussion on oral history in Chapter 5.)

African-American Heritage

"Many genealogists estimate that 90 percent of African-Americans have white ancestors in their family tree. That may not surprise you. But did you also know that 80 percent of you are just as likely to have a Native American ancestor in your family tree?" (Donna Beasley, *Family Pride: The Complete Guide to Tracing African-American Genealogy* [New York: Macmillan, 1997], 59–60).

History Timeline of U.S. Slavery

1619 Dutch introduce first slaves, in Virginia

1700 Slaves are 5 percent of the colonies' population

1774 Slavery abolished in Rhode Island

1776 Slaves are 20 percent of the nation's population (500,000 slaves), but 40 percent of the South's population

1793 Eli Whitney's cotton gin revives southern slavery

1804 New Jersey becomes eighth northern state to abolish slavery

1808 Congress bans slave trade into United States, but a quarter million slaves illegally imported 1808–1860

1820 Union accepts Missouri as slave state but bans slavery west of Missouri River

1831 First abolitionist newspaper, the *Liberator*, starts Nat Turner slave rebellion in Virginia which kills fifty-seven whites

DIEU ET MON DROIT

Helpful Agencies, Handbooks, and Internet Sites

A valuable guide is Paula K. Byers, ed., *African Genealogical Sourcebook* (Detroit, MI: Gale Research, Inc., 1995). An excellent survey handbook for those doing African-American genealogy is Donna Beasley, *Family Pride: The Complete Guide to Tracing African-American Genealogy* (New York: Macmillan, 1997). The book has its own homepage on the Internet aimed at students' genealogy work. Its address is:

http://www.oryxpress.com/authors/a00230.html

There is a national organization created to assist and further African-American genealogy. You can join it and/or receive help from its national center and affiliated state chapters by contacting:

Afro-American Historical and Genealogical Society
1700 Shepherd Street, N.W.
Washington, D.C. 20011

The AAHGS has chapters in Arizona, California, Florida, Illinois, Indiana, Louisiana, Maryland, Missouri, New Jersey, New York, North Carolina, Ohio, Pennsylvania, Tennessee, Texas, Virginia, and Washington, D.C.

Other organizations devoted to black history and genealogy, or to particular groups of blacks in U.S. history, include:

Buffalo Soldiers Historical Society, Flagstaff, AZ
Black Military History Society, San Francisco, CA
Black Genealogy Search Group, Denver, CO
AAHGS Chapter, Chicago, IL
Fred Hart Williams Genealogical Society, Detroit, MI
North Carolina Afro-American Heritage Society, Raleigh, NC
Afro-American Genealogy Group, Philadelphia, PA
Rhode Island Black Heritage Society, Providence, RI

In addition, several black genealogy Web sites are on the Internet (see Chapter 2). Your best starting point on the Net is the

Genealogy homepage, which deals with all aspects of genealogy research and records, and provides help for African-American research. The address is:

http://www.genhomepage.com

Slavery and Genealogy

Slavery impacts severely on our ability to trace African-American family connections. Slaves were given first names in place of their African names, and their surnames, if any, were those of the white family who owned them. Also, slave codes forbade slaves from learning to read or write, so their version of a written life story or journal was oral, passed from one generation to the next by tellings and retellings from memory.

Because slaves were property, transactions involving them produced property records. Bills of sale were recorded. The buyer received a copy, and a copy was filed in the county's deed books. Tax collectors assessed the individual taxable value of residents' personal and real property, including the value of their slaves.

Plantations, being farm businesses, also produced business records. Those that survive include financial ledgers with entries regarding slaves bought and sold, and who died. Check for plantation records with reference librarians in the state historical societies in the states where your relative was a slave.

Runaway slaves caused owners to post notices and obtain warrants for arrests, naming the slaves being sought. Some of those documents can be used to trace ancestors. Freed slaves, or manumitted slaves, had to be legally certified as such in order to prove they were freedmen. This was a property transaction, so the manumission record was recorded in the county deed book. Two archives are the main ones in America with copies of manumission records:

Pennsylvania Abolition Society, Philadelphia, PA (in the
    public library)
Schomburg Center for Research in Black Culture, New York City

(continued)

1846 Slavery had disappeared from the north
1850 Compromise: California a free state, Utah and New Mexico territories can be free or slave, fugitive slave law toughened, Washington, D.C. slave trade banned
1852 Harriet Beecher Stowe's novel *Uncle Tom's Cabin* inflames public against slavery
1856 New Republican Party's platform includes anti-slavery plank
1857 Supreme Court *Dred Scott* decision: blacks are not citizens
1861 Outbreak of Civil War, slaves number 4 million out of 12 million southerners
1863 Emancipation Proclamation frees slaves in United States
1865 Union defeat of Confederacy and end of Civil War
1865 Thirteenth Amendment abolishes slavery

Wills can be excellent sources for finding names and ages of slaves. In their wills, slaveholders often mentioned slaves by name and indicated to which white relative or associate they were leaving the slaves, or that the slaves were to be sold. If a slaveholder died without a will, or intestate, probate courts probably handled the estate. If so, the court had to make an appraisal of the estate, including the slaves by name and their market value. This appraisal, or *return*, was filed with the court records, so look for the returns as well as the probate records themselves.

Some slaveholders were religious and cared about the salvation of human souls. They therefore allowed ministers to perform baptisms, marriages, and other church ordinances for their slaves, and some records of these religious rites name the slaves who received them. Blacks who attended church services did so at a church fairly close to their home. Some white churches kept records of their slave members.

Post-Slavery Records

Before, during, and after the Civil War, black churches sprang up in order to serve free blacks, in both the North and South. The African Methodist Episcopal Church became the most popular. You can contact its church headquarters in Williamstown, MA, to find out how to access its records. Two other churches to contact are the National Baptist Convention, USA, in St. Petersburg, FL, and the Christian Methodist Episcopal Church in Memphis, TN.

After the Civil War, former slaves had to find ways to earn a living. Many became sharecroppers; that is, they farmed on someone else's land, paying in return a share of their produce to the landowner. Some of these share-cropping account books survive. To find them you must look in local records and in the small collection in the National Archives.

At the end of the Civil War, the federal government established the Freedman's Bureau to assist former slaves, or freedmen. This agency set up offices in the southern states and the District of Columbia. These offices established schools; provided food, clothing, and medical help; assisted former slaves to get married; helped black war veterans to apply for pensions; and set up employment

programs. Freedman Bureau records are a major collection now housed in the National Archives.

In 1865 the federal government established a banking system for freedmen throughout the South, which lasted a decade. The Freedmen's Saving and Trust Company ledgers, which detail deposits and withdrawals, are in various national, state, and local libraries. Have a librarian show you how to look up the agency's records in the National Union Catalog of Manuscripts.

African Research

For more than two centuries the slave trade between West Africa and North America was big business. Slave traders, some of them black, bought or captured blacks in Africa and shipped them like prisoners across the Atlantic to America's east coast and the West Indies. The enslaved men, women, and children were from many different African nations and tribes.

To trace one's ancestry back through slavery to people and villages in Africa is possible only for a fortunate few. Some succeed, like Alex Haley, because of oral stories that include African names, words, and traditions. Others manage to track the genealogy back to the bill of sale of their African immigrant ancestor in America.

Another source that might prove fruitful is the logbook of slave ships. Identify the closest port of entry to the earliest location you have for one of your ancestors. Search for ship logs and records for that port in state archives and ship museums.

In terms of Africa itself, and records there, Donna Beasley's *Family Pride* and other guides to African-American genealogy contain addresses of historical libraries and record collections in various African cities and countries.

Jewish Genealogy

Today's Jewish families in America, like those with European or African backgrounds, are comprised of both those who have been in this country for many generations and those who have arrived recently.

To find genealogies for those who have been here a long time, you must follow the basic genealogy steps outlined in Chapters 1

Timeline: Jewish Presence in America

1654 First Jewish settlement in America, in New Amsterdam

1790 Jewish population in United States: 1,500

1840 15,000 Jews in America

1860 150,000 Jews, increase due to Jews emigrating from Germany

1880 280,000 Jews

1920 5,500,000 Jews, increase due to Jews emigrating from Eastern Europe

and 2. For recent arrivals, you will need to research records in foreign countries from which your people emigrated or copies of such records that are here in America.

Non-Jews must become very conversant with Jewish customs and the Hebrew and Yiddish languages before they can have much success conducting Jewish genealogy research. Several features of the Jewish culture illustrate the complexities the researcher encounters, such as religious rites and practices, synagogue customs, and the Yiddish language. Old Mohel books contain records of circumcisions. Some families save a ketubah, or marriage document, and pass it on to the next generation. Tying into a rabbinical family might connect you to genealogies reaching back centuries.

Large collections of Jewish records exist in a number of libraries and archives, such as the American Jewish Archives at Hebrew Union College in Cincinnati, OH, and the American Jewish Historical Society in Waltham, MA. A basic source of information about Jewish families in the United States prior to 1840 is Malcolm H. Stern's *First American Jewish Families*, rev. ed. (Baltimore, MD: Ottenheimer Publishers, 1991).

New as well as experienced researchers need to consult the Jewish genealogical quarterly, *Arotaynu*, which was first published in 1985. Its articles deal with Jewish genealogy not just in the United States but throughout the world. The journal features a "Family Finder" section in which you can ask for readers' help regarding specific family lines. Publishers of the *Arotaynu* also market a number of helpful Jewish genealogy research books and microfiche sets. Researchers need to examine the *Encyclopedia of Jewish Genealogy* (Northvale, NJ: Jason Aronson, Inc., 1991) as well. A small, helpful guide is Warren Blatt's *FAQ: Frequently Asked Questions about Jewish Genealogy* (Teaneck, NJ: Arotaynu Inc., 1997).

Dozens of Jewish historical societies exist in the United States. They include the Southern California Jewish Historical Society in Los Angeles, the Chicago Jewish Archives, the Jewish Historical Society of New York in New York City, and the National Museum of American Jewish History in Philadelphia.

Similarly, there are Jewish genealogical societies throughout the country. Here is a sampling of these: the Jewish Genealogical Society of Los Angeles (Sherman Oaks, CA), the San Francisco Bay Area Jewish Genealogical Society (San Mateo, CA), the Jewish Genealogical Society (New York City), the Jewish Genealogical Society of Philadelphia, and the Jewish Genealogy Society of St. Louis.

A number of professional genealogists specialize in Jewish genealogy, and they can be hired to do research. For a list of names of professional researchers, write to the following address:

Committee of Professional Jewish Genealogists
Association of Jewish Genealogical Societies
P.O. Box 11234
Teaneck, NJ 07666

Native American Genealogy

It is possible in many cases to trace Native American genealogy back several generations. A number of records contain useful information. However, as with any ethnic group, the researcher faces several unique problems.

You must know the tribal affiliation and learn about the historical background and customs of that tribe. You need to consult histories of the various tribes to know when they lived where. Then, you must know or find out about naming customs among the various tribes. Kinship systems of the various tribes must also be understood. Federal records divide Native Americans into two categories—those who participated in government programs and supervision, and those who did not.

The basic genealogy sources about Indians through 1830 are church and land records. The federal government became vigorous in transferring Indians to reservations between 1850 and 1887. Census records are sometimes helpful for the Reservation

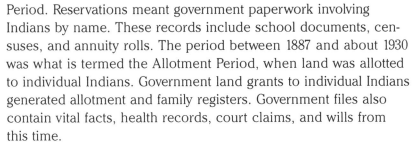

The National Archives

To learn how to best use the records in the National Archives, request from the National Archives for the information booklet entitled "Using Records in the National Archives for Genealogical Research." This useful bulletin is published each year.

The address of the National Archives is:

National Archives
700 Pennsylvania Avenue. N.W.
Washington, D.C. 20408

To reach the Order Department of the National Archives by phone call (202) 501-5235.

Period. Reservations meant government paperwork involving Indians by name. These records include school documents, censuses, and annuity rolls. The period between 1887 and about 1930 was what is termed the Allotment Period, when land was allotted to individual Indians. Government land grants to individual Indians generated allotment and family registers. Government files also contain vital facts, health records, court claims, and wills from this time.

The National Archives has many records relating to Native Americans who kept their tribal status. Most of the records, arranged by tribe, are dated 1830–1940. These records include:

Lists of Cherokee, Chickasaw, Choctaw, and Creek Indians and others who moved west during the 1830–46 period. Each entry on the list usually contains the name of the head of the family, the number of persons in the family by age and sex, a description of property owned before removal, and dates of departures from the East and arrival in the West.

Annuity payrolls, 1841–1940. These show for each person in a family the Indian or English name (or both names), age, sex, and relationship to the head of the family, and sometimes to another enrolled Native American. Rolls sometimes contain supplementary information, such as names of persons who died or were born during the year. The National Archives will search the records if you provide the Indian's name (preferably both the English and Indian name), the tribe, and the approximate date of association with the tribe.

The Eastern Cherokee claim files, 1901–10. These usually contain the applicant's name, residence, date and place of birth, name and age of spouse, names of father and mother and children, and other genealogical information. For a search of the claim files, it is helpful if you can identify some or all of the following: name or claim number of the claimant, age when the claim was filed, name of spouse, and names of parents or children.

After the Indian Reorganization Act of 1934, several individual tribes began to keep their own records.

For Native Americans not linked to reservations, oral information from living relatives is your best source. Then the usual genealogy research steps outlined in Chapters 1 and 2 should be followed.

At times various religious groups have worked among the Native American tribes. Records of the Quakers, Moravians, Presbyterians, Baptists, Catholics, and the LDS Church (Mormons) can contain useful information filed by their mission agencies and missionaries.

Several universities also have record collections relating to Native American tribes. A number of oral history projects in various states have tape-recorded Native American interviewees, supported by the Doris Duke Oral History Project.

Researchers need to search the basic Internet sites for genealogy to see updated information as well. They should also study Paula K. Byers' edition of the *Native American Genealogical Sourcebook* (Detroit, MI: Gale Research, 1995).

Other American Ethnic Groups

Much genealogy research involving ethnic and nationality groups in the United States must follow the same basic genealogy steps outlined in Chapters 1 and 2. If the ancestors lived in America, the basic genealogy sources, such as vital records, city directories, cemetery records, military documents, and censuses, need to be checked.

In addition, records kept by the Immigration and Naturalization Service can be helpful. Consult the Internet for constant updatings of lists identifying finding aids, guidelines, and source materials for conducting genealogy research for Asian Americans, Hispanic Americans, and other ethnic groups. Also, refer to two other fine guidebooks edited by Paula K. Byers and published in 1995 by Gale Research in Detroit: *Asian American Genealogical Sourcebook* and *Hispanic American Genealogical Sourcebook*. For Hispanic Americans, Catholic Church records are a fundamental source of genealogy information.

Foreign Country Research and Records

When your family lines extend back to and beyond the immigrant ancestor, your research shifts into records of a foreign country, assuming you know approximately when the immigrant ancestor came to America. You may need to travel abroad, or you may possibly find copies of many of that country's religious and civil records on microfilm in an American library, particularly the LDS Family History Library in Salt Lake City.

But, whether using the country's records here or abroad, you will need foreign language skills (even with British Isles English because meanings of some words vary); awareness of the country's customs and history; comprehensive maps; and a good education regarding the country's archives, libraries, maps, and genealogy records. You will need to consult genealogy handbooks such as *The Source* that provide detailed guidance for foreign-country research. Other guidebooks are available for specific countries. Also, the LDS Family History Library produces inexpensive *Resource Outlines* for many countries of the world.

Names and Naming Practices

Naming patterns vary from country to country and from one time period to the next. In Colonial days, most men did not have middle names. As proof, we have two-name patriots like Thomas Jefferson, Patrick Henry, John Hancock, and Paul Revere. By the 1800s it became the custom among some Americans to give their sons and sometimes their daughters the mother's maiden name as a middle name. All the children in one family, in such cases, had the same middle name. From Colonial times until the 1800s, it was not uncommon for families to give a son or daughter the same name as a son or daughter of theirs who had died.

Two strong currents have influenced American naming trends. One is to name children after famous people. In the early 1800s, for example, many families had sons with first and middle names of such heroes as George Washington, Andrew Jackson, and Francis Marion. In the twentieth century, parents have often given their children the first names of stage, radio, movie, and TV stars. A second

current is internal to the family—naming the children after a grandparent, uncle, aunt, or other favorite relative.

In biblical times, people had only one name: Adam, Seth, Noah, Abraham, Rebekah, Moses, Isaiah, Daniel, Ruth, Naomi, Amos. Through the medieval period in Europe, people still had but one name. William the Conqueror, when he invaded England from France, had no last name. As evidenced by the title attached to his name, custom grew during the period between 1100 and 1500 to assign a descriptive term to a man. When talking about him, then, or sending someone to see him, people could differentiate him from another man with the same name. "Go see James the smith" or "John the short one" or "Richard living in the oak trees" or "Henry with the beard." In time, such names became James Smith, John Short, Richard Oaks, and Henry Beard.

Surnames have definite meanings. Originally they were attached to one of our ancestors to identify him. The identifying word that became the surname referred to either a physical characteristic of the man, his relationship to another person, his employment, where he lived, or some accomplishment for which he was known. The prefix "Mac" means "son of." The addition of "son" to the end of a name means "son of," so Johnson means son of John. For fascinating reading, read a book devoted to names and their meanings.

British Records

In England, parish registers were instituted in 1538 to keep records of baptism, marriage, and burial. Huguenots and Quakers and Jews kept their own records. Information regarding baptism, marriage, and burials of Roman Catholics was kept by the Catholic Record Society.

In 1837 in England and Wales the registration by the government of all births, marriages, and deaths became law. The records are located at St. Catherine's House, London. As of 1858, wills had to be validated in the Probate Court and these can be found in Somerset House in London.

Recent records of births, marriages and deaths can also be found at Somerset House. Census returns exist from 1841 and are available in the Public Record Office in London.

European Surnames, Source, and Meanings

Aaron	Hebrew	Lofty, exalted one
Barnes	Old English	Owner of barley storehouses
Clinton	Old Norse	Farmstead on a headland
Decker	German	House roofer
Espinosa	Spanish	Thornbush-covered property
Flowers	Old English	Arrow maker
Grant	Old French	Large or great man
Houghton	Old English	Farmstead on a bluff
Irons	English	Strong-willed one
Jesse	English/Hebrew	Wealthy one
Kennedy	Irish, Scottish	Son of the helmeted one
Lang, Lange	Various European	Very large man

Monroe	Scottish	Lives by a red swamp
Noyes	French	Owner of nut trees
Owens	Old Welch	Well-born one
Presley	Old English	Priest's meadow
Quinn	Old Gaelic	Descendant of intelligent man
Ryan	Gaelic	Descendant of the young ruler
Seymour	Old Gaelic	Victorious and famous one
Talbot	Old French	Pillager
Underwood	English	At the foot of the forest
Valenzuela	Spanish	Young, valiant one
Wasserman	German	Water carrier
Xavier	Spanish	Owner of a new house
Yates	English	Home at the town's gates
Zuniga	Spanish	Man who frowned constantly

From one generation to the next, the spelling of surnames has varied, particularly during the era of verbal rather than written information. Names were spelled phonetically, according to how someone pronounced them. Thus, Smith was recorded alternatively as Smith, Smyth, Smythe, and Smits, and a name like Pearce was spelled variously as Perce, Peirs, Pierce, Peirce, Peirse, or Pearse.

Names sometimes became transformed merely through pronunciation. Those beginning with a vowel or with *h* or *wh* could end up starting with another vowel instead. Aiken could become Eakin. Harbach might change into Arbach. Whitmore could end up as Whetmore or Wetmore.

Very often, immigrants with an Old Country surname anglicized it after they arrived in America. German names like Braun and Schwartz became translated into English as Brown and Black. The Italian surname Roberto became Roberts.

Scandinavian Patronymic Naming Customs

A Swede named Christian had a son he named Peter. Peter was known as Peter Son-of-Christian, or Peter Christian's Son, or Peter Christianson. When Peter had a son he named Nels, Nels was known as Nels Son-of-Peter, or Nels Peterson. Then, when

Nels had a son, he named him Frederick, and Frederick was known as Frederick Son-of-Nels, or Frederick Nelson. For girls the name ended in "dotter" instead of "son," for example, Petersdotter or Nelsdotter.

This practice, whereby the surname of the child is derived from the given name of the father, is called patronymics (*patro* meaning "father"). Until late in the nineteenth century, the patronymic custom for naming children prevailed throughout the rural and common classes in Denmark, Norway, and Sweden. In the higher social classes, fixed surnames emerged much earlier.

Old Spelling, Archaic Words, and Strange Handwriting

Reading old records is sometimes difficult because of poor spelling, lack of punctuation, strange words not in our vocabularies today, and unusual forms of handwriting.

America lacked a widely available book of words until 1828, when Noah Webster published his first popular dictionary. But it took two generations after that before standardized spelling became the proper thing to do. The norm until then was for people, educated or not, to spell phonetically. They might even spell the same word five different ways in the same letter, such as wagon, waggon, wagun, wagin, or waggen. Also, many wrote without using punctuation—at best they would skip and leave a space to indicate a new sentence or what we now call a paragraph.

When trying to read old handwriting, use a magnifying glass so that you can closely inspect the lines and loops. When a letter in a word is hard to decipher, look for other words in the document containing that same letter. This can help you determine what the letter is. When you find a strange word, pronounce it out loud. That way, if it was spelled phonetically, you can understand what the word is.

One main handwriting problem is the double *s*. Prior to the 1870s, writers would make the second *s* normal but the first *s* to look like a huge, swirling *f* or *p*. As with present handwriting, the letters *a* and *u* in old handwriting can be hard to differentiate, as well as the letters *m*, *n*, or *r*. The letters *o* and *e* are often confused with each other. The old handwritten capital *L* often resembles our handwritten capital *T* or *S*; the capital *I* resembles a *J*; and the capital *T* and *F* look alike. A helpful book that explains early handwriting peculiarities is Harriet Stryker-Rodda's *Understanding Colonial Handwriting* (Baltimore, MD: Genealogical Publishing Company, 1986).

The meanings of words change over time. Some words used in the "old days" are no longer in use. If you find words not in our modern vocabulary, you can look them up in old dictionaries, which major libraries can provide.

A more challenging problem than extinct words, however, are words in use today that had radically different meanings in former years. Particularly misleading are terms dealing with family relationships. Today's terms like "in-law" and "cousin" or "stepchild" have specific and clear meanings. Before the 1800s, however, they did not carry our present meanings. Take the word "cousin," for example. In those days it meant anyone who was not a brother, sister, son, or daughter. A woman's nieces and nephews, and even her grandchildren, were considered to be her cousins. In his will, a man might term his wife's children by a former marriage—his stepchildren—as his "son-in-law" or "daughter-in-law"! And, the actual son-in-law or daughter-in-law according to our meanings were called "son" or "daughter." The word "brother" could mean a brother, brother-in-law, stepbrother, or fellow member of the church. "Mother" and "father" referred not only to parents but also to the mother-in-law and father-in-law.

Junior and Senior after a person's name did not necessarily mean son and father. The terms, instead, applied to two men of the same name, the older one being senior and the younger one junior. The terms "Mrs." and "Mistress" had meanings different than ours. The title "Mrs." referred to a woman of high social standing, not to marital status. "Mr.," in turn, is an abbreviation for "Mister," which refers to a gentleman of high social class.

The Calendar Change

In 1582 Pope Gregory XIII, head of the Roman Catholic Church, ordered that ten days be dropped from western society's calendar. His decree also changed the beginning of the new year from March 25 to January 1. The new system, still known as the Gregorian calendar, brought the old Julian calendar into synchronization with the sun, so that the equinox occurred on March 21, as it was supposed to do. Catholic countries immediately adopted the new calendar, but England held out until 1752. Until then, the calendar in English-speaking countries and in Russia was eleven days different from the Gregorian calendar the rest of Europe was using.

However, some Colonial American records contain double dates—the date written correctly for both calendars. For the January to March period, the years differed by one because New Year's was January 1 on the new calendar but not until March 25 on the other. Thus, in Colonial records February 3 might be written as 1680/81—it being 1680 by the English calendar but 1681 by the Gregorian calendar. A person might write a letter dated March 23, 1664 and another one five days later was dated March 28, 1665.

You can also become confused when using records in which the month is written not by name but by number. On the new calendar April was the fourth month, but on the old calendar it was the second month. So, when you read a record dated something like "the 10th daye in the third month," you must determine if that means March 10 or June 10! Usually the day was given first and then the month, but not always, which exacerbates the confusion sometimes.

When England adopted the new Gregorian calendar in 1752, it had to drop eleven days from the calendar. Thus, the day after September 2 that year was September 14!

George Washington was born on February 11, 1732, but when the English changed the calendar two decades later, he adjusted his birthday to the new system and redated it as February 22. Rather than get into the business of doing what Washington did and adjusting all old dates to fit the new calendar, genealogists use the original date with "(O.S.)," initials standing for Old Style, after it.

Heraldry, Coats of Arms, and Tartans

The Lancaster family steps inside a store specializing in family shields and coats of arms. They find an array of items bearing what claims to be the official insignia for the surname of Lancaster. They see wall plaques, crystal glasses, sweatshirts, ties, spoons, and pins carrying the Lancaster crest. Mr. Lancaster buys a wood wall plaque displaying a metallic shield brightly painted with a medieval-looking design, with "Lancaster" printed on a scroll beneath it. "We're Lancasters," he says proudly, "so this is our family shield." He displays the plaque prominently on a wall in the family's living room.

Many Americans are delighted to find objects containing their family name and its English coat of arms. Shops in malls as well as mail-order houses cater to our interest in obtaining objects bearing the coat of arms of our family line. Commonly, the terms "coat of arms," "family shield," and "family crest" are used interchangeably—revealing a total lack of understanding of heraldic realities. These popularly purchased display items are in fact fluff and pretend, out of touch with serious, legitimate, authorized hereditary rights to heraldic symbols. Nevertheless, they are fun to have and allow us to show a sense of pride in our family heritage.

The simplest way to make sense of medieval English crests, shields, and coats of arms is to imagine a medieval warrior or knight, dressed in armor, going forth to battle. How can this guy be recognized in an army of knights likewise dressed in shiny metal armor? If the face guard is up, they can recognize his face, but with his face guard down, who is he? As early as 1150 he incorporated four elements in his battle gear in order to identify himself:

1. His coat that wrapped around the armor, called his "coat of arms," to protect the armor from cold, heat, and rain. This coat was decorated with a design uniquely his.
2. His shield, used to block sword thrusts, arrows, and spears. On it he painted the same design as on the coat covering his armor.
3. The unique crest (meaning "on top of") atop his helmet. This was a figure—like a leopard, eagle, or horse—or just a

distinctive shape modeled from wood, leather, metal, or parchment. It could incorporate feathers and other protrusions. This crest gave a top-side identity to the knight during a crowded hand-combat situation when shields were engaged in battle and not visible.

4. A rope-like wreath ("torse") of silk, with one to three colors twisted in it, that attached to the top of the helmet and the base of the crest.

(The Scots displayed these same basic elements but used slightly different arrangements.)

The knight's design on his coat and his shield was not haphazardly created. Rather, each section of the design—each symbol, each color, and later, each design's motto—had a definite purpose that met precise standards of the day. Among popular symbols emblazoned on the shields were variations of the Christian cross; all or parts of leaves, sheaves, and flowers; animals such as lions, leopards, horses, and deer; eagles and hawks; fish; bees; lizards; and such mythical creatures as unicorns and monsters.

The total "armory" design became incorporated into the knight's seal, which served as his signature. Some knights also used the design elements on their banners (the trappings on their horses), on bed curtains and coverlets, on ship sails, and to decorate their tombs.

The knight's armor, helmet, torse, coat, and seal passed to his firstborn son, but not to every son. Other sons used the design with slight alterations, so that each could be identified individually in battle and not be confused with the firstborn son.

The term *heraldry* refers to the heralds, or announcers, at tournaments who had to introduce the warriors and knights who were competing. The heralds had to be able to tell which designs belonged to whom. Hence they became the experts and arbiters of who could display what symbols—almost like grantors of copyrights. In time a central authority emerged to approve the use of "heraldic" designs and the introduction of new ones. The English monarchy established a College of Arms to handle heraldic authorizations, and this is still the official agency today.

Roman Genealogies

During the reign of the Roman Empire, genealogies of pedigrees were common at the courts of the Roman emperors and in the halls of the Roman patricians. There was a tendency to assume identity of blood from identity of name and claim a semidivine descent. Julius Caesar, for example, was supposed to have descended from the Roman goddess of love, Venus.

With the advent of firearms, the face mask disappeared, and so did the need for quick identification by simple symbols. As a result, designs increased in detail and complexity since their purpose was now show rather than identification. Also, designs began to incorporate words, which were not used earlier (when even the nobility was illiterate).

Based on the knight's fighting regalia, then, a drawing of the family's "armory" incorporates the shield, with its unique patterns, colors, and symbols, topped by the helmet, on which sits the wreath, and a crest or crown. The shield usually adds a cloth draped from the crown down to and around the shoulders and down the sides of the shield—representing the mantling (cloth) the knights wore to protect their helmets in hot and cold weather.

The insignia or design painted on a shield, called the armament, often included design elements from another armament. For example, a knight might combine his own insignia with that of his wife's father.

A rendering of all of the elements of a complete coat of arms—crest, crown, mantling, shield, and motto—is called an "achievement."

Your library has books on heraldry and the *Encyclopaedia Britannica* which provide good descriptions of heraldic symbols as well as generous and beautiful illustrations.

Those who hope to authenticate that they are entitled by birth to use a recognized and registered coat of arms must apply to the College of Arms. They must prove through documented pedigree charts their direct descent through male lines from the original bearer of those arms. Then, if declared eligible, they must pay a hefty fee for the right to display the decoration legitimately as their own. (Daughters had some inheritance rights in cases where there was no son, but rules governing female use of heraldry symbols is a complex matter that you can study in official heraldry handbooks.)

When you come across a coat of arms assigned to one of your family names, you will be tempted to claim it as your own family's coat of arms. Technically, of course, that is not true, unless you are the authenticated legal successor in the long line of firstborn sons. To be correct, the best you can say is that it is the coat of arms of someone with your surname.

Elements of a Complete Coat of Arms or "Achievement"

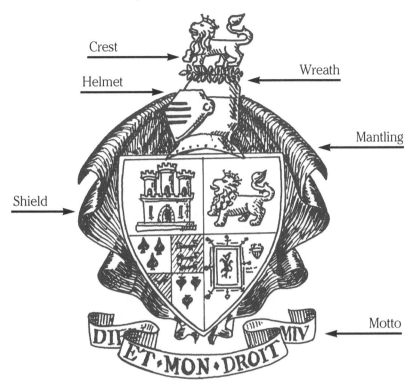

Crest

Helmet

Wreath

Mantling

Shield

Motto

Anglo-Saxon Records

Most students of Anglo-Saxon genealogy of the British Isles have found that except for royal lines, no genealogy can be taken back to more than three or four generations before the Norman Conquest in 1066.

According to some historians, only three families: Arden (The family of Shakespeare's mother) Berkeley, and Swinton are the families whose genealogies can be traced to Saxon stock in the pre-Norman Conquest period.

Tartans

McKenzie, McDonald, McPherson, Stewart, Fraser, Forbes, Campbell: All are great Scottish surnames. People today who are descendants of these and other Scottish families or clans like to find the tartan plaid pattern belonging to their surnames.

Tartans are alternately striped or checkered designs in cloth, claimed by Scottish clans to give distinguishing identity to principal portions of their costume. By the 1700s, each clan had adopted its own distinctive design pattern in its dress, including its kilts. The tartan for the Campbell clan, for example, features a green background with black and blue half-inch crossings and a yellow overcheck. The MacGregors' tartan has a red background with wide and narrow crossings of green and a white overcheck edged in black.

To help suppress Scottish Highlanders after their rebellion in 1745, the English parliament passed acts to disarm the Scots and to prohibit the use of their distinctive tartan-based Highland dress. The ban was repealed a generation later, and since then the clan tartan has become popular again in Scottish fashion.

As with family-name heraldry items, Americans feel some pride when they discover a tartan design attached to a Scottish name that is part of their heritage. Woven ties and skirts are especially popular, but kilts seem to have limited popularity on this side of the Atlantic. Admittedly, cloth manufacturers have also invented many tartan designs in order to market more clothing items to those Scottish named people.

Lineage Societies in America

The Daughters of the American Revolution (DAR) is perhaps the best-known lineage and heredity society in America. Its headquarters are at 1776 D Street, N.W., Washington, D.C. 20036. To belong to the DAR, you need to provide proof that you are a woman who descends from someone who served on the colonists' side in the Revolutionary War.

The leading heredity and patriotic societies in America are:

General Society of Colonial Wars
General Society of Mayflower Descendants
Holland Society of New York
National Society of Colonial Dames of the XVII Century
National Society, Daughters of the American Revolution
National Society of New England Women
National Society, Sons of the American Revolution

There are dozens of other such societies in America. Here is a sampling of some of the lesser known groups, just to illustrate the range of interests displayed by these units:

Children of the Confederacy
Descendants of the Signers of the Declaration of Independence
General Society of the War of 1812
Heredity Order of the Descendants of Colonial Governors
Order of First Families of Virginia, 1607–1624

Order of the Stars and Bars
Pennsylvania German Society
Pilgrim Society
Sons of Confederate Veterans
Sons and Daughters of Pioneer Rivermen
Sons of Union Veterans of the Civil War
United Daughters of the Confederacy

These societies require applications for membership, supported by genealogical records showing that the applicant is related to an ancestor involved in the cause the group honors. These applications and accompanying genealogies are a rich pool of genealogical information. So, if you know of an ancestor whose activities relate to a cause on which one of these organizations is founded, contact them to see if that relative is in their database. If so, that database will also tell you of descendants of that person.

The DAR publishes a multivolume index to the Revolutionary ancestors of its applicants, the *DAR Patriot Index*, which libraries can help you locate.

Employing Professional Genealogists

Genealogists, with skills ranging from amateur to professional, gain their expertise by taking classes or through hands-on experience conducting genealogy research. Several hundred professional genealogists work full-time and earn their living by doing genealogy research. Most of them achieve certification from recognized genealogy societies by taking qualifying examinations. Families occasionally need to call on these experts to pursue the really tough genealogy searches.

Hired research is expensive, however. If following this course of action, you will probably need family members' help to finance it. Some families create family organizations, obtain nonprofit status, and solicit donations in order to create and maintain a family genealogy research fund.

Professional genealogists charge $15 to $50 per hour or more, depending on the difficulty of the research problem. Even at the higher rates per hour, though,

they rarely can make a living. Being self-employed, they must pay both the employer and employee portions of Social Security tax and the full costs of their own medical insurance.

Usually, hired genealogy research is not a lump-sum, package arrangement. Rather, it is work done in installments. You hire them as you can afford to pay for the work, a few hundred dollars at a time. Many genealogists insist on payment in advance for a certain number of hours of work; they cannot afford to spend weeks of work for various clients and then not be paid for months—or end up not being paid at all. In addition, they charge you for travel, phone calls, photocopying, and computer supplies used for your case.

The National Genealogical Society in Washington, D.C., and the LDS Family History Library in Salt Lake City, Utah, maintain lists of accredited genealogists who do research for hire. Also, the *Genealogical Helper* annually publishes a list of professional genealogists. The Association of Professional Genealogists produces a *Directory of Professional Genealogists*, obtainable from their offices at 3421 M Street, N.W., Suite 236, Washington, D.C. 20007.

To hire a genealogist, you must write up a specific prospectus of what you want a hired researcher to do for you. Then, find three or four professional genealogists, if possible. Send each of them an inquiry letter containing your prospectus. When you receive their bids and responses, choose one. Write up a working agreement that spells out the pay rate and work schedule. Insist on timely reports that summarize work done, sources consulted, findings, and what the next research directions are. Stipulate that the genealogist fully document the source of each bit of new genealogy information they provide you. Also, be sure to inform the genealogist what sources you have consulted, so that he or she doesn't do research work you've already done.

Part 2
CREATING A FAMILY HISTORY

CHAPTER FOUR

Collecting, Preserving, and Displaying Family Records

Lucky is the person who possesses some records and objects important to the family's heritage. Generally, families will keep records and objects important to their heritage. But, it's almost a miracle that any records survive more than two generations. Most disappear! They are tossed out, damaged, lost, or destroyed.

To make family records last, you need to take proper care of those in your possession. Then, you can widen your search and obtain copies of the records other relatives have. Every family needs a caring relative who will make sure the important records are located, preserved and stored properly, and made available to the family in useful ways.

Collecting Family Materials

In some cases, one member of a family will become the record keeper, the authority about the family's genealogy and kinship network. Most often, though, one family unit has some records and another unit has others, and no one really knows what all the records are or who has what.

You can perform a great family service by seeking, obtaining, and preserving the family's heritage materials. When you find a relative who has a life sketch of a family member, some genealogy charts, a fistful of old family letters, or photographs a generation old, try to obtain copies for yourself. By doing so, you can make two vital contributions: You can create a backup, duplicate copy for insurance purposes in case the original is destroyed or lost, and, you can create a central collection of family materials for all the members to know about and use.

Ask your relatives about such records as genealogy charts, diaries, letters, portraits, photographs, scrapbooks, clippings, and certificates, as well as objects that are heirlooms. A "law of family physics" says that one object will be in only one set of hands at a time. Only one relative, for example, will have a great-great-grandparent's Civil War sword, locket or ring, citizenship certificate, eyeglasses, straight-edge razor, churn, or flat-iron. You will need to do

detective work and contact relatives—even distant cousins—to find out who has such objects.

Another "law of family physics" says that people don't write letters to themselves—they write to people a distance away. Again, by being a detective, you can ask yourself, "Was there a friend or relative to whom that ancestor might have written letters?" Then, contact descendants of those who were recipients of these letters to see if their families saved and passed them on to descendants living today.

A similar "law of family physics" is that we don't take pictures of ourselves—others take pictures of us. Who might have taken pictures of Grandpa or Grandma? Perhaps a best friend, a work associate, a neighbor, a school, or an organization to which he or she belonged. If so, who today might have such photographs?

How to Obtain Copies of Family Records

How can you convince relatives to let you keep, borrow, or copy their records and family keepsakes? Here are some suggestions:

1. *The "insurance copy" argument.* If they have the original item, remind them that it could be gone forever in a house fire or other disaster, or lost. By letting you copy it, the family gains a backup, security, insurance copy.
2. *Broker.* Offer to make them a copy when you make you a copy.
3. *Trade.* Offer to exchange copies of records or items you have in return for their letting you copy their materials.
4. *Family Project.* Design a family project—biography, photo collection, newsletter—for which you need to copy and use their materials. This links your request to a family cause rather than just being personal.
5. *Purchase.* If the person's reluctance to share is because of the monetary value of the items, consider buying the material, or at least part of it.
6. *Take Pictures.* They might have an heirloom locket or Civil War uniform, or other valuable items they won't let out the door. If they won't let the items out of the house, take

10 Major "Sins" Against Family Records (in Random Order)

- Making scrapbooks using rubber cement.
- Using "magnetic" (press-down) page photo albums.
- Not labeling/identifying photographs.
- Dividing up diaries or letters among the relatives.
- Keeping old letters in rubber-banded bundles.
- Storing family records in attics or basements.
- Not making photocopies of valuable records as backups
- Not making backup copies of computer files
- Throwing away old records when moving or when someone dies
- Storing paper records and photos in cardboard boxes

pictures of them. Offer them a copy of each of the pictures in return.

When borrowing a relative's items to copy, here are some helpful suggestions to prevent serious problems:

1. Make two copies of a list of everything they loan you: you keep one and give them the other. Then, when you return the materials, be sure both of you check off each item. If you don't check off the list and they are ever missing any record, even one you never borrowed, they may blame you for having had it and for having not returned it.

2. Schedule a date on which you will return the items you borrow.

3. Photocopy as much as you can, rather than transcribing the information. Make as good a photocopy as possible. If one photocopy center's equipment is making light copies that day, go somewhere else.

4. If a written item you want to photocopy is written in pencil, put a transparent yellow plastic sheet between the document and the photocopy machine glass. Usually this will enhance the pencil marks, making the copy easier to read than the original.

5. When borrowing photographs to copy, have the owner explain each one. You or the owner should write identifying information on the back of the photograph (names, place, date, activity) in soft pencil.

6. Take photographs or slides to a reputable camera store and pay to have copies made. Or, you or someone else who is a serious photographer can take pictures of the pictures. If your computer has the capability, you could even scan the pictures into a computer file.

7. Tape-recordings are best copied by using two recorders connected by a "patch cord." One recorder plays the tape while the other records it. Copying by simply playing the tape out loud while another machine records it is workable but risky— all other noises must be kept out of the room during the recording session.

Why So Few Records Survive

Not many family records survive. Most people have few if any items that once belonged to a grandparent or great-grandparent. Rarely is a descendant lucky enough to have inherited a locket or comb or watch or Bible or lock of hair, let alone any old letters, diaries, or photographs.

What happens to all those items that belonged to people living three or more generations ago? Almost all of it probably was thrown away because it became broken, unusable, or unwanted. And most of it, no doubt, didn't deserve to be saved.

Generally, those bits of material with family heritage value that do manage to survive are not saved in proper ways, so they deteriorate or become damaged or ruined. The bottom line is, your family records must be valued or they risk being thrown away, and they must be protected so as not to become damaged, ruined, or lost.

Two Main Enemies

Paper and objects face two destructive enemies: people and nature.

People

People can damage, ruin, and destroy the family's records, intentionally or through carelessness. Too often, people decide not to save some of these important items. They clean house and throw away old stuff, including several things that, if they survived, would be cherished by later generations. Landfill workers often see old photographs, letters, books, and finance records churn up in front of earth movers.

A grandfather once favored a captain's chair that he always sat in at mealtime. Someone in the grandchildren's generation sawed off the back, put new upholstery on the seat, and made it into a stool. What could have been an heirloom was instead destroyed.

If items are not thrown away, damaged, or destroyed intentionally, people often allow them to become damaged through neglect. Instead of carefully storing items, they casually toss them in drawers, grocery sacks, shoe boxes, and on attic or garage shelves, where the

Junk or Heirloom?

The difference between a piece of junk and an heirloom or antique is simple: one generation of time. If items can survive the junk stage for one full generation, they will become curiosities and then valuable family keepsakes and heirlooms.

Family Records

People throw items away at two crucial times in particular: when someone dies, and when someone moves. These are red flag moments—extremely dangerous situations—for family records.

items become dirty, bent, torn, damp, moldy, or otherwise damaged. Also, people leave items where direct sunlight can strike them, or close to fluorescent lights that fade their color.

We often see color portraits of important people displayed in public places, such as the U.S. president's portrait hanging in post office lobbies, or the likeness of a homecoming queen in a campus student union building. Very often, such portraits have washed-out colors and a bluish appearance. This is because fluorescent lights nearby caused the portraits to fade.

When a California congressman died, the family's situation was so rushed and so emotional that the deceased's daughter-in-law hired someone to clean out his house from attic to basement. The congressman's career papers were sent to the garbage dump.

Moving can be so awful that bodies become tired of packing and loading, and boxes are in short supply. Harried movers seem glad to throw away old materials that have no immediate usefulness. When people move into smaller housing—when parents move from the family home into a condo or apartment, for example—they are forced to get rid of a lot of their belongings. Out go piles of unorganized papers, broken or unused items, and old stuff that seems more like clutter than anything valuable. When a relative dies or moves to a different residence, you or someone who cares about family records should be involved in the decisions about what to throw away, what to save, and who should receive what.

Nature

Wind and water erode. Dust and dirt cover things. Sun dries out materials. Gravity pulls matter down and breaks it. Fire destroys. Metal rusts. Silver tarnishes. Paper oxidizes. Leather dries and cracks. Ink fades. Dirt stains. Photographs fade. Worms and rodents feed on paper, glue, cloth, and leather. Pencil lines smear and rub off. Book bindings crack and break. Staples and paper clips rust. Transparent tape yellows and cracks. As a consequence, family records in our homes are hurt by window sunlight, water pipes flooding a basement, high humidity, a fire, dirt, car exhaust, and other results of nature's processes.

An Arizona woman had several family letters written in the nineteenth century. When someone asked her for copies, she wrote that "we had a fire out at the house. We did save most of our genealogy books and I hadn't looked for those letters until I received your letter. I just can't find them. So much was burned up." An Idaho family possessed a valuable diary kept by an ancestor who crossed the Plains in the 1850s. They made a typescript of it, which a publisher was preparing to print. The Teton Dam suddenly burst and flooded thousands of homes in the valley. The original diary washed away and was lost forever, but the publisher had the typescript copy and published it.

A woman in her nineties kept a small white trunk beneath her kitchen table in a tiny basement apartment. In the trunk were a dozen of her immigrant father's diaries, written first in German and then in English, in purple indelible pencil. This woman bottled fruit every summer, and steam from that cooking permeated the trunk and diaries, causing the purple pencil marks to bleed through the pages, making both sides nearly illegible.

Even if we could keep our records totally safe from nature's outside agents, they are still in danger of disintegrating. Many paper products contain acid from the manufacturing process, in which it is used to break down paper fibers. Cardboard boxes, paper grocery bags, binder paper, computer paper, manila folders, and cheap scrapbook paper have high acid contents. Products made from vegetable or animal ingredients (organic) do not last very long; mineral products (inorganic) endure much longer.

Recently, there have been numerous reports on the deterioration of books in the Library of Congress. Officials regularly appeal for money to deacidify paper in the library's books. They say 75 percent of the books need the treatment but that 25 percent can't be saved. The books, instead, must be microfilmed and then taken out of use or destroyed.

Inks also contain damaging acid. Photographs have chemicals coating their surface. These chemicals are in turn subject to interaction with other chemicals and moisture. Audio and video recording tapes become brittle over time and lose the clarity of their images or audio recordings. Paper and nonpaper items have short natural

Quiz: Lifetime of Family Records and Objects

What is the standard lifetime of the following types of records or objects before they seriously deteriorate?

1. newspaper clippings
   _____
2. computer printer paper
   _____
3. modern book paper
   _____
4. bond, high rag content paper _____
5. magnetic (press-down) page photo albums
   _____
6. color photographs
   _____
7. slides _____
8. Polaroid, instant-print photographs
   _____
9. scrapbooks made with rubber cement
   _____
10. video cassette
    _____
11. audio cassette

lifespans, which are sped up by carelessness and which can be extended a little if properly preserved.

Preservation Suggestions

Though we lack the money, skills, products, equipment, and storage space that professional archivists have, we can take several simple steps that will help preserve our family records and heirlooms. The more of these we apply, the longer and better our records will last.

Many stationery departments in major bookstores sell archival-quality materials, meaning acid-free or low acid items, including diaries and journals, blank-page books, computer paper, scrapbooks, photo albums, file folders, tape, glue, ink pens, plastic sheet protectors, and picture-mounting materials. *Use archival-quality products for preserving your valuable records whenever you can,* even though they cost more than their non-archival-quality counterparts at the discount supermarts.

Too often, those who close down a house are too efficient at house cleaning and discard valuable records. When records are organized in files or boxes and are clearly labeled, they stand a much better chance of being saved than records that look like disorganized clutter.

Storage Places

Collections of family materials deserve to be housed responsibly. You will need some drawers, a file cabinet, shelves, or cupboard space suitable for these items. Your storage place should be safe for records, ideally with the following conditions:

1. Medium temperature between 40 and 68 degrees.
2. No major swings in temperature, such as can happen in garages and unfinished attics.
3. Medium humidity—not too dry, not too humid. Keep records away from steam coming from bathrooms and kitchens, and from humidity produced by air conditioners and washers and dryers.

4. No direct sunlight or fluorescent lights. Light does more damage than either water or fire. Ultraviolet rays from the sun and from fluorescent lights cause photographs to fade and paper to yellow and become brittle.
5. Away from water pipes that might leak.
6. Out of contact with floors that could be flooded if water pipes break, a roof leaks, or a sewer line backs up.
7. Not touching basement cement floors from which they will draw moisture.
8. Dirt-free, and relatively free of dust.
9. In an area where the air is not stagnant (so that mold doesn't grow).
10. Away from car exhaust, which mixes with humidity to create sulfuric acid.
11. Safe from mice and other rodents, worms, and insects. Books contain the cellulose of paper, as well as proteins or carbohydrates in the form of gelatin sizing, glue, paste, leather, and other organic substances that are attractive to insects and to rodents.
12. Safe from children.
13. Safe from spilled drinks or food.
14. For audio tapes, away from magnetic fields caused by magnets, motors, light switches, and TVs.
15. Where they can be rescued reasonably easily in case of fire or natural disaster.
16. In a safety deposit box or fireproof vault if containing extremely valuable items.

(continued)

Answers:
1. a few days
2. 5–10 years
3. 50 years if properly housed
4. 50 years or more
5. 4 years
6. 20 years
7. 15 years or more
8. 2 years
9. 10–15 years
10. 10–20 years
11. 10 years

Plastic Covers, Protectors, Bags

Most plastic covers, sheet protectors, and bags are highly acidic. Plastic-covered binders and folders contain PVC plastic coatings which lift the print from pages. Photocopied print rubs off easily, as does computer printer ink. Generally, the more flexible the plastic, the more damaging it is; the more it smells like plastic, the more acidic it is. Exceptions to the stiffness test are the better-grade sandwich, food, and Ziplock bags that are very flexible but made from polyethylene (which doesn't smell like plastic).

Paper

Since 1860, most paper has been manufactured by a chemical process. These chemicals, when exposed to air, high temperatures, or auto exhaust, form sulfuric acid in the paper. This process then makes the fibers that hold the paper together deteriorate, and the paper becomes brittle. Therefore, paper records should be stored flat—not folded or rolled up.

Newspaper Clippings

Newspaper is inexpensive to produce and highly acidic. Clippings will also discolor any paper next to them, again due to their high acidic content. Instead of mounting a newspaper clipping in a scrapbook, make a photocopy of it and mount that instead.

Typing and Printing

Anything you want to save for the long term should be typed or printed out in dark, clear characters. Regular computer paper has a short lifetime. Thus, printouts designed to last a long time should be printed on acid-free computer paper or bond paper with a high rag content, or else photocopied onto normal-quality photocopy paper.

Ink

Most inks in fountain pens, ballpoint pens, and markers are damaging—but ballpoint ink is the least damaging of the three. Large bookstores, in their scrapbook sections, sell pens that are safe to use. Currently, pens containing "pigma ink" are recommended for archival work. Look for ink that is fade-proof, waterproof, and won't bleed through the page or transfer to the page next to it.

Glue

Stay away from rubber cement. Because it is highly acidic, it will damage both the object being glued and the page it's attached to. Also avoid using liquid white glue. Instead, use a white or purple glue stick that is water soluble, such as those marketed by Dennison, Scotch (3-M), or Eberhard, Faber Co. These are the safest glue products available and can be found in most school, office, or stationery supply stores.

Tape

Cellophane tape is not a good product to use on paper that you want to save for a long time. It yellows; it absorbs printing or writing taped under it; it discolors; and its adhesive side is acidic. Also harmful are vinyl tapes that many people use to repair book spines, brown shipping and packaging tape, strapping tape, and masking tape. The biggest problem with them is their acidic adhesives content. Art and library supply stores market tapes that are archivally acceptable.

Page Protectors

School- and office-supply sections in stores offer plastic page protectors for use in 3-ring binders. Packages indicate what kind of plastic the protectors are made of, and those that are polyester, polypropylene, or polyethylene are the best ones to use. These plastics are clear and rather stiff. The protectors have openings that do not seal the page shut, thereby letting them and the items inside breathe.

Encapsulating

Very old and valuable documents need to be covered to protect them. To properly preserve them, use a process called encapsulation. Archival supply houses provide the materials needed—good polyester plastic sheets larger than the item to be saved, and special tapes to seal the edges—in kits or as separate items. Once encapsulated, the document itself is safe, does not stick to anything, and can be removed if necessary without damaging it.

Lamination

Another practice widely popular but terribly damaging to records is lamination, or covering them with clear contact paper. To laminate, you place an item between two sheets of mylar plastic and run that "sandwich" through a heat machine. The heat seals the plastic to the item. While the records are protected from spills and tearing, these coverings will cause discoloration, blurring of writing, and deterioration of paper fibers. Any item that is laminated but not deacidified first will continue to disintegrate inside the lamination. In time,

An Archivistis Tip

For archivists, the general rule of thumb for preserving records is not to do anything *irreversible* to a record. That means no gluing, taping, or laminating, for example, that cannot be undone without damaging the record.

the lamination or contact paper will curl and warp. For immediate display purposes, make a photocopy of the item and then laminate or use contact paper on the copy, not the original.

Mold

Microorganic spores are always present. They grow when temperatures are above 80 degrees, humidity is above 70 percent, and air is stagnant. Brush mold away when it appears. If you don't, it will digest the paper it grows on, stain it, and weaken its strength.

Duplicate, Backup Copies

Duplicate all valuable old paper documents and photographs, and computer files. Make duplicates to serve as backup copies—replacements in case the originals are damaged or lost. Store duplicates in a separate building than the originals.

Old Letters

A woman now in her fifties remembers that when she was a little girl, her family had a cherished collection of family letters written in the 1850s. The letters were kept in their envelopes in a shoe box. In order to read them, family members had to open the envelopes, pull out the letters, unfold them, read them, refold them, and slide them back inside the envelopes. This constant handling tore the letters along the creases, and little chips of paper would crack off whenever opened. After forty years, they were in pieces. The family destroyed the letters they loved so much, by reading them.

In order to avoid similar consequences with your own family letters, take them out of their envelopes, unfold them, and flatten them out. Put each separate page inside a clear plastic page protector that is open (unsealed) on at least one end. That way, both sides can be read but also protected from skin oil, spills, and tears.

Collections of letters should not be divided up among relatives. You can make photocopies for your relatives instead. Or, you

can give away the original and make a photocopy for yourself, so your collection stays complete.

Diaries and Journals

Acting on generous impulses, some people who have an ancestor's collection of letters or set of diaries divide them up so that others can each have a part. This sharing makes the recipients happy, but it breaks up and scatters materials that should be kept together. Copies can be made and shared, but sets of original records should be maintained.

If the journals are getting very fragile and their ink is fading, they should be donated to a good library where they can be stored properly. In return for the donation, you can ask the library to provide you with a photocopy or microfilm of the journal.

Tape-recordings

Tape-recorders, as the name says, record sound on magnetic tape. Recording heads arrange microscopic magnetized particles on the magnetic tape, and playback heads transform the patterned particles into sound. Some of us grew up using reel-to-reel tape recorders, but the current recordings are done on cassette tapes.

Several steps will extend the life of tape-recordings that you make or have in your possession:

1. Obtain a good quality recording in the first place, and always label your tape.
2. Punch out the two tabs on the back of the cassette to prevent the tape from being recorded on again.
3. Record with cassettes that run no longer than sixty minutes total, or thirty minutes per side. Tapes that run longer are too fragile and should not be used.
4. Use name-brand cassettes instead of inexpensive, generic ones.
5. Store the cassettes in protective boxes, to keep dirt and dust away. Boxes should be stored flat rather than on end.
6. Keep tapes away from magnetic fields caused by motors, TV sets, magnets, and electrical switches.

Storage Containers

From best to worst: steel file cabinets or shelves, wooden file cabinets or shelves, plastic bins and shelves, and cardboard boxes. Archival supply businesses sell sturdy, flap-lid cartons and containers for just about any kind of paper, photographic records, and heirloom objects (see the list in Appendix 3).

7. The spools of tape must not be left tightly wound for long periods of time. Play them every year or two. Don't store them after fast-forwarding or rewinding, both of which wind the tape tightly.

8. Tapes should be dubbed so that there is more than just the original tape. Use a copy (copies) for playback instead of the original.

9. Store them at room temperature and away from extreme heat or moisture.

10. Make a transcript of what was spoken on the tape, so that if a tape becomes lost or ruined, a copy of what was on it will still exist.

11. Clean the tape-recorder's heads occasionally by using a cassette cleaner kit. Heads sometimes need to be demagnetized, too, using a demagnetizing wand sold at audio-visual stores.

Videotapes

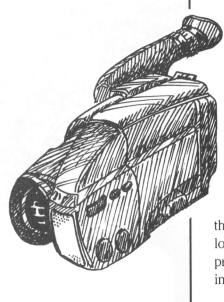

Videos are easy to shoot and enjoyable to watch. As is seen at soccer games or school assemblies, increasing numbers of proud parents are videotaping their children's performances rather than shooting pictures or slides of them. Family events such as birthdays, weddings, holidays, and vacations are often videotaped.

A problem with videotape is its questionable life-span—fading can be noticeable after ten years. Copies made from original videotapes are less sharp than the originals. Also, each time a tape is played, the video recorder's heads wear off some of the image material.

Videotapes need to be kept in their original boxes to protect them. They should be stored vertically, not horizontally. Experts no longer recommend that videotapes be rewound periodically to help preserve them, as each rewinding removes some magnetic particles, increasing "snow" on the screen when the tape is played.

Experts recommend that copies be made of very valuable video-tapes. The copy should be played instead of the original, in order to save the original from wear and tear.

Slides

Slides stored in dark, dry, cool places will last a long time. Kodachrome slides last up to 100 years and Ektachrome half that time. But, when stored under the wrong conditions, slides can deteriorate rapidly.

Slides are affected by light and heat. Therefore, the longer a slide stays in the projection beam, the worse that light's effect. Experts say to project the same slide no longer than sixty seconds, and preferably no more than thirty seconds at a time.

Slides need to be stored in projection trays and kept in the tray's box. Or, you can keep them in slide binders with special plastic pages that have indented wells designed to hold the slides and keep them from touching one another.

Experts recommend we replace our most valuable slides with duplicates after a few years, and then use the duplicates instead of the originals. Duplicates, of course, are of a slightly lesser quality than the originals.

They also need to be properly identified: Who is in the picture? Where and when was it taken? What is the event? This information can be recorded on the cardboard frame of the slide or listed on the tray box's index. Another approach is to number the slides and list the numbers and identifications in a notebook. Slides should be organized and grouped together, so that slides of the same event are together in one section.

Like photographs, slides that are not identified become worthless to future generations. A man once went to a major library and offered to donate his deceased father's collection of 5,000 slides. None were labeled, so the library declined to accept the collection.

Slides can be made into prints very easily and placed in photo albums. You can also transfer your slide collection onto videotape so that you can watch the images on your television, rather than setting up a projector and screen. If you do this, save the original slides, because videotape will not hold up well for very long. Another method which will soon be available is to transfer prints, slides, and videotape onto compact disks. These could then be watched on a computer.

Books

Bookcases and shelves should be in safe places, away from heaters, air conditioners, water pipes, and windows. Don't cram your books into a bookcase—pack them loosely so that books can be taken out and put back easily. Books should be shelved standing upright, not at an angle. Heavy volumes should be shelved with the spine down so that the weight of the pages won't pull the book away from the cover. Tops of spines break easily. Therefore, books should be removed from shelves by grasping them by the middle of both sides rather than pulling down from the top of the spine.

To mark a page, use a bookmark instead of bending the page corner or attaching a paper clip. Don't mend pages with everyday transparent tape; instead, use only archival-quality clear tape.

Leather Book Covers

Leather is an organic product that will dry out and become brittle and powdery if untreated. Never wash leather book covers. To keep leather bindings soft and flexible, condition them periodically with a leather dressing that is a mixture of lanolin and neat's-foot oil. (Baseball mitts, boots, and leather bags need the same care.)

Work the dressing into the leather with a pad of cheesecloth or cotton, using several thin coats. Wipe off excess liquid, and then shine the surface lightly with a soft, absorbent cloth. If the leather covers are already powdery, the lanolin/neat's-foot oil treatment won't do much good.

Obsolete Film and Computer Equipment

Word-processing programs are constantly upgraded. Old files need to be converted by being copied into the new programs.

Reel-to-reel recorders have become obsolete and have been replaced by cassette recorders. Super-8 mm movie cameras were phased out when video cameras became popular. You will need to convert your tapes and film products to each new system. That way, they can be played and used on new equipment. You should still save the original tapes and films, though—even when the newer playback equipment can't play them. University libraries and historical societies keep older equipment in working order to play and use materials recorded on old technological formats.

Responses to Water Damage

When a fire, flood, or any other disaster strikes, some damaged records can be salvaged. Items damaged by water from broken pipes, a flood, or the fireman's hose must be dried within forty-eight hours, or else mold will begin to grow.

The simplest way to dry items that are not dripping wet is to set them out on a table to air dry. First put plastic down on the table, and then newspapers that will absorb the moisture. Change the newspapers when they dampen. You can also hang papers, photographs, booklets, and file folders from a fishing line strung up like a clothesline.

Flatten paper or photos warped by water by pressing them on blotter material, putting a plastic mesh over the top, and then placing a weight on the mesh.

Photographs and Photo Albums

Caring for Photographs

Photographs combine chemical surfaces with paper backings. Keep the chemical surface away from contact with almost everything, including the oil on your fingers. Handle photographs by their edges; do not touch the heart of the picture.

Keep photographs away from light as much as possible, and away from extremes of temperature and high humidity. Avoid any surface contact with water or liquids as well.

Labeling Our Photos

Pictures need to be identified as to *who* is in the picture, *where* and *when* the picture was taken, and *what* the event or occasion depicted was.

It is best to write on the photo's back, as close to the margins as possible, using a #1 soft lead pencil or an archival-quality pen. Ballpoint-pen writing digs impressions into the back that become protrusions on the front. Felt tip pens' fluids can bleed through the photograph to the front.

If photographs are in an album, you can write the identifications on the album page or on a list that is attached to the page. As with slides, photographs can be numbered and a list made by number identifying each photograph.

Computer Disks

Who has not "lost" information on a computer? To avoid that, make backup copies of what you are writing.

Computer disks can be damaged, making information stored on them unreadable by the computer, so backup copies are essential.

Displaying Pictures

Photographs can be displayed or shown in frames and in albums. They can be copied and given away as gifts. They can even be transferred onto T-shirts. Photographs can also be copied onto videotape. Soon you will be able to scan your photographs into your computer to store on compact disks.

Because light fades pictures, those mounted and displayed on your walls should be duplicates, not originals. Portraits, likewise, should not be displayed near fluorescent lights or where direct or indirect sunlight will shine on them.

Photo Albums

Don't use magnetic-page photo albums (those with clear-plastic press-down pages that self-stick). So easy to use, they seemed like a dream come true when they first came on the market, but they are very bad for photographs (and scrapbook items). The sticky materials that hold the plastic pages in place are acidic. Damage is caused to the face of the photographs as they are pressed against it. The tacky texture on the pages deteriorates within a few years, as well as leaving them discolored and sticky.

Another mistake to avoid is gluing photos into a photo album. Glue ruins anything written on the back of a photograph. If you need to remove the photo for any reason, you will destroy the album page that you pulled the photo from, and also damage the photo itself. Glue is acidic, as well, and will damage both the album page and the photo.

Two methods of securing photographs in albums are recommended. One is to use an archival-quality scrapbook and mount photographs in it by using acid-free photo corners. Photo corners have been used for generations as a way to mount photographs in albums, and they work rather well. Be aware that photographs positioned across the page from one another run the risk of sticking together when the album is closed. To avoid this, insert a thin sheet of acid-free paper between the "kissing" pages.

The second recommended way to mount photos is to buy albums that have non-flimsy plastic sleeves—polyester pockets—into which the photos are inserted. Some have six pockets on one page, each pocket with an open end in which to insert the pictures. Others are layered, much like slats on a louvered door or a row of fallen dominoes, and each sleeve flips up so that you can look at the next photo.

Recently, a new technique that combines these two methods seems promising. You can now buy clear self-stick archival-grade photo protectors. These are loose plastic sleeves that have adhesive material on the back under a peel-off layer. You can insert a photo into the plastic sleeve, decide where you want to position it on a traditional photo album page, peel off the back protector, and press the sleeve down on the album page, where it will stick.

Photos to Share

Photographs can be shared by being copied. Reprints can be made from the original negatives, or a photograph of the photograph can be taken. Also, many quick-copy centers have special machines that make excellent copies of black-and-white photographs, as many per page as you want and very inexpensively. These machines also make color copies of photographs for about $2 each. You can create sets of family pictures for other family members. One daughter, for example, compiled a selection of the best photographs that her mother had saved in a shoebox for decades. The daughter then mounted the selected pictures one by one on blank paper, using a sticky-tag-type gluestick. Then she printed captions or labels and sticky-glued them either at the top or the bottom of the pictures.

The daughter then took these pages of pictures to a quick-copy center. She had a dozen copies made of each page, mostly black-and-white copies. She took each set of those pages and put them in order inside plastic protector sheets for 3-ring binders, two pages per protector sheet (back to back). The daughter then gave a binder full of these wonderful pictures to each of her mother's children and grandchildren.

Scrapbooks and Memory Albums

Creating scrapbooks is a labor of love. A mother creates a scrapbook for each of her children when they graduate from high school, containing items from their childhood and youth. A son makes a scrapbook about his father's career and presents it to him at his retirement party. A new mother creates a baby book and places in it items from the baby's first year or two—a lock of hair, footprint, birth certificate, photos, and statements about the baby's first word, first tooth, and first steps. A couple returns from a memorable vacation to England and puts together a memory book filled with postcards, photographs, a menu, a recipe, currency and stamps, ticket stubs, a list of English equivalents of American words, and other objects. A public official or performer saves newspaper clippings about his or her career and glues them in a scrapbook.

"Scrapbookers" is a term now used to refer to people who enjoy making creative scrapbooks. "Scrapbooking" is a new verb. Scrapbookers even have a magazine, *Creating Keepsakes* (published bi-monthly and available at [888] 247-5282). Some bookstores now carry archival-quality scrapbook materials—scrapbooks, photo albums, pages, adhesives, and decorating materials.

Specialized keepsake books, in addition to scrapbooks, include several types of *memory albums*. The most popular are baby books, followed closely by wedding albums. We also see a lot of trip or vacation albums, Scout albums, and even clipping collections.

Scrapbook—what an unfortunate name! That's why some people prefer to call them keepsake books or memory books. In common usage, the word *scrap* applies to things leftover, discarded, rejected, or unimportant, like scrap metal. A less used meaning, which applies to scrapbooks, is "fragment."

Many people create scrapbooks mainly for photographs, and occasionally add nonphoto items they like. However, most "scrapbookers" insert more paper items than photographs. Scrapbooks can contain such items as birth certificates, baby announcements, diplomas, sports block letters, greeting cards, graduation and wedding announcements, report cards, locks of hair, congratulatory letters, newspaper clippings about the person, some of the person's childhood drawings and writings, Scout badges, cloth fragments from a

favorite piece of clothing, printed programs, old driver's licenses, old passports, membership lists or rosters, and stubs of theater tickets,

Scrapbooks are priceless family records. They contain important and valued bits and pieces of history that don't quite fit anywhere else—not in diaries or journals, and not in photo albums. Because they are memory books, scrapbooks are treasures. Rarely do families throw away scrapbooks that they have inherited.

Unfortunately, many scrapbooks are created by using poor-quality materials that are not durable. A look at others' scrapbooks reveals several valuable dos and don'ts that determine how long and how well scrapbooks will last.

Scrapbook Materials

In the past two generations, manufacturers of scrapbooks created books more like workbooks rather than treasure books. They gave them attractive covers but made the pages and refills out of cheap, poor-quality paper that is textured like construction paper. Highly acidic, this paper causes deterioration of the items placed on it. Only in the past few years have stores started carrying archival-quality scrapbook materials.

Stores now sell two basic kinds of scrapbooks or albums: expandable-spine albums (sometimes with tie cords through the left edges that holds the cover and pages in place) and 3-ring binders. The expandable-spine albums come with standard pages, usually white. The 3-ring binder albums contain clear-plastic page protectors, which allow the scrapbooker to place any color and stock of paper inside the protectors.

Scrapbook display areas offer buyers a range of scrapbooks and of papers and cardstock to use for pages. Some bookstores sell vibrant colors of archival-quality scrapbook paper, and also paper with tiny dots or patterns for use as pages or as background paper behind an item being mounted in the scrapbook. They also offer paper that is textured or specially coated. Many of these items are available by mail order as well.

Here's what you need to get started scrapbooking: a scrapbook with pages of acid-free scrapbook paper or cardstock, scissors, a sharp knife or razorblade, a ruler, acid-free adhesive glue or tape,

Memory Books

If proof is in the pudding, a scrapbook or memory book is one of the best and most popular ways in which families store and try to preserve items for the next generation.

and an acid-free permanent-ink pen. Scrapbookers prefer cardstock or heavy-grade paper for mounting photographs and flimsy papers.

Scrapbookers like to add creative lettering, designs, and drawings to make their displays attractive. Some like to use calligraphy for lettering. For titles and labels and for writing in scrapbooks, you should use permanent-ink pens. Pens containing pigma ink are close to archival quality; you can find these in the scrapbook or craft section of stores.

Creative scrapbookers add style and decorative touches when positioning items on scrapbook pages and titling them. You can create designs with crinkle scissors and stencil decorative patterns onto the pages. You can also cut shapes out of colored paper or use colored marking pens (acid-free). You can even use the new confetti paper punches now available, with which you can punch out little shapes of all kinds of things—animals, plants, cars, hearts, etc. You can then glue these onto the pages like sprinkled confetti, for borders around objects, or around the edge of the page to add color and excitement.

Scrapbookers also use clip art to decorate and illustrate scrapbook pages. Clip art designs can be found in books of cut-and-copy clipboard art with assorted themes such as school, babies, sports, or holidays. Computer software packages that generate clip art are also available. Rubber stamps are available in all sorts of designs as well, and they can be used with permanent, acid-free ink.

If stores in your area don't sell archival-quality materials, you can order them by mail from archival supply firms and scrapbook supply dealers. Check Appendix 3 for descriptions, addresses, and phone numbers.

Light Impressions, an archival supply firm, sells a Memorabilia Album Kit by mail order. It is a scrapbook starter kit that contains an album in a protective slipcase, acid-free paper pages, top-loading sheet protectors, and mounting corners.

Scrapbooks on Videotape or CD

You can videotape scrapbooks so that they can be shown on your TV set. Videotaped scrapbooks can include a soundtrack that tells about the items being shown. In the near future, technology will make it easy for you to scan anything flat in your scrapbook into your computer so that you can see it on the monitor and print out copies.

Objects, Keepsakes, Heirlooms

People like to save objects that once belonged to their ancestors. Some of these objects are textiles such as a wedding dress, World War I army hat, keepsake quilt, old lace handkerchief, embroidered pillow case, flag, or cape.

Like paper products and photographs, textile items need to be stored in moderate environments, away from light and high heat and humidity. They also need protection from bugs, worms, and small animals.

Some cloth items need to be stored flat, in boxes, while others are strong enough to be hung from padded hangers in a closet. Conservators who care for fabric items in museums advocate not covering textile items with plastic garment bags. These will decompose and harm the object inside them. Instead, they suggest wrapping textiles in muslin. Also, fabric should be stored so that it is not in contact with wood.

Store noncloth heirloom objects in acid-free boxes, with acid-free tissue inside to protect them.

Consulting with a Conservator

If you need advice on how to preserve a family heirloom, contact a large museum and explain your problem. They should have a conservator who can help you. Or, to find a qualified conservator near you, contact:

Conservation Referral Service
Foundation of the AIC
1400 16th Street, N.W., Suite 340
Washington, D.C. 20036

Passing the Records On

You need to find someone to take care of the records after you no longer can do the job. You need either to pass the records on to them before you die or else spell out in your will exactly who is to inherit what out of your family heritage materials.

Memory or Treasure Box

Some parents help their children create small boxes for storing childhood "treasures"—seashells, feathers, carved wood, souvenirs, Pogs, baseball cards, rings, etc. As children outgrow this stage, these boxes can be saved for when the child grows up.

CHAPTER FIVE

Tape-Recording Personal and Family Oral Histories

Gold the Easy Way: The Magic of Oral History

At rare, fortunate, unexpected moments, people share their fascinating life experiences: a grandmother reminiscing about her childhood on an Iowa farm; a grandfather recalling life as a railroad conductor on passenger trains in New England; an old man on a bus telling a stranger the engrossing story of his brush with fame; a young girl in an airplane excitedly talking about a recent accomplishment. Such people have something important to share. But, all too often, experiences shared by voice die with the teller because they are not written down or recorded.

Because most of your very special older relatives won't write down their life stories, they need your help. They often lack the writing skills or health, or perhaps even energy to spend weeks putting their lives on paper or computer. What a blessing it is, then, both for them and for you, to be able to tape-record their life histories.

Through the magic of a good-quality tape-recorder, adequate preparation, and proper interviewing techniques, you can capture vivid reminiscences exactly as described by the person who remembers them. Then, at the touch of a button, you and generations to come can recall the hopes, fears, joys, and disappointments of a very real life that you will cherish as part of your heritage.

Sample Page from a Transcribed Oral History Interview

A: This is an interview with Grandpa Brown—Arthur J. Brown—by his granddaughter, Kathryne Allen, on September 26, 1970 at the Brown residence, 123 Fourth Street, San Diego, California.

Let's start out, Grandpa, by having you tell us your first memories about your boyhood.

B: Well, as you know, my father moved around a lot because he worked for the railroad. When I came on the scene the folks were in Texas. Of course, I don't remember any of that because they moved to Montana when I was about three.

Butte, Montana. Quite a mining town, Butte was, and quite a place for a boy to grow up in! Yes, sir! (*laughs*)

Main things I remember about growing up there are hunting and fishing. And the winters! Funny how the snow seems so deep to you when you're a boy, but we spent many a winter day at the ice rink, which was really a flooded football practice field. Used to build a big bonfire, especially when it got below freezing, so we could warm up.

'Course the mines were the big thing in Butte, all over the place. And lots of Irish there, and lots of drinking. My pals in the neighborhood all had Irish names like Conway and McGowan and Sullivan—anyway, they showed me how to hit up drunk miners coming out of the bars, for money. I can remember getting $10 from one old guy. So what else do you want to know?

A: What was grade school like?

B: Now that was a long ways back! (*laughs*) Seems like I went to an old, yellow-brick, three-story school on Broadway Street. As I recall, all we had was old-maid school teachers. Strict. Every year we had to learn and recite poems, and one year—I think it was fourth grade—my mother, your great-grandmother, made me practice and practice this one poem. When the day came, my mind froze and I couldn't remember even one verse of it. Lincoln School, that's the name.

A: What were your teachers like?

B: Well, let's see. I think I liked Mrs. Simpson the best. She was my fourth-grade teacher. Old maid like the rest. I liked to help her clean the blackboards and make posters after school. So, when school got out for the summer, she gave me all the marbles she had taken from the boys that spring. Opened her desk drawer, and she had hundreds of marbles in marble bags and little boxes. What a great collection I had after that! We boys played a lot of marbles back then. Shooters. Purees. Cat's eyes. We used steel ball bearings for shooters, ones that kids got from their dads who worked in the mines.

Transcripts

One hour of tape-recorded conversation, when transcribed, equals about twenty double-spaced typed pages.

Tape-Recording

In a nutshell, you have two simple objectives when you tape-record an oral history interview with a relative:

1. Obtain a good-quality recording
2. Have the interviewee talk, not you, about the subjects you want discussed.

Oral history is popular in America. Hundreds of oral history programs—funded by universities, historical societies, and organizations—are busily interviewing people all across the country. A national Oral History Association holds annual conventions and publishes journals, newsletters, self-help booklets, and training guides to help anyone conducting oral history interviews. Since the 1960s, interest has mushroomed among families who want to record the life stories of their older relatives.

Tape-recording oral histories involves four simple steps: (1) selecting someone to interview (and obtaining a tape-recorder); (2) setting up the interview and creating questions to ask; (3) conducting a good interview by following some tested, useful techniques; and (4) transcribing the recording and making the history information accessible to others.

There is no one, sure way to conduct oral history interviews because each person being interviewed is unique, with a personality and experiences distinct from everyone else. Still, experienced interviewers offer several proven dos and don'ts that you should consider.

Audio and Video Recording
Audiotape Recording

Audiotape recorders have built-in recording and playback heads that can "read" the cassette tapes. If you could look super-microscopically at the dull side of a cassette's thin, dark tape, you would see a coating there of millions of magnetized particles. When something is recorded, it means a tape recorder head magnetically arranges the tape's particles into patterns that playback heads can "read" and turn into understandable sounds.

How recorder heads do this is not important, but what is vital to know is that audiotapes are greatly affected by magnetic fields that can alter the magnetic particle patterns. So, if we place a recorded tape on a TV or near a strong motor or magnet, the sound will "garble." Also, on very thin recording tape, such as that found in cassettes that run more than thirty minutes per side (sixty

minutes total), tape when wound tightly can cause sound "print through" from layer to layer.

Videotape Recording

Isn't it better to videotape an interview with Grandma rather than audiotaping her? The answer is 20 percent yes, 80 percent no. Videotaping certainly has pluses, but it has even more minuses.

Videotaped recordings capture the face, the body expressions, the hand gestures, and therefore more of the personality and the reality of the person than an audio recording can. But, *to record someone's complete life story often takes four to eight interviews or more.* If we videotape Grandma sitting in her living room chair, talking for eight to fifteen hours or more, we create a nonaction, "talking head" video. This is so boring to watch that no one will actually view it from beginning to end. It's a good idea instead to videotape perhaps a half-hour segment after a normal sit-down-and-talk interview is finished, just to capture the person's appearance and personality on film.

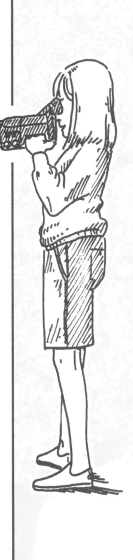

Video is designed to record action and movement. Therefore, to do a video oral history right, one needs to be not only an interviewer but also a producer and cameraperson doing creative filming. This type of interviewer might zoom in on her face, then back; pan wide to show the living room, and then go back to her face; come around behind her and videotape over her shoulder while she explains the pictures in the photo album on her lap; and occasionally tape the face of the interviewer (if the interviewer has another cameraperson along). To videotape an interview requires much more work and planning, therefore, than does an audiotape-recorded interview.

Some older people are intimidated by the small cassette audio recorders used for normal oral history interviews. So, an interviewer does his or her best to help them forget it is there during the interview. A video camera in front of them on a tripod or held by a cameraperson, however, is not as easy to ignore. Additionally, most people do not like to hear their voice on tape, but many dislike even more how they look on film—elderly people often more so than others.

Videotape has particularly good oral history value in a few specific situations: when someone is explaining family photographs, belongings, or heirlooms; when someone is demonstrating a skill such as canning fruit, plowing, painting, welding, playing a musical instrument, knitting, or playing a sport; when someone is at a family home and is explaining what is being shown; and when the person being interviewed is at a family reunion or gathering where he or she can talk with other relatives who can be filmed while they share family stories.

(A great videotaping project is to make a video of someone's life that is based on a mix of materials such as audiotape interviews, still photographs, video clips of sites and people, and family objects. To make it a successful video "program," there should be a script and the video should be shot as a carefully planned sequence of voices, sounds, still pictures, and live action.)

Be cautioned that, until the approaching digital revolution changes things, videotape has a short life span. Estimates are that videotape's sharpness and color will start to fade within twenty years, much like color photographs do, or even sooner if played often (see preservation facts in Chapter 4). So, videotape lacks permanence and "staying power" as a family record.

Even though this chapter is designed for audiotaping interviews, most of its suggestions also apply to videotaping interviews.

Step 1: Selecting an Interviewee (Narrator) and a Recorder

Selecting a Person to Interview

You need to decide which of your relatives needs to be interviewed first. Who has the most information about the family? Who knew the previous generation, or earlier ones, best? Who knows a lot of the family's history but because of age or ill health might not be around too much longer? Whose life story do you urgently care about recording? You should select a person you know has something significant to tell, who has a fairly alert memory, and whose full recollections are not already written down or recorded.

Opportunities pop up sometimes that you can capitalize on. For example, if someone you'd like to interview is coming for a visit or if you will be spending a vacation with him or her, you could take advantage of the contact and conduct an interview or two while fate has you together in the same place.

The best interview situation is with one interviewer and one narrator—one-to-one. Sometimes an additional person, such as a sibling or spouse, can benefit the interview by reminding the narrator of details or adding information of their own. However, in 50 percent of the cases, the extra person ruins the interview by disagreeing with, contradicting, or dominating the discussion.

Your choice of interviewee, or narrator, might be determined by what types of information you want to obtain. For example, do you want a complete life story of the person or a particular episode in that person's life? His or her recollections about deceased relatives? Or, that person's version of a particular family controversy? Or, is your goal merely to learn genealogical data?

Selecting a Tape-Recorder and Tape

You need to make a good-quality, audible recording, so the quality of the tape-recorder you use makes a big difference. You can buy a decent tape-recorder or borrow one from a friend or a library. There are too many brands and styles of recorders on the market to recommend any particular one—by the time this book goes to press, any models suggested here may not even be available anymore. Interviewers should test-record on a recorder before they decide to use it. If the sound quality of that recorder turns out to be poor, a better unit is needed.

When selecting a recorder to use during oral history interviews, consider these suggestions:

1. Test your recorder to see how well it records the human voice. Position it about four feet away and talk normally into it. Then, play back the recording for a few people in a somewhat large room. If all the people in the room can understand what is said on the tape, it is a good recording.

Taping a Group Discussion

Occasionally, taping a group discussion such as a gathering of relatives around the dining room table can be useful. Very often, though, when listening to the tape of that discussion, you will not be able to tell which person is saying what—voices mingle and sometimes one voice will cover over what another person was saying.

2. Many inexpensive cassette recorders have poor-quality built-in microphones that record the machine's "engine noise." This adds a humming sound to the recording, which is not good.

3. If the recorder has an input hole for an external or plug-in microphone, buy or borrow an extension microphone and record with that instead of the built-in mike. In most cases, using an external microphone will double the audio quality. If you do use an external mike, never hold it in your hand to record; instead, set it down on a table or chair arm. If you place it on bare wood or metal, cushion it underneath with a handkerchief or pillow.

4. Mikes that clip onto people's lapels are very distracting and bothersome to narrators forced to wear them.

5. Recorders used during interviews should operate on electric current and not batteries. Batteries can easily run down (even new ones).

6. Select a recorder that uses standard-size cassette tapes; microrecorders that require mini-tapes are not recommended. If you do use a microrecorder that has great recording quality, you *must* immediately copy the contents onto standard-size cassettes to preserve the recording and make it useful for others.

Cassette Tapes

For durability, experts recommend using name-brand cassettes that have recording times of sixty minutes total (thirty minutes per side), called a C-60 cassette. Tapes that run longer than sixty minutes are too thin. They can develop jamming and tangling problems and suffer print-through distortions that garble the recording.

The tape in a cassette starts with a clear or white leader that runs for five to ten seconds before the magnetic tape begins. You cannot record on the leader. So, when you start recording on a new side, you should count to about eight before you start talking.

What If They Don't Want to Be Interviewed?

People who decline to be interviewed do so for a variety of reasons. Some of these are:

1. They have family information they want to keep secret and are afraid they might reveal.
2. They feel unsure about their memories and don't want to be embarrassed by saying wrong things on tape.
3. They are deathly afraid of tape-recorders and freeze up when facing one.
4. They are modest and believe that talking about themselves is egotistical.
5. They are too busy.
6. They have personal and family history materials that they want to study before they respond to questions on tape.
7. They distrust the interviewer and his or her motive.
8. They are afraid they must carry the interview and do all the work while the interviewer just listens.
9. They are uncomfortable being interviewed in their home.

Some of these objections we cannot overcome. But a few approaches do sometimes work. Here are some ideas:

Inform Them the Workload Is On You, Not Them

Promise them that they have the easy part—just answering the questions that you ask—and that you will guide the interview.

Appeal to Their Conscience

"You are the only one who remembers our great-grandfather, and we need you to tell us about him." "My brothers and sisters have asked me to plead with you to share your memories with us. We need your help."

Stress That Talking Is Easier Than Writing Things Down

"Mom, you've got all that family history in your head. You've either got to write it down for us or tape-record it. Let me help you do it the easy way—you just talk and I'll record."

Record Them Over the Telephone

People reluctant to face a tape-recorder can often be convinced to talk to you by telephone while you record them.

Ask Them to Talk About Their Parents or Grandparents, Not About Themselves

Once they start talking about others, you can gradually introduce questions about their own childhood contacts with those people. From there, it is easy to shift the conversation toward their own lives as youngsters.

Capitalize On Occasions When They Talk About the Past

If the relative is at someone's home for dinner or a visit and starts telling interesting stories, you can grab a recorder and turn it on. "Let me turn on the recorder while you're telling that story, Grandpa—it's such a good one."

Arrange for Them to Be Jointly Interviewed With Another Relative

"Uncle Manny, I'm going to be talking to Uncle Ramos about the family. Why don't you join us and share what you know, too?" In this case, having an extra person in the interview might be the only way someone will agree to be recorded.

Bribery By Trade or Barter

If you have a photograph collection or a written life story of a relative—or any other kind of record the prospective interviewee might like—you could barter with it: "Aunt Maria, I've got copies of Dad and Mom's history. I'll make you a copy and give it to you if you'll let me interview you about the family."

Send Them an Account of the Family's History That Will Make Them Want Them to Tell Their Version

A man could not gain his aunt's permission to interview her. So, one day he gave her a copy of her brother's (his father's) oral history transcript, in which the father talked about their parents and family. The aunt found several wrong statements in it, so she asked if she could tell the story "right."

Step 2: Preparing for the Interview

Pre-interview preparation is easy to slight, but it spells the difference between a so-so interview and a good one. You should do some background fact-finding about the interviewee, and then create a fact sheet/question sheet to take with you to use during the interview. Also, it's a good idea for beginners to do a practice interview with someone close to them who'll agree to be a guinea pig. You also need to become familiar with how your tape-recorder works before you use it at the interview.

Background Homework

The more you know about the individuals you are interviewing, the more able you will be to make sense out of what they tell you. The more family genealogy you know, the better you can understand who the people you are interviewing are talking about. It helps, too, to talk to others who know the interviewee and hear their suggestions about what to ask during the interview.

Create a Fact Sheet/Question Sheet to Use During the Interview

If at all possible, you should have in front of you during the interview key facts and dates—a life-outline or chronology—relating to the person and events to be discussed. Based on your homework about the person, you need to create a list of questions and topics to raise. (For ideas, see "A Full-Life Story: Topics and Questions" in Appendix 1.)

One key to good life-story interviews is to *ask open-ended questions, not closed questions*. Closed questions are very specific and can be answered in a word or two, such as:

"What year were you born?"
"What were your parents' full names?"
"What city was that?"
"Did she go to school?"

By contrast, open-ended questions require the narrator to explain and discuss, rather than merely to give a name or date, or a yes or no answer. Open-ended questions ask *what was it like*, or *how* was something done, or *why* something happened. So, in preparation for the interview, write down a dozen or more open-ended questions to ask.

The fact sheet/question sheet gives interviewers confidence during the interview and helps them keep the narration moving in the direction they want it to go. However, the question sheet should not become an inflexible blueprint for the interview. Interviewers need to be ready and willing to explore any new topics the narrator introduces.

It's okay to inform the narrator ahead of time what general topics the interview will cover. However, the actual list of questions should *not* be given out ahead of time, because this often suggests to the narrators that they cannot discuss subjects not on the list. Also, the question list sometimes causes the person to write out a formal statement to be read during the interview.

Sample Interview Questions

CLOSED	OPEN-ENDED
(Questions requiring specific, limited answers)	(General questions calling for fairly broad answers)
What was your grandfather's name?	What do you remember about Grandpa Chambers?
Where was your first law office?	Why did you decide to become a lawyer?
How many children did you have?	When your children were all young, what was a typical day like as a housewife?
Did you like working for that company?	How was the tool-and-die shop organized back then?
What year did you move?	Why did the family move to Michigan?

CLOSED

Was there prejudice against Hispanics living in your town?

How much money did you sell the family home for?

Did you attend church regularly?

Did you like Franklin D. Roosevelt as president?

Do you mean there were no doctors in the area?

How many blocks away was the baseball diamond?

OPEN-ENDED

What kind of reception did the Hispanics receive when they moved into town?

How did the Great Depression affect the family?

What role did religion and church play in your teenage years?

How did you feel at the time about the New Deal?

What were some typical medical practices when you were a young girl?

What did you do for recreation?

Do a Practice Interview

Do a dry run with a spouse, relative, or roommate. This will help you get the feel for the interview situation before doing the actual interview itself.

Learn How to Use the Tape-Recorder With Ease

You need to practice with your recorder until you are thoroughly familiar with how it works and can sense when it does not sound right or function properly. You need to know which buttons to push to record, how to load and eject the tape in order to turn it over or add a new one, and perhaps how to hook up an external microphone.

What to Talk About

Scores of topics can be explored during oral history interviews, depending upon what purposes you have in mind. In Appendix 1 of this book is a section called "A Full-Life Story: Topics and Questions." These topics are appropriate for biographical-type interviews, and by reviewing them you will think of many other subjects to discuss with your relative. You should develop a list of topics tailored to your own purposes and to the particular individual you will interview.

In view of the historical value of this oral history interview, I, _____ knowingly and voluntarily permit _____ the full use of this information for whatever purposes he or she may have, in return for which I will receive a copy of the cassette tapes and a typed copy of the interview.

Signature _____ Date _____

As the topics and questions in the appendix show, most people's lives are filled with experiences that have been many years in the making. So, you need to record your relatives' memories slowly and deliberately. Several hours of interviewing is a bargain price to pay for the rich materials you'll obtain by taking the time to be thorough.

Written Agreements

You and your narrators need to have a clear understanding about what will happen to the taped interview. You need to tell them what you intend to do with the cassette and the information on it. Will there be a transcript? Will they be allowed to proofread it? Will they receive their own copy of the tape? Of the transcript? Will their information be used as source material for a written history?

Universities, historical societies, and other groups who sponsor oral history projects require narrators to sign written agreements that spell out what rights both parties have in terms of the taped interviews. Most family projects, however, because of family bonds and trust, don't demand such signed agreements.

If a narrator seems legalistic about the taped interview, you can draw up a simple agreement. In it you should obtain the narrator's permission for you to have full rights to use the interview in any way you wish. Those rights will be given in exchange for a copy of the tape or transcript, or both. If those terms are not acceptable to the narrator, draw up a more restrictive agreement that he or she can feel good about.

Step 3: Conducting the Interview

Preliminaries

Make an Appointment

Schedule the time with your relative, allowing 1 1/2 to 2 hours for the interview. (After two hours, an interview declines drastically in quality, because both the interviewer and narrator become weary.) Conduct the interview in a place as free from interruptions as possible. It also helps to interview on territory familiar to the narrator.

Don't Hurry to Do It All in One Interview

If at all possible, plan to do several interviews. A reasonably full life story can require five to ten interviews or more, so don't try to cover everything during the first interview.

One-to-One Interviews Work Best

The best interview situation is one-to-one. It may require more effort to keep on the subject if another person is present, and it almost always produces less rapport between you and the narrator than could be developed in a one-to-one situation. Group interviews are not recommended, though if the narrator's spouse insists on sitting in, there are few tactful ways to avoid it.

Test the Recorder

Just before leaving for the interview, do a sample recording to be sure the machine is working.

Bring What You Need

In addition to the tape-recorder, interviewers should take along extra blank cassettes, the question sheet, a notepad, a pen or pencil, an extension cord, and, if the interview is in an older home, a two-prong adapter for the recorder's three-prong electrical plug.

Setting Up Seating

Chat informally with the person you are interviewing to establish rapport while you are setting up the equipment. (Try not to draw too much attention to the tape-recorder.) Don't prolong this warm-up, however. Rather, move fairly soon into the interview itself.

It is vital to establish a good recording situation. Both how and where you sit and where you position the tape-recorder make a big difference. For proper recording, and for good rapport and eye contact with your interviewee, you should sit within four to six feet of each other. If you need to move a chair closer to a sofa or bring in a kitchen chair to get this close, do so.

Position the tape-recorder so that you can see the cassette spindles turning and how much tape is left. It should also be close enough for you to easily turn the cassette over to side two or put in a new cassette.

If one voice is considerably louder than the other, move the external microphone or recorder closer to the softer voice. Put a pad underneath the recorder or microphone if you have placed it on a hard surface such as a table. Otherwise foot-tapping or finger drumming make for a disastrous recording.

Sample Oral History Agreement Form

In view of the historical value of this oral history interview,

I, _____,
(PRINT FULL NAME OF NARRATOR)

knowingly and voluntarily permit _____
(PRINT FULL NAME OF INTERVIEWER)

the full use of this information for whatever purposes he or she may have, in return for which I will receive a copy of the cassette tape and a typed copy of the interview.

_____
Narrator's signature

_____ Date

Here is a good seating arrangement:

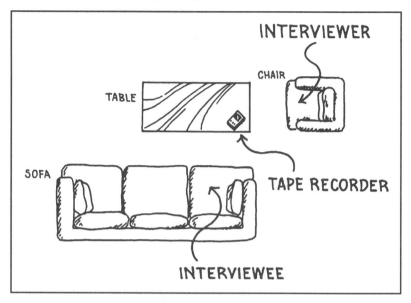

Arrangement A: Built-in Microphone

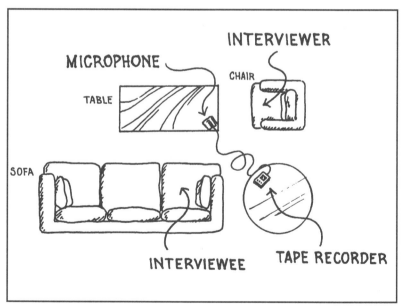

Arrangement B: Extension Microphone

It is important to reduce outside noise and interference as much as possible. If necessary, ask the narrator for permission to close windows or doors to block out noise from children, dogs, motor vehicles, TVs or radios in adjoining rooms, and dishwashers. Be warned that the ticking and chiming of grandfather clocks record very clearly, as do the hums of air conditioners, fans, and some heaters.

Basic Interview Techniques

Record a Heading on the Tape

Begin the interview by pushing the record button to start the taping, waiting eight seconds for the leader to run, and then recording a heading. A heading officially starts the interview, shifting it from conversation into something that is more formal.

To record a heading means to dictate on the tape the names of the interviewer and narrator, the place of the interview, and the date. Here's an example:

> "This is an interview with Maria Catale by her son Tony V. Catale on January 15, 1998, at Maria's residence at 3115 Ackman Avenue, Eastbrook, New York."

After recording the heading, push the recorder's stop button, rewind the tape a little, and play the heading back. This will tell you if the recorder is working and will give you an indication of how the rest of the recording will sound.

Start With a Question He/She Would Love to Answer

The opening question is critical to creating the mood and method of the interview. It therefore needs to be one the person really would like to answer. If necessary, you can ask about something not related to the interview topics but that is important enough to that person that he or she will enjoy talking about it. Your goal is to help the person quickly discover that you would like to listen while he or she talks.

Begin the Interview With Open-Ended Questions

Some people are so gregarious that no matter how you ask a question, they will talk a lot. Others, however, are uncertain and insecure when the interview begins, and they are afraid they will say something wrong. So, they watch the interviewer closely in order to "read" what is wanted. You need to signal clearly to them that they are there to talk and you are there to ask questions and listen.

Let's use a sports analogy here. Your goal is not to play Ping-Pong; you want rather to play open-field football wherein you hand them the ball and let them run with it. Guaranteed, you will play Ping-Pong for most of the interview if you start out with closed, short-answer questions like these:

You:	What was your father's full name?
She:	Thomas Walton McKinlay.
You:	When was he born?
She:	Ah, 1915, I think.
You:	Where was he born?
She:	Kirksville, Missouri.
You:	What was his mother's full name?
She:	Nancy Walton.

That back-and-forth routine is Ping-Pong—your turn, her turn, your turn, her turn. Instead, you need to hand her the ball and let her run with it.

Open-ended questions are ones that ask why, how, or what something was like. You obtain the same result by giving an instruction instead of a question, such as, "Tell me about the grade school you attended." That's a statement, but it carries an implied question: "What was grade school like?"

Another questioning technique that works well is a one-two combination of a statement and a question based on the statement. This helps you make transitions from one idea to the next. It also helps the narrator see clearly what you are asking. Here are four examples of one-two combinations:

You mentioned a few minutes ago that Aunt Elise divorced Uncle Stefan during World War II. Tell me more about that.

Cars today have air conditioning and stereos and automatic doorlocks. What was your '43 Ford like, compared to today's cars?

You said your grandma died at your Aunt Ardith's home. Why was she living with her?

My branch of the family seems to have a lot of musicians in it. What musical talent was in your grandparents' family and among your uncles and aunts?

Stifle the Impulse to Interrupt

In normal conversation we constantly interrupt one another. So, during an oral history interview, we need to stifle our normal, natural, conditioned impulses to interrupt. Normally, when we hear something said we want to know more about, we don't hesitate to jump in and ask about it right then. For example, if Uncle Ambrose made the short, simple statement, "We lived in Pennsylvania for awhile and then we moved to Florida," you would quickly think of several questions to ask as soon as he finishes the sentence:

What town in Pennsylvania?
What year did you move?
Why did you move?
How did you move?
What relatives were left in Pennsylvania?
What town in Florida?
How did you find a house?
What were your first reactions to Florida?

It's a major mistake, though, to ask even one of those questions right away. Instead, you need to jot them down on your question sheet to be asked later. The best thing you can do is to be a good

Sample Open-Ended Questions

What do you remember about your Walton grandparents?

When you were young, what contact did you have with your Walton grandparents?

Physically, what did your mother's family members look like?

Why did your parents move to Texas?

How did your parents earn a living for the large family?

What became of the farm after your grandpa died? What kind of farm was it?

listener who lets them talk while you jot down topics to explore later. While listening and taking notes, you need to encourage the narrator to continue by giving him or her approving nods of the head instead of vocal exclamations.

To simply listen to another person and say nothing more than "well, well" or "my goodness" or "hmmm" goes against our nature. But let the narrator "run" with the question without interruption for as long as he or she wishes. Only after the narrator has undeniably concluded his or her reminiscences about your initial question should you begin follow-up questions.

Let there be Pregnant Pauses

Another simple interview technique that is hard for new interviewers to learn is to "let the dust settle" from one question before asking another one. Let there be a pause in the discussion. This lapse might seem very awkward for the interviewer, but it is a "pregnant pause" for the narrator—a chance to quickly rethink the answer just given and to search the memory for more details to tell you. Silence does not necessarily mean he or she has finished the answer. You can say something as commentary or as a reaction, but not move on to a new question or subject. Say, "Well, well," "That's fascinating" or "I'd never heard that before," or even "hmmmmm."

Very often a narrator will provide highly significant information on subjects that you would never think to pursue. Such information, supplied by the narrator, can become the basis for subsequent lines of questioning. Even if, after a pause of a few seconds, the narrator says something like "Well, I guess that's all I have to say on that subject," you should offer a question that helps the narrator think harder about what he or she just said, rather than a question on an entirely new topic.

Save Questions About Details for Later

It's vital to establish the pattern of you asking a question and then listening while they do the talking. After the narrator has answered the broad, open-ended question and before you move on to the next broad question, ask the specific-detail questions you've

been dying to ask. Request that the narrator fill in some of the details of his or her reminiscences. If you hear what appears to be contradictory or wrong information, you need to ask for clarification. If a statement seems unclear, you should say it back to them in your own words and ask if that is what was meant. Even while asking for specific details, though, try to use as many open-ended questions as possible.

Do More Than Just Listen

While the narrator is doing most of the talking, you must be very busy doing several tasks simultaneously. Listen very carefully. Try to hear "clues" that the narrator gives of areas he or she would like to discuss. Digest and become conversant with the information you are hearing, much of it new to you. Keep track of what's been said so that you don't ask questions later that were already answered. Signal by eye contact and nods and "gurgles" ("oh," "uh-huh," "well, well," "my word") to the narrator that you are very interested in what's being said. Make notes on your question sheet regarding matters to bring up later. And, check the tape-recorder to be sure it is working properly and to know how soon the tape will need to be turned or replaced.

Pursue Truth and Accurate Information

The quality of an interview depends upon your ability to dig, to get the full story, and to obtain sequences and details. So, sometimes you will need to ask a question again in a different way that will make the narrator discuss the topic more fully. Also, you need to ask yourself constantly, "How does he know that? Did the narrator see or hear that himself or did he hear it from someone else?" Sometimes you have to ask point-blank questions like this: "How do you know that, Aunt Janice?" or "Did you see that with your own eyes?"

Allow Tangents

Tape is inexpensive, so it's all right to let the narrator stray from the main subject being discussed. Not only is this tendency very difficult to stop without hurting the person's feelings, but often their

While Interviewing

Oral history expert Dr. Gary Shumway often gives new interviewers this wise advice:

When there is a pause in the discussion, what do you do?
Nothing!
You pause; you wait.
Bite your tongue.
Dig in your toes.
But do *not* rush in with the next question.

replies are not tangents at all—the narrator has a purpose for pursuing these byways, usually contributing to answers you requested.

However, if recollections do get too far off-course, they can be stopped by asking a series of closed questions, one after another. This breaks the narrator's train of thought. You can then ask a question related to the one from which they originally strayed.

Keep Opinions to Yourself

If narrators ask for your opinion about a subject being discussed, don't give it. You need to explain that the interview is designed to record their views, not yours.

Save Sensitive Matters Until Late in the Interview

If you know there is a sensitive topic, problem, or scandal in the family, don't discuss it until after you have established good rapport with the narrator. Narrators need time to assess and trust your genuine interest and sincerity regarding their recollections. So, later in the interview is the best time to ask about sensitive matters.

Rather than pretending to be naive and asking, "Was there a problem?" you could tell what you know about the problem instead. Once they realize that you know about it, and that it's not a secret they would be divulging for the first time, they will be more willing to talk about it.

Let Them Show You Materials After the Interview, Not During It

If the narrator wants to find and show you pictures or documents, or wants to read something on tape, explain that it would be better to wait until after the interview to examine or add that material. Then be sure to give them this "show-and-tell" opportunity at the end.

Watch for Signs That It's Time to take a Break

Notice signs of fatigue. Be sensitive to needs for a drink of water or a bathroom break. If the narrator becomes tired, schedule a second appointment to finish up the interview. Usually 1 $1/2$ to 2 hours is long enough for one interview session.

Concluding the Interview

False Stops Can Be Very Worthwhile

When it seems that the interview is over, push the "stop" button but don't unplug the recorder or remove the cassette tape. That way, during postinterview time, when a narrator typically says, "Well, now, something I forgot to mention before was...," you are still ready to record.

Ask for Clarification

When the interview is over, ask the narrator for the correct spelling of names and places unfamiliar to you, and to clarify family relationships, births, and death dates. Write his or her answers down on your interview question sheet.

Find Out What Other Family Records They Have

A good time to ask them about the family's records is at the end of the interview. You can find out what they have—and what they know other relatives have—in terms of genealogy collections, diaries, letters, photographs, heirlooms, and other family records. While they are showing you the items, you could tape-record their comments about them, if it seems worthwhile.

Label the Tape and Its Container

While you are small-talking after the interview, or as soon as you are in your car or have returned home, label the tape and its container by writing the following on it:

> narrator's name, birthdate, and address (with zip code)
> your name
> date
> interview length ($3/4$ of side 1, 20 minutes on side 2, etc.)

Telephone Interviews

If personal visits are not possible, you can conduct an interview by telephone. Most electronic stores or even electronics sections of larger department and discount stores sell telephone adapters for

Telephone Interviews

A word of advice for phone interviews: Turn off the call-waiting feature so that you are not barraged by beeping interruptions during the interview.

cassette recorders. They range from simple suction-cup adapters that stick on to the receiver above the ear part to little units that connect between the telephone cord and the wall plug. And, it is often possible to switch the phone to speaker and put the recorder in front of the speaker to tape.

Step 4: Preserving and Transcribing the Tapes

Preserving the Cassette Tapes

Interview tapes themselves have much value in simply preserving the voice of the narrator for posterity.

For permanent storage the recording should be on a quality, name-brand tape that runs no longer than sixty minutes total. Microcassette recordings should be copied onto standard sixty-minute cassette tapes.

Tapes need to be kept in their protective plastic boxes and stored at room temperature, away from high humidity, dampness, heat, or machines that create magnetic fields. Knock out the two little tabs on the spine of the cassette to prevent it from being recorded on again.

At least once every year or two, you need to play your oral history cassettes to loosen up the winds of tape, and then store them again. Don't get the cassette ready to store by rewinding or fast-forwarding, however. That packs the tape too tightly. Instead, *play* the tape through to loosen it up and then put it away.

You should also make copies of the original tape(s), and listen to and use only the copies, not the originals. (See Chapter 4 for more on how to preserve your family records.)

Verbatim Transcripts of the Tapes

Typed/word-processed transcriptions of interviews are easier and more enjoyable to use than tapes. And, the transcripts can be photocopied so that others can have their own sets.

Although transcribing takes time, it is worth the effort. An excellent word processor or typist takes approximately four to eight hours to transcribe one hour of a taped interview. Longhand transcription, of course, is a slower alternative. One hour of speaking on a tape produces about twenty typed pages—so three interviews that run two hours each become 120 pages. Some families have relatives who will volunteer to transcribe oral history tapes during off-hours at work. Also, most typing services listed in the *Yellow Pages* offer transcribing at a standard rate per page or per hour.

The *exact transcript* needs to be an accurate copy of what is on the tape. So, you need to transcribe as nearly verbatim as possible. You must preserve the question-and-answer format. However, false starts, stammering, and insignificant repetition need not be included. Also, murmurs such as "well, well" or "is that right?" or "my goodness" or "how about that" serve as encouragements during an interview but are left out of the transcript. "Uh huh" and "yeah" should be transcribed as "yes," and "nah" and "nope" should be changed to "no." This transcript serves as a guide for finding information on the tape.

The first version of the transcript needs to have adequate margins and be double-spaced so that corrections can be inserted. To identify the participants, use the initials (in capitals) of the respective last names, each followed by a colon, two spaces, and then the dialogue. (See "Sample of Transcript Editing" below.

Transcribers need to be very careful to spell names and locations properly. When a word is unclear, write what it sounds like and then put (?) after it, or leave a blank space in the transcript. Indicate laughter and body actions in parentheses, such as (laughs), (points across the street), and (pounds table).

The first transcript needs to be "audit-checked." That is, someone, preferably the interviewer, needs to listen to the entire tape, comparing it with what's written, and correct errors found in the transcript.

Minor editing of the transcript is necessary. You must insert basic punctuation and create sentences and paragraphs. Such modifications, needed to make the oral information readable and understandable, ought to be kept to a minimum.

Sample of Transcript Editing

Unedited transcript, typed as verbatim as possible:

A: Let's see, did you...why did you leave the farm? Was it...?

B: Did I tell you about the time the river flooded our corn? I did? Well anyway when the river flooded our corn we, you see, were not able to get more loans and so there was a store in town run by let's see was it Amos Wilson or George Jordan? George Jordan it was. Well anyway the store had an opening for a clerk and now my uncle also needed a...needed some workers on his farm near the town and so see we moved to Littleton and that's also where a car dealer just opened for business and so we maybe a month later we decided to buy our first car for a hundred dollars.

A: Is that right? Wow.

B: Yes and all the kids in town thought our boys were the luckiest in the world.

Corrected transcript, to add punctuation, make sentences and paragraphs, delete false starts and murmurs, etc.

A: ~~Let's see, did you...~~ why did you leave the farm? ~~Was it...~~

B: ~~Did I tell you about the time the river flooded our corn? I did? Well anyway~~ when the river flooded our corn we, ~~you see,~~ were not able to get more loans, ~~and so~~ there was a store in town run by ~~let's see was it Amos Wilson or George Jordan?~~ George Jordan, ~~it was. Well anyway~~ and the store had an opening for a clerk, ~~and~~ now my uncle also needed ~~a...needed~~ some workers on his farm near the town, and so ~~see~~ we moved to Littleton, ~~and~~ that's also where a car dealer just opened for business, and ~~so we~~ maybe a month later we decided to buy our first car for a hundred dollars.

A: ~~Is that right? Wow.~~

B: ~~Yes and~~ all the kids in town thought our boys were the luckiest in the world.

Final transcript:

    A. Why did you leave the farm?

    B. When the river flooded our corn we were not able to get more loans. There was a store in town run by George Jordan, and the store had an opening for a clerk. Now my uncle also needed some workers on his farm near the town, and so we moved to Littleton.

        That's also where a car dealer just opened for business, and maybe a month later we decided to buy our first car for a hundred dollars. All the kids in town thought our boys were the luckiest in the world.

After the transcript is audit-checked, corrected, and minimally edited, print out a clean copy. You should create a title page, table of contents, and a preface for it. The preface needs to explain the project: how it was done, why, who did it, and any unusual circumstances surrounding it. The preface should also carry a disclaimer that says something to the effect of: "Information in this oral history transcript is only as accurate as _____'s memory. We have not tried to confirm or correct information he/she has provided here."

By then you will have a finished, complete, original working transcript. Next, if at all possible, the narrator should proofread the transcript. He or she should review this audit-checked and punctuated version to make corrections, additions, and necessary deletions, and to clarify confusing parts and spellings that you have circled. Send them the transcript, but keep a copy for yourself in case theirs gets lost.

After the narrator has corrected and returned the transcript, you should have a final version word-processed or typed. Any additions the narrator made that are not on the tape can be included, but place them within square brackets []. (Inform readers in the preface that bracketed words are additions to the tape.)

To complete the packaging of the transcript, you can add maps, charts, and photographs. This final set can then be photocopied for others, and each set should be hardbound if possible. Send one set to the narrator, as promised in your agreement. Libraries and historical societies in your area may also welcome a copy.

A Popular Alternative: Revised Transcripts

Sad to say, few narrators like the transcripts of their interviews. They are horrified to see their speech patterns in print. The question-and-answer format also seems awkward. To reduce the narrator's negative reactions, many families make a new, edited version out of the exact transcript by restructuring it to read better.

First, questions are deleted by working them into the answers. This is a slight fudge, but it hardly compromises the integrity of the information. Second, they shift blocks of subject matter around so that all the information about one topic is grouped together and not scattered throughout the transcript as it may be in the exact transcript.

For example, let's say the narrator talked about subjects A to H in this order: A, B, C, A, D, E, B, A, F, G, C, H, etc. With word-processing, it is easy to group all the statements about subject B together, subject A together, etc., and even change the order in which the topics appear.

The result is an autobiography created from oral history interviews with that person. It reads much better in this restructured format and family members like it much better than the exact transcript version.

Oral History's Limitations

Taped oral histories are not histories in the sense of a well-researched and carefully told story. Rather, they are oral memories, or "memory claims" by someone regarding the past. You record the history "as so-and-so remembers it." But, the oral history, because it is based so much on fallible memory, contains inaccura-

cies. Sometimes it is downright unreliable. Oral history tapes and transcripts serve the family as material from which they can try to write a history—raw source material much like a collection of letters or a set of diaries. Oral accounts serve as one record of many from which history or biography can be written. No historian or biographer can accept an oral history uncritically until he or she has done proper research in other sources to confirm or corroborate what the oral history says.

Great Ways to Use the Tapes and Transcripts

Oral history tapes serve several functions. Mainly, the tapes and transcripts stand by themselves as historical documents. Copies of the tapes and of the transcripts can be given to family members and libraries. A tape of "highlights" can be made, containing the best stories and information from the tapes, and provided to the family. Transcripts can be packaged nicely and given to the family. For instance, they can be given a title page that includes a picture of the narrator, a preface, a table of contents, maps, pictures, and an attractive cover. Voices on a tape can be copied and edited into a slide/sound presentation or videotape history of the person or family, or they can be added to a tape containing other family members' recollections, too.

Tapes and transcripts can be used as source material for written histories or biographies From them you can draw information and colorful or meaningful quotations to enhance your histories. Oral histories open doors for other research, also, by raising unanswered questions or by providing leads to pursue and names of people to contact.

Finally, one "use" of oral history is really a by-product of interviewing. The oral history becomes the source of a bond between you and the individuals you interview. Oral history projects often create new friendships, strengthen family relationships, and make interviewers, narrators, and those who read or hear the oral histories cherish their family and heritage even more.

A Family's Treasures

Heirlooms we don't have in our family. But stories we've got.

Rose Chernin,
In My Mothers House

CHAPTER SIX

Your Personal Diaries, Journals, and Life Stories

T wo very popular personal history activities are keeping a personal diary or journal, and writing one's own life story or autobiography. No hard-and-fast rules determine how to do either project, but by looking at how others have done them, you can pick up some good ideas.

Diaries and Personal Journals

Of all the texts in the world, handwritten or printed, few are treasured as much as diaries or personal journals. We enjoy reading the personal journals of notable people like George Washington and Charles Lindbergh, and the famous diaries of obscure people like Anne Frank and Samuel Pepys. In family circles, we cherish an old diary passed down to us by a grandparent or other forebear.

Today the terms "diary" and "journal" mean essentially the same thing; clear distinctions between them cannot be drawn. A good definition of a diary or journal is:

A personal record, kept daily or quite regularly and by date, wherein a person tells about his or her own experiences soon after they occur.

The key words in this definition, the characteristics that make diaries and journals distinctive, are: "personal," "quite regularly," "own experiences," and "by date."

Nearly everyone who can write eventually toys with the idea of starting a personal journal. And the number who do try it is surprisingly large. Journal-keeping is popular. People of all ages are writing in diaries today for the same reasons people have done so for centuries. In our day we have readily available paper, pens, typewriters, and word processors—not to mention more schooling than people in the past—which make the activity much easier now.

What Is a Journal or Diary?

Libraries contain published and unpublished diaries that have survived the ravages of time. They are hand-printed, handwritten,

1773

Boston Tea Party

typed, legible and illegible, narrative and shorthand, tall, tiny, thick, skinny, and of various colors of paper, ink, and bindings. Their entries are impersonal, deeply emotional, mundane, exciting, aloof, conceited, literary masterpieces, and barely literate. There are long and detailed entries as well as brief ones, regular as well as irregular ones, and gaps and interruptions lasting days, weeks, or months. Some diarists penned thirty or more volumes during a lifetime; others wrote only a few pages.

Surviving diaries show that journal-keeping is a highly personal activity—journals are as unique as the people who pen them. Part of the satisfaction diarists receive comes from complete freedom to fill up the pages in any way they wish.

Two myths about diary-keepers are popular: first, that diaries are mainly the work of adolescents; second, that journal-keeping is primarily a female activity. To the contrary, library lists of published and unpublished diaries show more adult than juvenile diaries, and more men's than women's. Journals are personal thoughts penned by young and old of both sexes. Anyone who can read and write is a potential diarist. And, with the easy availability of tape-recorders, anyone who can talk can be a diarist without writing a word.

Why Keep a Personal Journal?

We are busy people. Journal-keeping takes time. Why, then, do people do it? Put simply, it brings personal satisfaction for a variety of reasons. There are several purposes or needs that journals fill.

Recording Special Experiences

Tourists at Gettysburg click cameras constantly. Photographs allow you to record special scenes. Diaries also record special experiences, but as word "pictures." And, as an advantage over photographs, words can quickly span a sequence of happenings, trace an experience from beginning to end, detail the role played by each participant, describe feelings and reactions, and explain complex factors invisible to a camera's eye. Innumerable diaries were begun because someone witnessed or participated in something special, unusual, or extraordinary, and wanted to remember it.

Journal Keepers

By way of name-dropping, some famous Americans who kept journals (or became famous because they did so) include William Bradford, Cotton Mather, Samuel Sewall, Martha Ballard, George Washington, John Adams, John Jay, Aaron Burr, Washington Irving, Brigham Young, James K. Polk, Mary Chestnut, Louisa May Alcott, John James Audubon, Harriet Beecher Stowe, Charles and Ann Morrow Lindbergh, Lewis and Clark, Francis Parkman, John C. Frémont, Samuel F. B. Morse, Henry David Thoreau, Ralph Waldo Emerson, Rose Kennedy, Thomas Edison, and Charlton Heston.

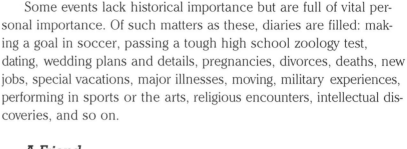

Mary Boykin Chestnut's Diary's Opening Entry, Two Months Before the Civil War Broke Out

"February 15, 1861. I have always kept a journal, with notes and dates and a line of poetry or prose, but from today forward I will write more. I now wish I had a chronicle of the two delightful and eventful years that have just passed. Those delights have fled, and one's breath is taken away to think what events have since crowded in."

Some events lack historical importance but are full of vital personal importance. Of such matters as these, diaries are filled: making a goal in soccer, passing a tough high school zoology test, dating, wedding plans and details, pregnancies, divorces, deaths, new jobs, special vacations, major illnesses, moving, military experiences, performing in sports or the arts, religious encounters, intellectual discoveries, and so on.

A Friend

A journal is a friendly, listening ear—something we all need. Robinson Crusoe needed Friday to keep from going mad. Diarist Anne Morrow Lindbergh observed, "In our family an experience was not finished, not truly experienced, unless written down or shared with another." Loneliness produces some of the finest diaries because people of all ages, away from loved ones or surrounded by others not interested in them, need to tell someone about their lives. Diaries, then, become their listeners.

Expressing Feelings and Emotions

Experiences can be powerful and deeply felt. Some events or emotions can be too overwhelming to share fully with other people. We could compile a long list of people whose journals served as emotional safety valves for expressing such emotions as anger, frustration, fear, worry, deep sorrow, pride, hope, and love.

A Record Book of Everyday Doings

Lawyers, sales reps, and businesspeople use appointment books not only to plan ahead but also to refer back to past work. Doctors and dentists keep records of their patients' health. Car owners have vehicle maintenance books so that they can know when to change the car's oil or get it tuned up. Parents record immunization histories of their children. PTAs, corporations, religious groups, and government agencies keep minutes of their meetings.

Diary-keeping is a personal application of this need to record normal activities. Diaries serve as minute books for the individual. Because memory is fallible, journals prevent the loss of information that could be caused by forgetting. In time, such a faithfully

kept record of everyday doings becomes a valuable reference book—a data bank filled with useful information about past experiences and associates.

A Family Record Book

Some parents keep journals to serve as their family unit's minute book or history. Important developments are noted therein, such as births, deaths, marriages, moves, vacations, and accomplishments and activities of the family members. As adults, the children often love to hear what their parents wrote about them in earlier days.

Useful Mirror of Oneself

A journal, if frank and forthright, provides you with a fairly accurate picture of what you are like. It records your personality, behavior patterns, habits, tastes, interests, and progress. It shows your strengths and weaknesses. Memory plays tricks on people. It sometimes blanks out negative things you do, making you see yourself in the most positive light. Or it does just the opposite: It focuses on only the bad and blots out your good qualities. Your journal serves as a record of how you change over time, offering you perspectives for judging development, attitudes, strengths, weaknesses, and worth.

The journal acts as a soul-mirror, offering strength in trouble times and recalling positive parts of your life during times of depression and self-doubt. For some it helps trace out the meaning and understanding of life's purposes. It therefore is a good place to make resolutions and plan improvements for oneself, and then to record how well those goals are reached.

An Enjoyable Hobby

As noted earlier, people keep journals because they enjoy it. Journal writing is like talking with a good friend, one of life's genuine pleasures. It involves creativity when artwork, poetry, clever narration, and word play are attempted. Diary writing is a quiet, private time, when the person is alone with himself and away from other demands. These peaceful moments provide healthy interludes for rethinking, self-assessing, planning, relaxing, and reminiscing. Good things are experienced twice when written about in a diary.

Emotional Diary Entry of a Colorado Father Whose 11-Year-Old Son was Dying of Diabetes

"Dec. 10, 1884. Oh dear God, I wish the doctors were smarter and could discover something to cure this awful disease. They will someday, but it will be too late to save my little boy."

Diary Entry of a Young Teenager

Helped grandma with the weekend shopping. She was dead fierce in the grocer's; she watched the scales like a hawk watching a fieldmouse. Then she pounced and accused the shop assistant of giving her underweight bacon. The shop assistant was dead scared of her and put another slice on.

From Sue Townsend's
The Secret Diary of Adrian Mole
Aged 13-3/4

Additional pleasure comes from reading the journal later. This is a person's very own creation, a personal contribution to literature and history, his or her own words, thoughts, and feelings. To read your diary is to relive old times, remember old friends, and see turning points in life that at the time seemed insignificant.

For Assignments

In some college classes, instructors use personal journals as learning tools to help students discover their own reactions and ideas about the course's subject matter. Military officers, ship captains, explorers, and foremen—involved in ventures that require strict accountability—keep daily journals for their professions. Ministers, missionaries, and church workers often feel obligated to keep a record of their stewardships. And more than one person became a diarist simply because so-and-so gave them a blank diary as a present, and they knew the giver would be checking to see if the receiver used the gift.

For Partial Immortality

Anne Frank is dead, but she still shares her thoughts with living people through her diary. Her case shows how diaries provide a degree of immortality. Some diarists write intentionally for unknown readers yet to be born. Parents sometimes record advice for children or grandchildren to read many years later. Wars, accidents, and sudden misfortunes force people into desperate situations in which hopes of escaping grow dim. Such despairing people sometimes use diaries to detail their plights so that others can know what happened to them.

For Whom Is a Journal Written?

Diarists seem to have in mind one of four audiences. These are:

The Private Journal

Probably most journals are written solely for the eyes of the diarist—no one else. Either the diarist believes no one else would be interested in it, or he or she is recording things others should not

see. The sense of privacy in journal-keeping allows for free and uninhibited discussions. A private diary, then, needs to be kept in a safe place where others cannot read it.

The Semi-Private Journal

Even if no one sees the journal but you, it has filled its purpose. Keeping a semi-private journal means that you don't mind if someone else reads it, but you are not really writing the journal for others.

The Semi-Public Journal

This type of diary is written especially for someone other than yourself: a spouse, child, friend, or unknown future reader. In writing a semi-public journal, you therefore tend to be careful how you tell things so that your self-image and the reputations of others are protected.

The Public Journal

Written for wide public consumption, even perhaps publication, a public journal tends to say too little or too much. It often says too little when it emphasizes the positive, gives satisfactory explanations for questionable behavior, and avoids negative admissions. Consequently, the full, unvarnished story is not told.

It may also say too much when more than the truth is told. Sensational materials designed to shock and excite the public are intentionally added, or lies are inserted to enhance the marketability of the journal or to damage an enemy's reputation. Even with the public as the intended audience, though, a diarist can write a reasonably honest account—and many do.

Not surprisingly, there seems to be a direct correlation between how private a journal is and how honest its content is.

Children's Diaries

Some five-year-olds have written simple diaries, but at age nine or ten is a more typical time for children to start keeping a diary. It is a good idea for parents to give a child a blank-page or lock-and-key

---

A Young Woman's First Diary Entry

"November 23, 1930. Yesterday I went to town and bought this book to enter scraps in, not a diary of statistics and dates and decency of spelling and happenings but just to jot me down in, unvarnished me...It seems to me it helps to write things and thoughts down."

diary as a gift. That may encourage the child to start a diary, or it may simply be there when some interest sparks awhile later.

Some parents keep a diary for a child who is too young to be able to write. They ask him or her what should be written down, and then they do it. In the middle grades, some teachers require students to keep some kind of journal containing reactions to reading materials or class projects.

Parenting experts overwhelmingly agree, however, that parents should never read a son or daughter's diary without permission. Respect their privacy. After all, that's what most journals are about.

Bound Blank-Page and Other Types of Journals

Journals today come in four forms: bound-book, loose pages, on computer, or tape-recorded. Each kind has advantages and drawbacks. Here are the pros and cons of each type:

Bound Blank-Page Journals

Store-bought journals are attractive and convenient. Their pages are of uniform size and quality, and they come with permanent bindings in a variety of pleasing colors. Books with sewn rather than glued bindings are best, as are ones that can be opened to lie flat. When buying a journal, open it and check the binding. Then feel the paper to test for quality; generally, the heavier the weight, the better the paper.

Small books are more portable, tucking easily into a purse or briefcase. Small daybooks and appointment books, however, provide only tiny spaces for each day of the year, so they serve poorly as journals. Even blank diaries with pre-printed dates rarely allow sufficient space for making lengthy entries. Usually undated books work best. Lined pages help keep handwriting legible. Although less portable, large books hold more entries and therefore may last months longer than smaller diaries.

Bound journals require handwritten or printed entries. Handwriting is more personal, and, unlike typing, it easily identifies the author. But poor or hurried handwriting makes this type of diary hard to read, so try to be neat.

The Loose-Page Journal

All you need to write a journal entry is a blank sheet of paper. You do not need to lug a diary book around with you. By using any available paper, you can make spontaneous entries anywhere and anytime. Good-quality bond paper should be used whenever possible, but if poor-quality paper is all that's available at the time (and most binder, typing, and computer paper is of poor quality), you can photocopy from it later onto the good paper.

In time, the loose pages need to be collected and housed so that entries do not get lost. Manila folders work best at first for this purpose, but eventually some kind of permanent cover needs to be added.

Unlike the bound-book journal, the loose-page version has no length restrictions. The diarist may use as many pages as needed to complete a year, and then he or she can start over, using a new folder for the new pages. Another advantage to loose pages is that items can be added to the journal that would make the bindings of bound books bulge out. Snapshots, postcards, clippings, membership lists, minutes of meetings, and anything you can photocopy can be inserted into a loose-page journal.

Because anything that can be photocopied can be included in the loose-page diary, it can become loaded with inserts that make it hard to find and follow the daily entries themselves. So, a very workable solution is to have two folders for each year: one containing the diary entries and one that is a "diary supplement," containing photocopied or loose materials.

Diaries on Computer

Word processors are rapidly replacing typewriters. People who once typed diary entries now do them on computer. Three cautions need to be heeded by those keeping diaries on computer: First, do a backup copy for each entry and make a backup copy of the backup copy. Second, print out the diaries after each month or two of entries, creating a hard copy on paper in case the disk becomes damaged. Third, when you upgrade to new word-processing software, upgrade past diary entries into the newer software from the old disks. Files on the old 5.25-inch floppy disks, for example, need

Children's Diaries

Unfortunately, very few children's diaries are preserved. Too often the child diarist grows up, is embarrassed by his or her juvenile jottings, and destroys the diary.

In your family, if possible, encourage children to keep their journals and diaries.

to be moved onto 3.5-inch disks. Computer technology changes so fast that in ten years you cannot expect your computer to still read a disk you made today.

Typists/word processors prefer loose-page journals. Typed entries are faster and easier to make than handwritten ones, so they tend to be longer and more detailed, as well as more legible. Typewritten entries, however, do seem less personal.

The main requirements for a journal are good-quality paper and some kind of protective cover. Spiral notebooks do not hold up well over time, since their pages are easy to tear and their paper is low-quality.

Tape-Recorded, Dictated Journals

Tape-recording a journal is a great idea, but it causes extreme difficulties if the tapes are not transcribed onto paper. Some people dictate entries into tape-recorders or dictation machines. Then someone else transcribes and produces a typed or word-processed final copy of the diary. Because talking is so much easier than writing, dictating allows for fuller and more detailed entries. But unless the transcribing person is totally loyal, the diarist will not be as frank and self-revealing as he or she would be if the diary was written privately.

Physically challenged people often find dictating the best way to do diaries. Children, too, can recite daily doings into a tape-recorder even though unable to read or write.

If not transcribed into writing, tape-recorded diaries are very hard to "read" later on. The information is in there, but it can't be located quickly. A careful index can solve some of that problem.

What to Write With

Paper

Newspapers yellow quickly when left in the sun. Most kinds of paper deteriorate easily. Paper with a high acid content (like inexpensive binder, notebook, or computer paper) becomes brittle and discolored in a few years. If you type your journals, use good bond or high-quality photocopy paper. Erasable bond, even if low-acid, is not recommended because writing on it is too easily smeared or erased.

For word processors, archival-quality computer paper is available and can work easily for single-feed printers. For consecutive-feed print-outs, most diarists can't easily switch from their normal, low-grade computer paper to the archival-quality kind and then back again. So, those with consecutive-feed printers should print the journal out on normal computer paper and then photocopy the pages onto more durable photocopy paper. (Photocopy paper, however, is vulnerable to plastic sheets and covers pressed against it that lift the print off the page.)

Writing Instruments

Old diaries teach crystal-clear lessons about what does and does not endure well through time. Pencil is a no-no because it easily smears and fades. Wide-point fountain pens and felt-tip pens conduct much more ink than normal pens, producing thick lines that bleed through the page and into the neighboring pages as years pass by. Medium-point pens with blue or black permanent ink work best. Some fine-point pens produce lines too thin to endure legibly through time. Any pens that leave smears or blobs of ink should not be used.

Letters as Substitutes

If a person does nothing more than write a letter to someone regularly (perhaps weekly or bimonthly), each summing up in decent detail the news since the last letter, and copies of the letters are saved, the collection becomes a pretty good diary.

How Often to Write

Daily journal entries are best. They tend to capture more of feelings and reactions. Details can be forgotten within a few days, so daily entries are more accurate. Habit helps in writing regularly. Some diarists sign off the day by reviewing it in their journals. Others use early morning hours or lunch breaks for the task.

Sometimes a daily entry seems unwarranted because nothing of importance happened that day. If so, the diary habit is maintained if you do nothing more than just jot, "Nothing of note happened today."

Journal Hints

It helps to compare a diary or journal to a newspaper. A newspaper has sections or subject areas: national and local news, society, entertainment, editorials and opinions, etc. Your diary can deal with similar matters as well, and not just big-news items.

Dear Diary: Ideas for Writing

A few journals are specialized, focusing on only one aspect of a person's life. There are single-subject diaries dealing with such things as a childbirth experience, a military career, a political campaign, a love affair, a vacation, a writer's thought processes while creating a novel, and a business operation. But instead of specializing, most journals treat a wide range of subjects, often randomly.

News of Your Day

You may ask yourself when ready to write: "What was new today?" Some days deserve but one line, others many pages. Write about the sort of things you readily share with a close friend or relative. But also tell important developments that are too personal to tell anyone else. Some events, though not historic, are of vital personal importance, and diary after diary is filled with them. It sometimes helps to select a half-dozen categories that cover your main daily activities—work, school, personal matters, family happenings, leisure, finances, etc.—and to review each one every time you make a journal entry.

Writing about big events seems obvious, but that task bedevils many diarists. The problem is, the more important events in our lives occur at the times when we have the least chance to write about them. Yet those are the very happenings that most deserve diary treatment, the ones which, if preserved, produce lasting value for your journal. Those fast and busy times are the ones which really merit being recorded. This is because the mind is so busy then that the memory misses much, and too many details of that major happening are quickly forgotten.

Travel

Travel is exciting for most people, whether for business or pleasure, and a journal record of the trip often is appreciated later. Write in a travel journal such things as transportation methods, accommodations, travel mates, sites you see, people you meet, new customs encountered, new foods you taste, and what you really like and dislike about your visit.

Current Events

Journals often disappoint when they fail to pay any attention to major national or local news events. If happenings of the magnitude of the Kennedy assassinations, man first walking on the moon, presidential elections, Watergate, the collapse of the Soviet empire, or the abortion and gay rights debates trigger responses in you, why not describe your reactions in your journal? Tell about the broader forces that are disturbing your personal world, such as national economic trends, local protest movements, government regulations that affect you, matters being decided in current elections, local celebrations, new construction or demolition, crime in the neighborhood, and local natural disasters.

Religious Experiences

A person who is in love has a dimension added to his or her life that was missing before. Likewise, a religious believer has a world of thoughts, feelings, and experiences that nonbelievers lack. Religion, like love, being a more private than public matter, is a topic many diarists write about.

New Ideas and Insights

New knowledge, new ideas, new "truths" of which diarists become aware deserve some notice. School situations produce many new insights through science, philosophy, history, and other classes. Speakers stimulate minds, as do books, magazine articles, discussions with friends, and quiet moments of meditation. Being a parent triggers much thought about what that role means and how to fulfill it. Being a leader or having contact with large groups of people is enlightening. Observations and conclusions about man, society, and the world make good ingredients for thoughtful journal entries.

The Routine, Everyday Life Matters

Something need not be new and exciting to merit journal attention. Even newspapers carry "non-news" items about everyday living like those found in feature articles. If a journal deals only with the unusual or exciting turn of events, and makes no mention of normal, routine, everyday type doings and contacts, it presents an incomplete picture of the diarist's life. While it might be absurd to tell in detail what the breakfast menu is every day or how the business is run hour by hour, it seems equally foolish to write a journal without at least once detailing the commonplace activities and everyday acquaintances occupying so much of your time and concern.

Opinions

Like the editorial page of a newspaper, why not take the time now and then to express your opinions about politics, religion, moral issues, the economic system, your boss or employees, your neighborhood, and current music or TV or movies? Newspaper editorials sometimes eulogize prominent people for accomplishments. Why not pay tribute to a successful close friend or relative? If you write an opinion letter to your local newspaper or congressional representative, why not copy that into your journal? Why not express some of your value system in writing in your diary? Why not editorialize sometime in your journal about what you stand for in life and why? Write about what you like and dislike about your life right now. Or, be introspective about life and its meanings and changes.

Want Ads: Hopes, Plans, and Goals

People who pound the positive-thinking drums tell us that the mere act of putting one of their goals into writing increases their determination to achieve it. If you are not today where you want to be, why not indicate in the journal what situation you are hoping for or working toward? You can also record there your resolutions to change—to live better, to lose weight, to take lessons, to control a temper, to get out of debt, to quit smoking, or whatever. Subsequent entries can trace how well or poorly such resolutions are fulfilled. This gives the journal a forward-looking, blueprint role in the diarist's life rather than only a backward-looking, recording function.

Humor

Some jokes are too much in bad taste to be written down. However, many jokes reflect our society's values, foibles, personalities, and mainstream concerns. So, why not include selected jokes and

humor in your diary? Many political cartoons also brilliantly capture opinions and values and current humor tastes, so why not photocopy a few favorites and include them?

Feelings

Humans are not emotionless machines or animals—we are creatures who feel and react. Feelings are the happenings inside the human soul. Therefore, a journal in which feelings are not expressed is seriously deficient. Too many journals are matter-of-fact about emotional situations: "I was fired today." "My daughter ran a 104 fever last night." "I had another date with Tom this weekend." In these cases, strong feelings are not being recorded. Why not use your journal as a place to tell off the boss who fired you? To worry or hope or cry over your sick daughter? Or to be thrilled or upset by Tom's romantic interest?

Autobiographical Flashbacks

Days when nothing particularly important happens are good times for writing non-news entries, such as expressing opinions or thoughts about everyday living. Another possibility is to record autobiographical information from the years prior to when the journal began. Some diarists try to begin their journals with a summary of their life up to that point. But all too often that task looms so large that it sinks the whole effort to keep a journal. Perhaps a better way to record autobiographical passages is to sprinkle them here and there throughout the journal whenever there is a "newsless" day.

Touches That Add Interest

A meal tastes better with salt, pepper, and seasonings. Likewise, a journal becomes interesting when some nonreporting kinds of "seasonings" are stirred in.

Details and Examples

Columbus, regarding his first day ashore in the New World, did not shortchange his journal by writing something brief like "Visited

Current Prices Listed in a 1970 Diary

"Eggs down to 41 cents this week from 53 a few weeks ago. Gas up 34 cent from 26.9 a month ago. Bread 44 cents, milk (2%) 1.03 a half-gallon, bacon 90 cents a lb., Life Savers 7 cents, 2 lbs. Hersheys cocoa 78–79 cents, margarine 31 cents, bologna about 80 cents a pound, hamburger low of 59 cents, usual 65 cents lb. Cold cereals lg. box like Wheaties and Cheerios near 60 cents."

new islands today and saw some strange natives." Instead, he recorded many fascinating details and descriptions (see the sidebar). Why not make your journal entries that detailed?

Conversations

Actual dialogue, as accurately written as possible, sometimes captures reality better than descriptions alone. Anne Frank provided this example dated March 13, 1944 in her now-famous diary:*

Peter so often used to say, "Do laugh, Anne!" This struck me as odd, and I asked, "Why must I always laugh?"

"Because I like it; you get such dimples in your cheeks when you laugh; how do they come, actually?"

"I was born with them. I've got one in my chin too. That's my only beauty!"

"Of course not, that's not true."

"Yes, it is, I know quite well that I'm not a beauty; I never have been and never shall be."

* From *Anne Frank: The Diary of a Young Girl* (Transalted B.M. Mooyaart, Doubleday) NY: Pocket Books, p. 166.

Drawings and Poetry

Many diarists doodle in their journals. Those with artistic talent put good samples of their work there, too. Poems, by the diarist or his or her own favorite poets, also add flavor to the diary.

Maps and Charts

Whether hand-drawn or pasted in, maps and charts provide valuable illustrations for a journal. These can be maps of the neighborhood, showing who lives where, or floor plans of a house, school, church, or office. Diagrams can show genealogy or how an organization is structured. Some diarists even include a mood chart, tracing highs and lows over time.

Letters

Either received or written, letters can be included on a limited basis. Most letters need to be kept in a separate letter file or folder if you are using a bound journal.

Problems and Dangers

Getting Behind

Rare is the diarist who does not fall behind! When this happens, you face three clear-cut choices. The first and easiest is to quit. A second choice is to catch up on the missed days and events, relying on memory and notes. The third choice is to leave a gap.

Most journals have gaps. Gaps are all right. They are certainly better than quitting the journal altogether. If catching up seems impossible, write down today's date and tell about today, skipping the missing days.

Honesty and Sensitive Matters

To be believable and reliable, journals must be basically honest. Honesty comes from telling what you know to be the truth, checking to get facts straight, and explaining other points of view.

Total honesty, however, can be damaging. Because even private diaries might end up being read, you need to be discreet when telling about sensitive matters, whether they be your own, your family's, or your friends'. Statements made in the heat of the moment may need toning down later if they are too damaging or inaccurate. There are some activities that, if known about by others, can ruin careers, tear apart families, smear basically good people, and even trigger physical retaliation. Such matters are best left undiscussed.

Balancing Moods and Tones

It's a fact that diarists record more about discouraging times than happy ones, so their journals present a distorted view of their personalities. Being overly negative as well as being overly positive misrepresents the truth. Seek balance and fairness.

Christopher Columbus' Diary, October 12, 1492

They are the colour of the Canary Islanders (neither black nor white). Some of them paint themselves black, others white or any other colour they can find. Some paint their faces, some their whole bodies, some only the eyes, some only the nose. They do not carry arms or know them. For when I showed them swords, they took them by the edge and cut themselves out of ignorance. They have no iron. Their spears are made of cane. Some instead of an iron tip have a fish's tooth....They are fairly tall on the whole, with fine limbs and good proportions.

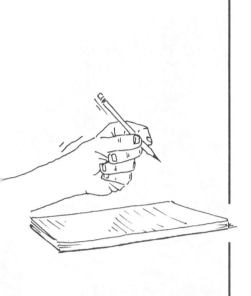

Writing Too Cleverly

Trying to write too well—in a clever style with carefully crafted sentences, meticulous organization, and judicious selection of topics—may make journal-keeping too tough a task. Most diarists, being in a hurry and not having to worry about others' critical eyes, write freely as ideas strike. Like making a vegetable soup, they dump a lot of different items randomly into their journal broth.

Writing Legibly

All diarists need to exercise some care in writing legibly when making journal entries. You will be glad for it when you can read your journal years later.

Full Identifications

To avoid confusion, later searching time, and the loss of name recognition, identify everything fully. Doing so is a simple but valuable habit to develop. Just include full dates, full names, children's ages, and your location.

The Completed Journal

While making entries or after the journal is filled, the diarist can greatly improve its readability and usability by adding several simple but useful touches:

Page Numbers

For easiest use, write page numbers on the upper, outside corner.

Table of Contents

Leave space in the front or back of the journal to create a list of contents once the diary is complete.

Underlinings

Underline the dates of entries, people's names, important events, or other key words so that the eye can easily spot these when scanning the page.

Captions

If there is room in the margins, write brief captions telling what subjects are covered on each page.

Index

If you have the ambition and patience, make a list of several names and subjects discussed in the journal along with the page numbers where those discussions occur.

Yearly Summary

On a few pages in the front or back of the journal, you can write a brief chronological list of the main happenings of the completed year.

Safety

Journals, in good covers, should be kept in safe places—away from curious children with crayons or scissors, and from dangers of leaky pipes, moisture, insects, and rodents. Diaries should be stored where they can be grabbed quickly in case of fire. Whenever possible, individuals would be wise to photocopy or microfilm their more valuable and irreplaceable records so that there are copies somewhere in case the originals are lost, stolen, or destroyed.

Inheritance

Great family problems can result if the fate of journals is not specified in legal documents. Children have fought over parents' journals, sometimes dividing up a set or even tearing pages out to be divided up among all the offspring. Journals also sometimes go to someone who does not want them, and the volumes end up at the garbage dump.

Diarists should consider donating their journals to a nearby university library or historical society. These agencies often accept journals, preserve them properly, allow family members to come there to view the materials, and sometimes provide a photocopy of the journals at cost to the donor in exchange for their donation.

Bookmark to Copy, Cut Out, and Keep in Your Diary

Anything Worth Saying About Any of These Today?

- Good humor, jokes
- Your health
- Emotional high or low
- Work, job, coworkers
- Homemaking, housework
- Happenings to family members
- Best friends
- Romantic interests
- Money, finances, purchases
- House, home, yard
- Pets, animals
- Neighborhood, neighbors
- Any visits? visitors?
- Weather, seasons
- Important phone calls

Writing Your Own Life Story

"By Myself, I'm a Book!"

You cherish life stories written by a grandparent or other ancestor. You can read them, however, only because those people took some time and wrote an account of their lives. Many people write their own life stories. By seeing how others have done it, you can gain some useful ideas about how to write your own.

When asked to tape-record his life story, an elderly immigrant thought a moment about his long and busy life. He then exclaimed: "By myself, I'm a book!" Like him, any of us could easily fill a book with our own life experiences if we wanted to or had to do it.

Why Bother?

Most people do not write their life stories. Writing workshop polls indicate that, on average, only two out of a person's parents and grandparents have written even one page of a life sketch or story. Indications are that, among the general public, probably less than one adult in ten writes even one page about his or her life.

However, in our age of inexpensive paper and pens, tape-recorders, word processors, and computers, more and more people are writing their life stories. And you can be one of them.

Life stories found in libraries and in families range in length from one or two pages to one or two volumes. They are handwritten or typed, polished or plain, brilliant or dull, honest or sugarcoated. Most run ten pages or less, but many are thirty to fifty pages. Some are even book-length. A good minimum length for a reasonably covered life story is forty pages.

People fail to write personal histories for three main reasons: lack of interest, lack of know-how, and discouragement caused by the amount of work such a project requires. The following are some reasons to overcome these hesitations in order to write a good personal history.

If you are reluctant, is it because you don't think your experiences are important enough to write about? *Every life is of priceless value.* So much time and resources go into making a human being become a healthy, capable person. Why not leave some accounting

of your life as a way perhaps of crediting those who helped shape you? Are there not some insights and lessons of life you can pass along to the next generation?

Another reason for doing a personal history is that the effort is *highly beneficial* to the one doing it. In the process of reviewing your life, you end up learning a great deal about yourself. You also remember things about your youth that may help you better understand and raise your own children. You discover things about your parents that can enhance your relationship with them in their older years. You review old friendships and may even renew or deepen old ties.

Writing a life story is also an *enjoyable experience*. It can be a creative, fun hobby because it combines the best elements of detective work, collecting, nostalgia, and creative writing.

If you record your history yourself it will be *more accurate* than accounts others might later write about you. You can save your life story from errors of commission and omission that may be inflicted upon it by well-meaning descendants who will try to tell—and may end up mis-telling—your history.

(continued)

- Mail sent or received
- Church or religious beliefs
- New insight, idea
- Sports result
- Community service, good deeds
- Anyone help you?
- Witness historic happening?
- Today's headline news
- Decisions made
- New plans, goals
- TV, radio, movies, music
- Clothes
- Habits
- Hobbies, talents, sports
- Celebrations
- Travels, tours
- Deaths, birthdays, weddings, divorces

What Type of History?

Whether long or short, a life story can be prepared in a number of ways. Here are the options:

Written

This is the standard form for a personal history. The end product may be a fine printed book, a typed or word-processed product, computer file, or a handwritten manuscript.

Tape-Recorded

Tape-recorders, which are easy to use, make it simple to effortlessly *dictate* memories onto tape. Speaking your history is much easier than writing it. You can produce a fine history simply by talking into your recorder for a half hour or so at time, regularly. Or, you could have a relative or friend conduct an *oral history interview* with you (see Chapter 5 for suggestions). Having someone else ask you

questions about your life is often better than dictating because you will enjoy the history-producing task much more and you will discuss many topics you wouldn't have remembered to include on your own.

Multimedia

Multimedia histories require extra time, energy, expense, and creativity, but they can be extremely valuable and interesting. They involve weaving three elements into your history: a story line you script just for this project, visual images and film footage you choose to illustrate the story you script, and a soundtrack of spoken words, sounds, and music that shares the story with the narrator. Even without sophisticated equipment, three types of multimedia histories are possible:

1. A very basic history is a *tape-recorded explanation of photographs or slides*. With this option, your collection of pictures or slides shapes and determines the story. You put your personal pictures in chronological order, and then explain the pictures while tape-recording comments. In this case, pictures determine what you tell about your life.

2. Rising fast in popularity are *videotaped life stories*. For these histories, you start with a script telling the life story and then select visuals to illustrate the narration. Visuals come from your or others' photo collections, slides, and video, and from video film you shoot of people, places, and objects just for this history. Sound for the history comes from your voice as the narrator, tape-recorded or videotaped voices of people in the history, sounds that are important in your life (church bell in the neighborhood, a daughter's piano performance, a clattering typewriter, etc.) that you record to enrich what you are showing and telling, and background music.

3. Also popular are *slide-sound* histories. Unlike the narrated photo album or narrated slide collection above, this history starts with a script—the life story—and then tries to come up with slides of people, places, and objects to illustrate that story. Like the videotaped version, this history has a soundtrack featuring narration, voices and sounds of others, and background music, if desired.

Starting to Write a Life Story

Writing your life story is a very personal enterprise. Only you can decide what to tell and how to tell it. However, you can learn much from seeing how others have written their life stories. What follows are tested methods used in workshops and classes.

Even very short life stories have great value. When such histories are less than five pages, they are not so much a story as a chronicle or listing of the main facts and happenings—somewhat like an encyclopedic summary of your life. Certainly, the longer the life story, the more information it will contain.

Let's consider some ideas for writing a fairly full life story of maybe thirty pages or more. This history should contain at least a handful of interesting sections or small chapters.

Begin by making a *time-line outline* of your life. List on paper or computer the major events of your life with dates. This outline will become more detailed as you further explore your life story.

Next, create a very simple *filing system* in which you can organize bits of information you collect. Possible filing systems include binders, with sections set off for particular categories; manila folders, each one labeled for a specific subject or topic; and index cards similarly divided. If you are using a computer, you can create the same kind of files in your computer file systems.

The keys to a successful filing system are the categories or sections of your life into which you divide the pages, folders, or cards. Each of the following useful categories could later be the subject of a separate section or chapter of your final history, such as "Life Stages":

    roots and family heritage
    childhood
    youth or adolescence
    early adulthood
    middle or prime adulthood
    later years

Some people file by geographic location. This division is extremely useful if you have moved a few times a decade or two. Set up a separate file for each place where you lived, and put into it information about that time period in your life.

You can also create files for special topics. These may be separate files even though they may cut across chronological or geographical periods. Such topics could include work experiences or careers, parenting, religious beliefs and experiences, influential people, humorous experiences, and health and medical matters. (See the lengthy list of memory triggers later in this chapter.)

Rounding Up Information

With a filing system in place, you can start gathering information about your life—from your memory and from other sources. Jot down brief notes whenever important memories come to mind. Some people keep index cards in their pockets or purses for this purpose. Then, put the notes into each appropriate file.

Your memory is your primary source of information, but it's not the only one. Because the memory sometimes muddles the facts, other records may need to be checked to ensure accuracy.

Memory

An amazing instrument, a person's memory contains a conscious and unconscious record of everything that individual ever did, thought, or experienced. However, only bits and pieces are ever recalled easily and readily. Other memories require some work to dislodge, but such efforts pay off royally. Here are ways to mine your memory:

Brainstorm by Yourself

Devote short blocks of time—during a bus ride to work, just before falling asleep, while doing dishes or mowing the lawn, sitting at your desk or kitchen table—simply thinking hard about only one topic. Brainstorm like this a number of times on each topic. Note ideas that occur.

Use Memory Triggers. Appendix 1 is entitled "A Full-Life Story: Topics and Questions." For people writing their own life story, that list provides memory triggers with hundreds of questions and ideas to loosen up your memory and help you recall items you'd perhaps

otherwise forget to consider. The numerous topics are designed to trigger a flood of memories as a person carefully ponders each one.

In workshops one memory trigger is picked, such as childhood play, and questions are discussed about the topic. Workshop attendees then write for five or ten minutes about only that topic. Then they try another memory trigger the same way.

Find items of interest to you in Appendix 1. The list, hopefully, will help you recall lots of things you otherwise might forget to include in your history.

Brainstorm with Others. Talk with others who can give you information about your life and experiences: parents, siblings, old school friends, neighbors, coworkers, former roommates, or your own children. If necessary, set up a meeting just for this purpose. Again, jot down ideas that are generated by these meetings and file them.

Visit Places You've Been. Visit old sites such as childhood homes, schools, and stores (and take pictures while there). Listen to old songs. Read books and magazines that tell about past decades. Watch movies that re-create older time periods. In attics, family trunks, storage boxes, or museums, examine objects common to your youth, such as toys, clothes and fashions, furniture, and cars,

Documents and Records

Some records exist and are usable; others have to be created, located, or made usable. Such records as the following may be your own or belong to relatives or friends:

Diaries. These are probably the most accurate source of history that you can use, especially for names, dates, and feelings. Locate any diaries (those you own or those kept by close relatives or friends) that might tell about your world at some time or other. Select key quotes to include in your written account or to read on tape.

Letters. Any letters you have received and saved will contain data useful to understanding your past, as will letters you sent. See if you saved copies of letters you sent or contact someone who received and saved them (such as old boyfriends, girlfriends, or relatives).

Snapshots, Photographs, Slides, Movies, and Videos. Sort through your own pictures in order to label, date, and group them. Have others look at pictures or films with you to help you recall

Diary Entry of a New York Teenager

"October 8, 1943. I feel self-conscious. I don't want to be handsome, but I hate my present appearance. Weak, pale small ears, big nose, 'peach fuzz,' weak chin. Now my mouth is out of shape and I cannot smile for Dr. Singer put my braces back yesterday."

events, names, and feelings. Arrange to look at similar collections belonging to friends or relatives.

Scrapbook Materials. Thumb through scrapbooks or any envelopes, boxes, or drawers containing such materials as clippings, report cards, samples of school work, special event programs, certificates, cards, and letters.

Official Records. Many organizations keep records that may include you or your activities. You can consult local, state, or federal government records, military files, church records, organization membership lists and minutes, medical records, and family genealogy charts.

Published Materials. Examine old school yearbooks, newspapers, magazines, printed histories about your community and about organizations to which you belonged, and yearly almanacs that list current affairs.

Tape-Recordings. Locate and listen to recordings of letters, family gatherings, current events, and oral histories.

Autobiographies and Life Sketches. If relatives or friends have written some of their life stories, their writings could tell about you or about relatives or events that were important in your life.

Putting the History Together

When writing up a life story, it is easiest to do one section at a time. Select one of the topic files and thumb through all the notes you have deposited there. Organize and group them. Develop a tentative outline to follow when writing or tape-recording your remembrances about that subject.

For example, let us assume one of your files is labeled "teenage years," and that you have in it a variety of notes about your life back then. These notes can be grouped into sections dealing with high school, family, friends, work, hobbies, or religion. Using the notes and ideas you've jotted down, just start writing.

Never try to make your first version of your written history be the final version. The first version needs to be a working draft, not a

perfect product. In working drafts you should try to get your facts and details straight and the basic information told adequately rather than perfectly. Polish comes later.

To make your story alive and interesting, give details about what you did. (For example, in addition to saying you worked for a drug store as a teenager, share some of your experiences while working there.) It is important that you tell not only *what* occurred but also *how you felt* about it as well, and some explanation as to *how* and *why* things happened.

Avoid the temptation to leave out problems or unpleasant events. Deal with them if they are important in your life's development. To sugar-coat your history is to be dishonest. Everyone has problems, and your history should show that you did too. Treat sensitive matters with great empathy and tact, however.

If you are willing, let another person or two read the first draft and make suggestions for improvements. Then begin your revision.

To polish up the working draft, rewrite to improve its organization, punctuation, grammar, and content. Strive for better sentences and paragraphs, and for a fuller, more interesting story. Missing information needs to be located and added.

Helpful Finishing Touches

Illustrative materials make your history more attractive and interesting. Consider adding pictures, maps, or a selected excerpt from a letter or diary. A time-line outline of your life, placed before your first chapter, is also helpful.

Add a title page with a picture of you on it. Include a table of contents and an introduction in which you explain when, why, and how you created the history. At the end of your history, as appendix materials, include such things as genealogy sheets, lists and charts, letters, poems, speeches, or important certificates.

You can make photocopies of the histories, put covers on them, and share them with close family or friends.

Family History

Within our family there was no such thing as a person who did not matter. Second cousins thrice removed mattered. We knew—and thriftily made use of—everybody's middle name. We knew who was buried where. We all mattered.

From Shirley Abbott's
*Women Folks: Growing
Up Down South*

Dictating and Recording a History

Your life story told on audiotape should be in your own voice. You can record it a little or a lot at a time, depending on your circumstances.

It's possible to include other voices and sounds in your history. If you have access to other tapes with voices of important people in your life, copy excerpts onto your history's tape. Or, go out and record the voices of important people in your life, such as teachers, neighbors, coworkers, children, or your spouse. Copy onto the history tape recordings of your voice as a child or as a performer or speaker. You might also include everyday sounds such as the chiming of the living room clock, the singing of a pet bird, or popular music of significance to you.

A taped history, whether a monologue or an interview, can be expanded into an effective multimedia history (see explanation earlier in this chapter). Excerpt parts from your tapes and connect the narration with appropriate videotape footage or with slides of pictures, places, or people important in your life.

Updating a Finished History

On occasion, you may want to update your "finished" history by writing or tape-recording new information. If your personal history is printed and bound, then your updating will possibly take the form of chapters for a second volume.

Any efforts to update your finished history later will be greatly enhanced if you start now to collect and enrich the following personal source materials:

Diaries or Journals

Consider keeping a journal regularly. It is one of the best sources you will have for your personal history. Rather than simply listing facts, however, give explanations of how and why things happened, and include your own feelings and reactions.

Letters

If you did nothing more than write a detailed letter every week or two to a relative and save a copy, in time you would have a

diarylike collection of tremendous value. In folders, keep copies of your outgoing correspondence, which tells about personal things, and retain your incoming letters. Writing and saving an annual family newsletter is a less satisfactory option but still a good idea.

Pictures

Regularly take pictures of such things as your family, home, place of work, pets, close personal friends, and important occasions. Label all your slides, snapshots, prints, and videos by listing names, dates, and other explanations so that someone other than you can identify them. Periodically ask friends and relatives to let you see their pictures, and arrange to obtain copies of those useful to you.

Tape-Recordings

If a camera is standard household equipment, why not a tape-recorder? Voices are at least as valuable as visual images, if not more so. Record performances of music or drama performed by you or your family. Regularly tape the voices of your children, friends, neighbors, spouse, and other relatives. Put some of your own observations and thoughts on tape, too. Through interviews, obtain personal histories of your parents, grandparents, uncles and aunts, spouse, and children.

Scrapbook Materials

Be conscious of saving such personal and family items as membership lists of clubs, churches, and organizations; clippings about family, work, or local or national events of note; announcements of weddings, graduations, and promotions; certificates of award; minutes of important meetings; financial records; and creative items such as samples of your poetry, speeches, artwork, and designs (See Chapter 4 for more information on scrapbooks.)

Genealogical Information

Collect family data about immediate relatives, and keep accurate records of your family's births, marriages, divorces, deaths, and other important events. Encourage relatives to do their own personal histories, and arrange for a detailed history of your family to be written.

Your Life Story

If you've dictated your life story onto tape, make copies of the tape for relatives, friends, or local historical societies. Consider having transcripts made from your tape as well, so that you have a written as well as a taped version.

CHAPTER SEVEN
Writing Family Biographies

People write life stories of their relatives for several reasons, ranging from obligation to recreation to curiosity. Some people have good collections of records and source materials, and decide they should write a history based on them. Others write for the opposite reason—they have no source material, know nothing about a relative, and want to do research to find out about him or her. Sometimes a special occasion prompts such a project—a major family reunion, a fiftieth wedding anniversary, an eightieth birthday. Or, a person just finds he or she has extra time and chooses to spend that time putting together a history of the family or a relative.

Sometimes the productive genealogist finds him- or herself getting bushwhacked. To find and record genealogy information is satisfying, but it is also a bit dangerous. Just when you deserve to feel contented about finding the birth, marriage, and death details you've been seeking, you might start to feel a new and rising discontent. You start wanting to know more about the lives of the people listed on your charts: What kind of people were they? How did they live? What was life like for them, compared to your own life? You know their names, and now you want to know who these people really were. You wish you could find written biographies and life stories about them. Then you start to suspect that if their life stories are ever to be written, you might need to be the writer.

To write a biographical history about a relative is one of life's most rewarding—but also most challenging—projects. Unlike the genealogist, who is a finder and compiler of facts, this project requires that you put on the historian's hat and become not just a collector but a teller, or narrator, of the family story or a relative's biography.

Although the advice that follows is designed for a book-length history, it can be applied to essay or chapter-length histories, as well.

Biographical History Versus Biography

Technically, life stories of relatives are biographical histories, not true biographies. So, whenever the term "family biography" is used here, it really means a biographical history.

Biography experts have very precise ideas about what constitutes a genuine biography. Their how-to books about biography writing are not designed to help you write a personal family biography. The true

biographers assert that a biography must get inside the mind and soul of the person, and reveal his or her motivations and near-total personality. To do that, true biographers must have access to extensive introspective writings by the person or do many in-depth interviews with him or her.

True biographers write about famous people in order to earn money or enhance their journalistic reputations. They craft biographies requisitioned for sales potentials. Therefore, when giving advice, these biography experts deal with a type of writing that has minor, not major, application to family biography writing.

True biographers assert, for example, that you must not choose for your subject someone you really like. If you do, you will not be unbiased and objective but too laudatory. Personal family biographies, however, are written out of family loyalty and love. Biographers warn against throwing in every detail about the subject, and they advise you to selectively use only the important information. But, those who write family biographies are usually so glad to find any details at all about their relatives that they feel no hesitancy in including almost all of what they have discovered.

One lesson to learn from true biographers, however, is that you should do all you can to find and explain the "essence" of the person you are writing about. In other words, what is or was that person like? If at all possible, you should let the reader know what the main personality traits of your subject are or were.

History Is More Than Compiling Facts

Just like 1 + 1 = 2, good history happens when you add good records to a good explanation of what the records say. Written as an equation, this is:

records + interpreter = history

Therefore, your task as a family biographer is twofold. First, you must search diligently and locate records that contain history information about the person. Second, you must study those records, decide what they tell you, and then write well the story that your findings provide.

An Exercise: What Is the "Essence" of a Person?

If you had to describe your own mother by using only five adjectives, what ones would best do so? Not just any five adjectives—the very best ones. Then, using that list, can you tell a story about her or an experience of hers that illustrates each of the five descriptions?

When you do such an exercise, you get closer to what the true biographers say should be done—capturing the personality of the person.

Deciding What the Project Will Be

It pays to visit a larger library, browse through its genealogy and family history shelves, and find family biographies and life stories there that appeal to you. They may help you decide how you want to do yours.

Do You Want to Write an Essay or Book?

What final product do you envision? Do you hope to complete an essay or chapter-length history? Do you hope to produce a nicely bound book, a photocopied booklet, or perhaps a picture book with text?

How Many People or Generations Should You Include?

Do you intend to write mostly about just one particular relative? About one couple and their family? About two or three generations of one side of the family?

Who is Your Intended Audience?

Are you writing just for the family insiders, or also for the community beyond the family? Are you writing for the adult readers in the family, or do you want your history to appeal to teenage readers or even children as well? Your choice of audience will shape what and how you tell the story.

Once you've come close to answering those questions, you are ready to put on the historian's hat and get to work.

A Chronological or Topical Life Story?

When writing about someone's life, you have to figure out when to deal with his or her life in chronological order and when to deal with it by topics. These two concerns, chronology and subject, constantly intersect through a person's life. For example, normally you would tell a life story in life-stage order, with each stage serving as a separate chapter:

1. Roots, or the person's family heritage up to his/her birth
2. Birth, including family setting into which the person was born
3. Pre-school childhood
4. Childhood, perhaps through grade school
5. Adolescent years
6. Coming of age as a young adult

7. Young parenting years
8. Later parenting years
9. Empty-nest years and retirement
10. Death and legacy

However, during each of these stages, a person is repetitively involved with the same types of life topics, such as:

A. Economics, income, work, career
B. Living arrangements
C. Family developments (birth of sibling, death of grandparent, etc.)
D. Extended-family involvements
E. Health
F. Education
G. Hobbies, interests, talents
H. Church/religion
I. Annual holidays
J. Vacations
K. Friendships
L. Current events

Normally, you would write a person's life story using the chronological approach, and in each time period you would cover most of topics A to L. That is, the A to L topics are a part of every stage in a person's life. However, you could make the topics the chapters. For example, work and income could be Chapter One. In it, you tell about the person's job and earning experiences from childhood to life's end—childhood allowances and chores, teenage part-time jobs, college training for a career, first full-time job, career changes, work accomplishments, spouse's income contribution, investments, lifestyles determined by income, etc.

You'll probably do most of the life story in chronological, life-stage order, with occasional short detours to deal with some particular matter or topic that involves several time periods. For example, in one section you might choose to talk about all of the person's contacts with extended family (grandparents, uncles, aunts, etc.) during his/her entire lifetime.

One approach is vertical, the other horizontal. In chart form, based on the two lists just given—the life-stage list (1–10) and the topical list (A–L)—here is what you face when deciding how to tell about the person's life:

STORY TOLD USING CHRONLOGICAL, LIFE-STAGE APPROACH

LIFE STAGE	LIFE TOPICS											
	A	B	C	D	E	F	G	H	I	J	K	L
1												
2												
3												
4												
5												
6												
7												
8												
9												
10												

LIFE STAGES

1. Roots, or the person's family heritage up to his/her birth
2. Birth, including family setting into which the person was born
3. Pre-school childhood
4. Childhood, perhaps through grade school
5. Adolescent years
6. Coming of age as a young adult
7. Young parenting years
8. Later parenting years
9. Empty-nest years and retirement
10. Death and legacy

STORY TOLD USING LIFE-TOPICS APPROACH

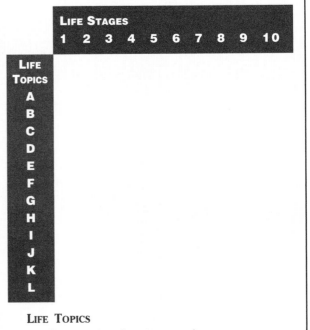

LIFE TOPICS	LIFE STAGES									
	1	2	3	4	5	6	7	8	9	10
A										
B										
C										
D										
E										
F										
G										
H										
I										
J										
K										
L										

LIFE TOPICS

A. Economics, income, work, career
B. Living arrangements
C. Family developments (birth of sibling, death of grandparent, etc.)
D. Extended-family involvements
E. Health
F. Education
G. Hobbies, interests, talents
H. Church/religion
I. Annual holidays
J. Vacations
K. Friendships
L. Current events

The "His Story, Her Story, Their Story" Approach

To write the history of a couple, a standard formula that has worked well in hundreds of histories is the following:

Opening	The couple's engagement and marriage
Chapter(s)	His growing-up years in his family
Chapter(s)	Her growing-up years in her family
Chapter	As newlyweds and starting a family
Chapters	Careers and child-rearing years
Chapter	Passing of the parents; summaries of the children as adults
Conclusion	Assessments and observations about their lives

History Research Basics

In school you learned some basics about how to write a general research paper. Most of those principles apply here. In addition, history classes teach several ideas that pertain just to history research papers. Drawing from both approaches, here are some useful recommendations for working on your family biography project:

Organizing and Filing Materials

Before writing the history, you must round up materials that contain family information. What do you do when you obtain genealogy charts, photocopies of obituaries, photographs, newspaper clippings, parts of a book chapter that tell about the family, tape recordings, and other source materials?

Your collection might start out as one pile of material, but sooner or later you need to divide the mass into separate groupings, each based on a separate aspect of the person's life you are researching. Typical groupings are by the life stages—childhood, teenage years, etc. Or, if the person you are researching lived in several places, you can group the records according to location.

Some people organize their materials into groupings by putting them in separate boxes. Most, however, favor the use of file folders, which can be kept in file cabinet drawers or in boxes.

Taking Notes

How does a record or source material become a history? That's where the historian, the interpreter, comes in. Records are not history—they are merely raw materials from which historians extract "the story" of what happened. So, at some point you will examine a letter, an obituary, or a life sketch; decide what information you need for the history; and write it down.

A generation ago, researchers wrote their notes down on index cards or half-sheets of blank paper. Today, many still do it that way, but growing numbers input their notes directly into computer files. Either way, you must read the source materials; ask yourself, "What does this tell me?"; and then summarize your findings.

Four general rules about notetaking are very useful. First, summarize rather than copy a quote. It saves time later and gets the writing process started sooner if you render the information in your own words. Second, in your note cards or computer file you need to carefully document where you found the information—copying down the bibliographic information of author, full title, publishing place, date, publisher, and the page number(s) you consulted. Third, when you do quote, copy the material exactly and put it in quotation marks. Fourth, when using note cards, write only one main idea per card and use only one side of the card. That way, your cards are easier to move from file to file, and you can see quickly what each card contains without having to refer to its front and back every time.

Sometimes the same note card has information that belongs in more than one file or section of your research. You can hand-copy or photocopy it and put it in several files. Computer notes are easy to copy and place in multiple files.

Constantly Backing Up What You Input on Computer

Because disks fail, computers crash, power outages suddenly make computers go dead, and tired people accidentally erase files, it is absolutely essential that every five or ten minutes you make a backup or duplicate copy of whatever you are inputting. For security reasons, it also is good policy to store the backup disks in a place separate from the originals.

Honest Research and History

History must be reliable, responsible, and committed to telling the truth. Dishonesty and errors can come from:

1. Improper reading of what the sources say
2. Not using all the sources available
3. Failing to know about contexts of time and place
4. Not double-checking family memories against other records
5. Censoring the story by leaving out pertinent information
6. Outright changing of the facts intentionally to mislead
7. Creating dialogue and fictionalizing an account

Handling Sensitivities

When you write about your own family, you often feel uncomfortable presenting information about them that is negative. Withholding information might seem noble, and little harm is done when it involves minor matters. But leaving out significant parts of the real story is an intentional act of dishonesty.

Because families have sore spots that they do not like to have touched, you face the problem of what you should or should not tell about yourself or your family. The historian must demonstrate tact and compassion when facing difficult family problems such as illegitimate births, desertions, child abuse, adultery, crimes, alcoholism, disfigurement, or mental illness. You should not be in the business of sensationalizing human failings in order to tell a good story, but you shouldn't write sugar-and-cream biographies, either. Too many family histories deal only with a relative's upright character, righteousness, and goodness, and don't portray the real person who also has flaws and shortcomings. A sugar-coated history isn't very palatable to most readers.

To mix together equal parts of honesty with decency is to produce a commonsense understanding that some problems need to be discussed and others do not. If a sensitive problem is not central to the history, you probably can ignore it. But if it played a key role in the course of the family, then you really should include it.

Most family sensitivities can be handled with tact and phrasing. When you need to deal with a sensitive matter, you can approach it from one of several directions:

File Categories

A typical file system contains a separate file for each of these kinds of groupings:

- Address file: names, addresses, and phone numbers for relatives, libraries, and contacts that are sources of information
- Leads to pursue, loose ends to tie down
- Genealogy charts and information (alphabetical order works best)
- File for each person or family unit in the study
- File for each place the family lived
- Map file
- Picture file
- File for certificates, documents, life stories, diaries, and letters

1. Tell the story in full detail. You should be as empathetic as possible, however—not necessarily justifying a behavior, but at least trying to indicate some understanding of why and how it came to be.
2. Include the story, but leave out names when appropriate so as not to damage someone else.
3. Touch on the problem generally and quickly, but don't give specifics. "Tom and Dorothy had a few rocky times in their married life, but...." "John got into a little trouble when he was a teenager." "She was ill for two years and could not work."
4. Tuck the problem into an endnote or footnote, assuming most readers won't read it.
5. Make no mention of the problem at all.

Reliability of Sources

You should have a natural skepticism about trusting family versions of the past completely. The most reliable accounts are those written or told by firsthand witnesses with sharp minds for perceiving and remembering. Less reliable are stories told secondhand by those who heard it from someone else. For example, if Grandpa tells you about his life experiences, that's firsthand knowledge and can be relied on (but only so far as Grandpa saw it right in the first place and remembers it correctly). When Grandpa tells you about things about his father that his father told him, however, you can expect some loss of accuracy in the transmission of the information.

Also, some people mistakenly think that because something is in print, it must be true. Much information printed in newspapers and books is incorrect, so always be skeptical.

In your mind, ask this question about each source you read or hear: "How does this person know this?" In families, different relatives have different versions or understandings of an event or family reality. Watch for those differences and weigh carefully which one to trust. Often, historians can't determine which of two differing accounts is the right one, so they say something to the effect of "According to Aunt Mary...but Uncle Aaron disagrees and says that...."

Balancing the Story

Even when writing about one particular person, you need to include the people who played key roles in each of his or her life stages. Histories too often slight the person's parents, spouse, or brothers and sisters. Sometimes a biographical history concentrates on the person's adult life and shortchanges the growing-up years.

Another imbalance comes from focusing most attention on spectacular, major happenings, and not including the everyday routine that was the heart of the person's life. In a similar vein, diaries often tell more about serious times and problems than happy and fun ones, so you must try to give a fairer, balanced view. Also, when dealing with controversial matters, be sure to let readers know of another explanation that a different family member may have.

Proving/Documenting What You Say

Document your assertions. Use endnotes, footnotes, or source notes to tell your readers where you obtained the information in your narration. Don't just expect your readers to trust you.

Raising Questions to Guide Your Research

Even with rich source materials about which a long history can be written, it is vital for you to stand back and ask commonsense questions about what any good biography of that person ought to include. Such questions will make you dig for new sources in order to find answers. What would you like to know about that person if a fairy godmother could grant you all your wishes? What should your readers know if your history is to be a complete and thorough one?

Cross-Examining Photographs for Information

Photographs are good sources if they are labeled and studied. Questioning a photograph can make you gain some good insights into the person you are researching. Go through the journalist's who, what, when, where, and why questions. Who is in the picture? Why was this photo taken? Who took it? When and where was the photo taken? What does the picture tell you about such things as the community, the way people dressed, and how they lived?

Accuracy of Accounts

As a general rule, firsthand accounts have the best odds of being accurate, and accounts recorded closer to the time the event happened are more accurate than ones recorded later.

Visiting Sites

It is highly useful to visit the places where the person you are writing about lived. You can better describe it for your readers if you've been there. Visiting a site, you not only learn about the landscape, vegetation, climate, and landmarks, but you can research in the local library and talk to old-timers in the area. While there, you can videotape or photograph the family's sites for a multimedia history.

Analyzing and Drawing Conclusions

Decide to go beyond just the facts of what happened—seek to know how and why things happened. Analyze patterns in the family—health, personalities, occupations, talents, standards of living, religiousness, hereditary traits, etc. Make comparisons between siblings or between generations.

Research: Find Out What the Family Has

Survey the Relatives

As for genealogy research, when you start collecting information for a biography, contact all your relatives to find out what they have. If the person or family unit you are writing a history about goes back more than two generations, do more than survey just your immediate relatives—track down "invisible cousins" who descend from a common ancestor. If researching great-grandparents, for example, don't presume your branch is the only true line of the family. Very likely, another line of descendants from those same great-grandparents has more information about that couple than your side of the family has.

A law of physics applies to family objects: An object only passes to one person at a time. That means that if great-grandmother had a bundle of letters received from her mother, that bundle probably went to only one of the children. If you descend from one of the other children, your family by now does not even know about the letters that one of your distant cousins has. So, you need to tap into those other branches of the family to find out what those relatives might have.

When inquiring about records, don't ask your relatives a general question like "Do you have any records?" They usually have no clue what kind of records you need, and they might think you mean only genealogy information. Spell out what kinds of materials you are looking for. Survey each relative and ask if he or she has such items as the following, or knows where any are. With each relative you contact, run through as much of this list as pertains to the relative you are researching:

genealogy information	obituaries
diaries	letters
scrapbooks	life sketches
marriage certificates	death certificates
photographs	deeds
wills	financial records
military papers	school records
tape-recordings	objects, heirlooms
clothes, uniforms	location of graves
naturalization certificates	passports

When you find that someone has source materials, you need to examine them to determine how they might be useful. If you need to use those materials, you have three choices: borrow them, have photocopies made of what you can use, or examine them and take notes at the person's home.

Materials Borrowed

When borrowing items, with pencil or a sticky tag, label each document with the name of the person to whom it should be returned. Give the person a list of what you borrow, and make a copy for you to keep. That way, you can be sure to return everything to the rightful owner. Use the materials and return them as quickly as you can. If necessary, ask the person for permission to make photocopies.

Tape-Record Oral Histories with Relatives

A seventy-year-old grandmother knows three generations of the living family, but she could also know two or three generations before her in time. This one witness could comment somewhat on six generations! It pays to tape-record the recollections of older members of the family, especially when you are writing about a person or family unit contained within those six generations. Often, interviews are your best sources of the human-story part of the family. See Chapter 5 for instructions on how to conduct an oral history interview.

Research: Looking Beyond the Family's Walls

Even if your family has a lot of information about the relative you are researching, you still need to look outside of the family for records that might have great information for your study. Family records are only half of the loaf; nonfamily records are the other half. It's amazing sometimes how much information community, government, and church records contain about individuals, perhaps including your relatives.

Let's assume you have family sources that give you only birth, marriage, and death information about a set of grandparents, and genealogy information about their children. These family sources allow you to write, at best, only two or three paragraphs about the grandparents' lives. What can records outside the family add to their life story?

Because your ancestors lived daily lives as part of and interacting with communities, records kept in those communities can be very useful—and often are absolutely essential—for you as a biographer. Federal censuses could show you where they lived and when. Grandpa's will might be found in a local courthouse. Military records would show where he served, what ranks he gained, and any pensions he or your grandmother might have received. A local library might have a diary kept by a neighbor or associate that tells about your grandparents or at least describes the community and the time in which they lived. In microfilm copies of old newspapers you might find a write-up about your

grandparents' fiftieth wedding anniversary, including a lengthy life sketch about each of them. A published history about their community would contain information about social, business, cultural, and political developments during their lifetimes. The county recorder's office should have a list of property your grandparents paid taxes on, year by year. If your grandfather joined a fraternal lodge, that organization might have his membership application in its files. If your grandparents belonged to a local church, its records probably can be found and researched. City directories (not phone books) are published annually, and they might list your grandparents year by year, giving their address and your grandpa's occupation. Old maps in the library can tell you what the area was like when your grandparents lived there.

Libraries and Archives

The starting places in looking for records not in family hands are libraries and archives. An archive is where official records are stored. A corporation's official records are kept in its own archive; local and state government official records are kept in the state's archives; and the federal government's official records are kept in the National Archives, which has several regional centers throughout the United States.

Libraries—town, county, university, private—house information about almost every subject, including local history. Most communities have a public library, which lets patrons use published local histories, newspapers, current and old maps, annual city directories, old school yearbooks, and life stories of local residents. University libraries usually have good collections of published and unpublished local history materials, too, as do large public libraries in bigger cities.

The federal government operates not only the National Archives but also a national library called the Library of Congress. Each state has both state archives and a state library. State libraries, located in capital cities, are part of state historical societies or departments. Every state has a historical society or history department, which operates a library that houses materials about the state and its people. These state historical libraries have great collections of published

Library of Congress

The Library of Congress main catalog for browsing can be reached on the World Wide Web at Marvel.loc.gov.

and unpublished local and state histories, life stories, photographs, letters, business records, maps, newspapers, and other useful materials.

Local Government Records

Many records found in county courthouses are particularly useful for would-be biographers. These include the vital records—of births, marriages, and deaths. County recorder's offices have deed books and property title records dating back to the county's founding, as well as old and current maps. County court records include wills and probate actions and adoptions. County assessor's offices keep track of annual tax assessments, although most tax records older than a few decades have been turned over to the state's archives for permanent storage. They are still accessible to the public, though. Decades-old school records also can be found at the official state archives.

Land Records and Property Titles

From the time Europeans first arrived in America, they worked out ways to own, buy, and sell land and property. Records of property transactions go back to the settlement of every state in the union. County recorders, and their earlier equivalents, kept property deed books that list changes of ownership. When someone buys a house, they must have a title search done in order to show that the seller has full ownership of the property. Title searches are recorded in the county's deed books, usually housed in the county recorder's office.

Property must be described by exact location and size in deeds or in sales transactions. In the early South, property descriptions often read something like "Beginning with the oak tree and continuing west for six rods, then at the creek continuing northeast for two rods, then northwest for sixty rods...." Today's property descriptions are in feet, but the early surveyors used measuring terms not familiar to the general public. They measured property boundaries in units relative to their measuring chains:

link = .92 inches
rod = 25 links, or 16.5 feet or 198 inches
chain = 4 rods
mile = 80 chains

Most of America's land is surveyed into "townships." Townships are six miles square, thereby containing thirty-six square miles. Each square mile is a "section" of land and has a number between one and thirty-six. Here is how the sections in a township are numbered:

Township
R2W T4N

6	5	4	3	2	1
7	8	9	10	11	12
18	17	16	15	14	13
19	20	21	22	23	24
30	29	28	27	26	25
31	32	33	34	35	36

T4N

R2W

Every township is identified by a north-south "township" number and an east-west "range" number. A township might be in Range Number 2 West, from a surveyor's main meridian, and Township Number 4 North, from another main meridian. So, the township's location is described as R2W and T4N. (In much of the East and Midwest, these townships not only are named by their R and T numbers but are given actual names, like Walker Township or Fremont Township.) Let's say your relative bought land in Section 27 in the above township grid. His property would be described in the property title as "Sec. 27, R2W, T4N."

Because most people did not want to buy or own an entire square-mile section, land dealers liked to work in terms of quarter-sections. So, Section 27 has a northwest, northeast, southeast, and southwest quarter. Let's say your relative owned only the southwest quarter of Section 27:

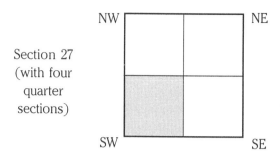

Section 27
(with four
quarter
sections)

Officially, his land, shaded in ...., was "the SW$1/4$ of Sec. 27, R2W, T4N."

Federal Government Records

Many kinds of federal records contain details about the lives of individuals. Government forms and paperwork seem like a curse when you have to fill them out, but the paperwork then becomes a record—usually a public record open to researchers—often containing valuable history information. Most often consulted are the federal censuses, taken every ten years since 1790. The latest census open to the public is the 1920 census.

Federal Homestead Records

These records are wonderful sources if one of your relatives took out a homestead anywhere in the late nineteenth century. To gain title to a homestead, the settler had to file for it. Once obtained, he had to live on the land for a period of time, make improvements on it, and prove he did both. Lots of paperwork is contained in those files, from a detailed application about the person to statements from neighbors spelling out what specific improvements the person had made on the land.

Military Records

You can assume that anyone who served in any branch of the United States military has at least one military record. The National Archives houses military records according to time periods, including a file for every U.S. war, and even some records for service performed during the Colonial period. Military records include service records, bounty-land records (the soldiers' bonus of a land grant when they finished their service), and pension files (veterans were entitled to old-age pensions, and their widows were eligible for widow's pensions). You can obtain a number of published guides to using U.S. military records at a library, or by contacting the National Archives by mail or via the Internet.

Immigrant Passenger Arrival Lists

During most of the nineteenth century, masters or captains of ships bringing immigrants into U.S. ports were required to file passenger lists as soon as they docked. These lists are in the National Archives and are grouped by entry port—New York, Boston, Philadelphia, Baltimore, New Orleans, San Francisco, and so on. The lists usually contain the immigrant's name and such things as age, place of origin, and occupation.

Naturalization/Citizenship Records

To become a naturalized citizen, immigrants had to file first papers (an application of intent) with a federal or state court authorized to handle citizenship cases. This application contained information about their birth, parents, country of origin, immigration, and current location. After the immigrants had lived in the country five years and had gained some basic knowledge about the American government and the English language, they filed in the same court for citizenship. If citizenship was granted, they received a naturalized citizen certificate, and the government filed their application materials. These records are now in National Archives branch repositories. Some states have indexes of naturalized citizens that indicate the particular court record books in which each immigrant's naturalization information is listed.

Other Federal Records

Tons of other records are available for research in National Archives regional centers. These include personnel records of government employees, private citizens' business transactions with federal agencies, documents regarding Native American land and tribal matters, hearings on land and resource use, and original government survey maps and notes (Government Land Office or GLO maps that laid out two-thirds of America's land so that settlers could reside on it and obtain titles to it). Visa and passport files are also available.

U.S. Census Information Gathered from 1790

Since 1790 when the U.S. Federal government began collecting census information, the *type* of information collected has changed. Below is a sample of the forms and the information gathered that have been part of census gathering since 1790.

1790 Census—United States

State				Call number						
				Free white males		Free white females				
Page	Head of family			16 and up including head	Under 16	Including head	All other persons	Slaves	County	City

1800/1810 Census—United States

State		County			City				Call number	
			Free white males			Free white females			All	
Page	Head of family	Under 10	10-16	16-26	26-45	45 and over	Under 10	10-16	16-26	26-45	45 and over	others	Slaves	Remarks

1820 Census—United States

State	County	City	Call number
Page	Head of family	Under 10	10-16	16-18	16-26	26-45	45 and over	Under 10	10-16	16-26	26-45	45 and over	Foreigners not naturalized	Agriculture	Commerce	Manufacturers	Free colored	Slaves	Remarks

Free white males / Free white females columns with category ranges.

1830/1840 Census—United States

State	County	City	Call number
Page	Head of family	Under 5	5-10	10-15	15-20	20-30	30-40	40-50	50-60	60-70	70-80	80-90	90-100	Over 100	Under 5	5-10	10-15	15-20	20-30	30-40	40-50	50-60	60-70	70-80	80-90	90-100	Over 100	Slaves	Free colored	Foreigners not naturalized

Free white males / Free white females columns.

1860 Census—United States

Family History Department

State	County	Town/Township	Post office	Call number
Page	Dwelling number	Family number	Names	Age	Sex	Color	Occupation, ect.	Value—real estate	Value—personal property	Birthplace	Married in year	School in year	Can't read or write	Enumeration date	Remarks

1880 Census—United States

State | County | Town/Township

Microfilm roll number | Date | Enumeration district number | Sheet number | Page number

Page	Dwelling number	Family number	Names	Color	Sex	Age prior to June 1	Month of birth in census year	Relationship to head of house	Single	Married	Widowed	Divorced	Married in census year	Occupation	Other information	Can't read or write	Place of birth	Place of birth of father	Place of birth of mother	Enumeration date

1900 Census—United States

Family History Department

State | County | Town/Township

Microfilm roll number | Date | Supervisor's district number | Enumeration district number | Sheet number | Page number

Street	House number	Dwelling number	Family number	Name of each person whose place of abode on June 1, 1900, was in this family	Relation to head of family	Color	Sex	Month of birth	Year of birth	Age	Marital status	Number of years married	Mother of how many children	No. of these children living	Place of birth	Place of birth of father	Place of birth of mother	Years of immigration to US	Number of years in US	Naturalization	Occupation	No. of months not employed	Attended sch. (months)	Can read	Can write	Can speak English	Home owned free or rented	Home owned free or mortgaged	Farm or house

Location | Personal description | Nativity | Citizenship | Occupation | Education

1910 Census—United States

State | County | Town/Township

Microfilm roll number | Date | Supervisor's district number | Enumeration district number | Sheet number | Page number

Street	House number	Dwelling number	Family visit number	Name of each person whose place of abode on April 15, 1910, was in this family	Relation to head of family	Sex	Race	Age	Marital status	Number of years married	Mother of how many children	No. of these children living	Place of birth	Place of birth of father	Place of birth of mother	Year of immigration to US	Naturalized or alien	Language spoken	Occupation	Nature of trade	Employer, worker, or own account	No. of months not employed	Can read and write	Attending school	Owned or rented	Owned free or mortgaged	Farm or house	Veteran of Civil War	Blind or deaf-mute

Location | Personal Description | Nativity | Citizenship | Occupation | Education | Property

1920 Census—United States

State | County | Town/Township/City and ward

Microfilm roll number | Enumeration date | Supervisor's district number | Enumeration district number | Sheet number | Page number

Street	House number	Dwelling number	Family visit number	Name of each person whose place of abode on January 1, 1920, was in this family	Relation to head of family	Home owned or rented	Owned free or mortgaged	Sex	Color or race	Age	Marital status	Year of immigration to US	Naturalized or alien	Year of naturalization	Attending school	Can read and write	Place of birth	Mother tongue	Place of birth	Mother tongue	Place of birth	Mother tongue	Can speak English	Occupation

Place of abode | Name | Tenure | Personal description | Citizenship | Education | Nativity and mother tongue | | Person | Father | Mother

Organizations' Records

America has been termed a "nation of joiners." Even in generations past, citizens have participated in businesses, trade and professional associations, farm co-ops, labor unions, churches and religious groups, fraternal organizations and sororities, immigrant societies, hobby and recreational clubs, and service and civic groups.

Depending on when in time the relatives you are studying lived, you should raise two starter questions to be answered: What groups might they have belonged to? And where might records of those groups be preserved?

Surviving records might be found at the organization's headquarters or records' center, if such a place exists, or at a library or archives to which they were donated. To find organization records, the first step is to contact the organization directly, if it still exists, and ask about its records. Large national corporations have official archives, such as the J. C. Penney Company (in Dallas, Texas) and Union Pacific Railroad (in Omaha, Nebraska).

Churches and synagogues traditionally keep good records. Christian denominations feel it important to record births, christenings, marriages, and deaths. Often, a present clergyman or rabbi can put you in touch with someone at the place where that congregation's records from former days are archived. Or, you can phone or write to the national headquarters for the various religious organizations and ask about records for specific local units.

Essential in your search for organization records are the standard reference books for genealogy research. Bigger guides, such as *The Source*, have chapters about how to locate records of businesses, religious bodies, and fraternal orders. For organization records already donated to libraries and archives, the basic finding aid is the Library of Congress's series of volumes called the *National Union Catalog of Manuscript Collections*, commonly known as NUCMUC.

Records of Your Relatives' Associates

Other people were a part of your relatives' lives—living next door to them, attending the same school, belonging to the same church, or serving in the same military unit. Sometimes your ancestors' associates kept diaries, wrote letters, or recorded their own life stories in which they tell about the place and time when your relatives were there, too. Those records often mention local people. Perhaps an associate of your relative wrote something about him or her by name. It takes a bit of work to identify who these associates of your relative were. You can check censuses, organization membership lists, and property tax records of the locality.

You then need to do some creative detective work to locate living descendants of those associates, and ask them if their ancestor who knew your relative left any diaries, letters, or autobiographical writings. Also check the library and the historical society near where the person you are researching lived, and find out if they have diaries, letters, or life writings for that location and time period.

National and Current Events

Many family biographies discuss relatives as though they lived in a vacuum. The histories fail to mention major current events of the ancestors' lifetimes—even those that had a direct impact on them. Published histories of the United States and chronologies of American history year-by-year identify the main events and developments in this country. Here is a short list of these events, dating from 1860 to the present. If any of them occurred during the lifetime of the relative you are writing about, they deserve some mention in the story.

Civil War
Reconstruction
depression of 1870s
advent of telephones
advent of typewriters
depression of 1893
urbanized America
Spanish-American War
electricity and electric
    appliances
first automobiles

first radios
World War I
flu epidemic of
    1918–1919
women gaining the vote
Great Depression
World War II
    rationing and shortages
    war prosperity
    Japanese internment
    military service

Cold War/fears of
  communism
prosperity of the 1950s
baby boom
suburbanization of America
interstate freeways
television

advent of youth culture
Civil Rights/race tensions
Vietnam War
two-income families
end of Cold War
advent of computers

Contexts of Place and Time

The times in which the relative you are writing about lived were different than life today. People back then did almost everything differently than we do now. The cliché that "the past is a foreign country" is more true than false. To tell the story of your relative accurately, you need to become familiar with what life was like back then. What was the town like when they lived there? The schools? The transportation?

It is possible to marshal facts together for a history yet not draw understanding from them. To get a sense of past people and events, it is essential to know about their historical contexts of place and time.

To find a context for your relative's biography, you need to research written materials that tell about it—either published histories about that time and place or newspapers or other firsthand accounts of what was happening.

Don't Throw Empty Words at the Readers

To use words without understanding them is to parade semi-empty facts. That applies to present vocabulary as well as to past usages different from today's. For instance, if your relative suffered from diphtheria, you can say that, but you and the reader both may end up not knowing what that means. What is diphtheria? What does it do to the victim? How does it spread? How long does it last? How was it treated? Simple research in an encyclopedia will help you inform the reader what it meant for your relative to have diphtheria.

Writing: How Do You Tell the Story?

First and foremost, you are the narrator of a story. You are not just a compiler who finds information and strings it together. Rather, you must digest the information you have rounded up and explain the relative's or family's life story.

Some family historians write the narration as a personal, first-person chat with the reader—"my grandfather," "my family," "I knew her when she was elderly," etc. Most historians, however, use the impersonal, third-person voice when talking about their relatives: "John's parents moved when he was seven," "Victor Powell married Sandra Davis on...," "They had five children...."

Write a Prospectus or Preface

You can't know what your history will be about unless you can summarize what it is you intend to do with it. Before writing, or at least while working on the first draft, you need to tell yourself and future readers what your history deals with. A prospectus is a preliminary preface, and it should specify:

who the history deals with
what the main developments are
where the history takes place
when or what time period it covers
why you've chosen to write about this person or family
what sources you will be using

First Draft and Working Drafts

Once you've done a reasonable job of finding records and source materials, you need to start writing. Whether it's a chapter or an entire book, you should write three drafts to make the narrative respectable. With word processors, often the first draft is revised as you go along, so it really is a second draft by the time you stop and read it critically.

Before sitting down to seriously work on the first draft, read through all of your research notes to get a feel for the "big picture"

Checklist of Source Materials to Research

Family Sources
- Poll immediate family and distant relatives to find:

  - Genealogy information, photographs
  - Life sketches, letters, diaries,
  - Certificates, wills, obituaries
  - Objects, artifacts, heirlooms
  - Scrapbooks, tape recordings

- Borrow, copy, or research at their place
- Visit family sites and locations

Sources You Create
- Ask relatives to write their recollections down
- Tape-record your relatives' oral histories
- Take pictures

the notes seem to portray. A nonjarring way to move into the writing stage is to outline your history, using a word or topic outline only. Then, when your outline seems workable, enlarge it by making it into a sentence outline. That is, instead of "Dad's childhood in Butte," you say "Dad's childhood in Butte was a rough experience for him and his parents." To move from a topic into a sentence is to begin the writing process.

The first draft should be your first attempt at giving the information in your files some kind of organizational structure. Try to put that information into semi-coherent sentences and paragraphs. Often you sample two or three different ways to say the same thing—you experiment with possibilities—before it seems to work.

This first working draft is where you try to present a running account of the person or the family factually. This lets you see gaps, imbalances, contradictions, and problems in the story. Here you really find out what your sources seem to be telling you, as well as what they are not telling you.

The best advice anyone can give you regarding this first narrative effort is to just do it—no matter how good, bad, or ugly it is. Write some kind of version. That gets your foot in the writing door, and after that the process becomes easier.

The first draft is a major threshold. Finishing the first draft should produce a great sense of accomplishment. At last you can begin to see the shape the next versions of the history will take.

Revise

Once you have the workings of a first draft, two things normally follow. You do more research to fill in gaps and to make better sense out of your story, and you start rewriting and revising.

The key to good writing is very simple: Revise, revise, revise. It's like sandpapering rough wood or polishing a stone. Rewriting and revising produces better organization, better paragraphs, and better sentences and choices of words. Computer spelling and grammar checkers are helpful at this stage of writing. Revising means to alter your organizational framework; to edit for proper sentences, punctuation, and spelling; to rewrite to state things

better; condense sentences, paragraphs, and sections that are too long; and to expand your discussion to fill in gaps.

If you are using a word processor to revise, be sure to save a copy of the first draft—don't revise it out of existence. Save the original as named, but make a copy of it with a different name to revise as your second version or draft.

Use Headings

Normally, a biographical history should flow chronologically. Such accounts have several natural segments and turning points that move the story along. These are like natural breaks or shifts in the narration, allowing the story to be broken into sections. So, divide your essay into such sections or minichapters, and give each section a heading, like a chapter title. These headings help you make the transition from one discussion topic to the next. They often match up with the categories you created for filing your information. And, section headings become entries in your table of contents.

Effective Writing Techniques

While revising, you need to move into a stage in which you work on writing the narration well. During this stage, you move beyond your earlier main concerns of the organization and factual content of your information. Several good writing techniques make all the difference in the world between a ho-hum narrative and a really interesting one. These techniques are well known to experienced writers, but the techniques are not very hard to apply. The more of them you use, the better your writing will be.

Goal: Be Reader Friendly

You write a history with a hope that people will read it. If what you write is hard to read, however, you do a disservice to yourself and to those who try to read it. Commercial industry tries to produce items that are "user friendly," and your purpose as a writer is to do the same. The history you write should be reader friendly in terms of vocabulary, sentence length, and story flow.

Library and Archive Sources

- Town and local histories, newspapers, directories, biographies, photographs, yearbooks
- Associates of your relatives (libraries, descendants)
- Government records

  - National: censuses, ship lists, naturalization, military, homestead
  - Local: censuses, deeds, property tax, wills, birth, marriage, death, schools

- Organizations: church, employers, social groups
- Context materials:

  - Histories and newspapers telling what it was like then
  - World events, local big events during their lifetimes

Word Tips

Here are some long words that are often used, followed by the shorter words that could replace them:

abandon	give up
ability	skill
accompany	go with
affectionate	loving
alteration	change
alternative	choice
considerable	much
deficiency	lack
demonstrate	show
employment	work
encourage	urge
frequently	often
manufacture	make
obligation	duty
procedure	way, method
remedy	cure
supplement	add to
uncertainty	doubt
unmistakable	plain
unfavorable	bad

Use Words and Language Correctly

In school you were taught the basics of English—proper spelling, punctuation, and grammar. To sharpen those skills, buy a comprehensive, easy-to-understand style handbook, such as Strunk and White's *Elements of Style*. [William Strunk, Jr. and E. B. White, *The Elements of Style*, 3rd ed. (New York: Macmillan, 1979.)] This is a small, basic style bible widely used in English classes throughout America.

Short Sentences, Short Words

Writing is an art—not all writing is *good* writing. Some writing is loaded with good information but is hard to read and understand. Other writing is easy to read but says little. What you need to achieve is a happy combination: simple writing that clearly communicates information.

A common fault of writing is wordiness. Writing that is too long or complicated causes readers to skip over it. That means writers should cut out unnecessary words and shorten their sentences.

Sentences become too long for two reasons. First, one sentence is made to carry two or three complete ideas within it. For example, here is a sentence that should be three or four separate sentences instead of one:

When the company, which started in business back in 1893, the year the Depression struck, diversified into the packing business, filling a definite need in Salt Lake City in 1903, the president was ready to turn the reins over to his son, who had shown no interest in the meat business until the Depression wiped out his lucrative real estate business.

A good sentence contain one basic idea, not two or more. Also, the ideal sentence is one the reader can understand the first time through.

Second, sentences become too long when the writer uses several words to say what a few words could say better. Here is an example:

Long: Initiate a savings program at your earliest possible convenience.

Short: Start a savings program soon.

Short sentences communicate better than long ones. Likewise, short words are easier to read and understand than long ones. If you use lots of long words, you cause readers to slow down and can confuse them.

English specialists have created "fog" indexes that measure how clear or foggy a sample of writing is by counting words per sentences and syllables per words. How many words should sentences have? How many words with more than one syllable should you use? Both of these considerations are determined by audience. *Reader's Digest* is a model of effective writing because it uses direct sentences and words that communicate as easily to adults as to youths.

Family biographies usually aim for the general audience. To reach that group without "fog," English experts say, you should write for someone with an eighth- to tenth-grade reading level. For that reading group, your sentences should average 17 words each and your words should average 1.5 syllables.

Say It Directly, Not Indirectly

"The ball was hit by the batter into left field" is a roundabout way of saying "The batter hit the ball into left field." Start with the subject, then go to the action. State directly who did what. Change "Sally would come for a visit every spring" to "Sally came for a visit every spring." Writers who lapse into using the passive voice or indirect statements tangle readers up unnecessarily.

Use Concrete Words Instead of Abstract Ones

Good writing allows the reader to visualize what is being described. Words that are too general and vague are less effective than concrete words at giving readers a picture. Vague words need descriptive adjectives and qualifiers to make them concrete enough

What Is Your Fog Index Reading?

To see how you are doing, take a sample from your second draft of 100 words. Divide 100 by how many sentences you count in that block of words and you will find out your words-per-sentence average. Then, count the number of syllables in that 100-word sample and divide it by 100. This is your average number of syllables per word.

for readers to visualize them. For example, a biographical history might say, "For Christmas, Aunt Mary gave the little boys a puppy." Try to visualize the word "puppy." You can't, because it is too abstract. But if the history says, "Aunt Mary gave the little boys a black and tan Cocker Spaniel puppy," you can visualize it. A biographical account might say, "In 1955, Oscar bought his family their first new car." Why not say instead, "Oscar bought the family a new Chevrolet Biscayne two-door blue and white sedan"?

Use Specific Words Instead of General Words

Loose, general, imprecise statements are not very informative. Specific statements tell your story better, and readers find them more interesting. Here are two general statements and their specific replacements:

General: His parents were emigrants from Sweden.
Specific: His parents emigrated from Trollhatten, Sweden, in 1935.
General: Mother did volunteer library work.
Specific: As a volunteer at the Whitmore Library, Mother helped refile books on shelves nearly every Saturday for two years, from 1955 to 1956.

Use Details and Good Description

Good writing, either fiction or nonfiction, is good because it is filled with details. Details make the material more enjoyable to read and easier to understand. And, details give the reader confidence that the author is well informed and knows what he/she is talking about.

Too many family biographies fail to provide physical descriptions of the people in the story—height, build, hair color, eye color, physical features, timbre of voice, and mannerisms, for example. So, whenever possible, be sure to include a physical description of the people whose life stories you are telling.

Likewise, give good descriptions of the places where the people lived. To say, for example, that the couple lived in St. Louis in 1850 is not adequate. The readers can only visualize St. Louis today, so you owe it to them to describe St. Louis as it was back then.

Use Short Quotes Instead of Long Ones

Quotations, used well, bring life and interest to the narration. Quotes from the time period you are writing about give readers a sense of the reality of the past that you, as the narrator, can't express. They also serve to reinforce or substantiate statements in the narrative. Quotations are one of the best "seasonings" you can sprinkle into your history.

Readers do not like long quotations, however, so keep each to a one- or two-paragraph maximum. Break up a long quote by inserting short statements of your own in between the parts of it.

Avoid Clichés, Overused Statements, Jargon, and Current Slang

Readers do not like overused words and phrases. "They were the best of times and the worst of times" might seem perfect for a situation you are describing. But if you use that now-trite phrase, the reader will say in his or her mind, "Oh no, not again! Can't this author do something original?"

Jargon and current slang pose generational problems: Some readers will know what the words mean and some won't. It is better to use standard expressions rather than offbeat ones so that you can reach a broader audience.

Use Words That Appeal to the Five Senses

Homemade bread baking in Grandma's oven. Your tongue licking melted white marshmallow stuck to your fingers. A church bell tolling eleven o'clock on a dark, moonless night. A bright yellow dandelion growing between two red tulips. Our minds and hearts react to these kinds of descriptions. Why? Because they appeal to our five senses. Writing that deals with sensory matters—seeing, hearing, touching, tasting, and smelling—carries instant appeal for readers. So, capitalize on every opportunity to use these sensory descriptors.

Capitalize on Feelings and Emotional Situations

Readers most enjoy and best remember writing that makes them feel something. A major failing in many family biographies is

Abstract Words and Their Possible Replacements

Abstract	Concrete
magazines	*Newsweek, Atlantic Monthly*
truck	pickup truck
store	Safeway
dog	Cocker Spaniel
kids	three girls
school	Lafayette Elementary
went	walked, drove
worked	sold, clerked, kept the books, repaired cars
friends	Bill Snell and Tom Conway

the absence of feeling and emotion. They are all facts, facts, facts. But human beings *feel*. Their feelings range from love to hate, fear to trust, funny to sad, pleasure to pain, excited to bored, hopeful to frustrated, peaceful to disturbed. Histories about real people should show that those people *felt*. Capitalize on any source materials about your relative or events in his or her life that convey or trigger emotion.

Craft Effective Openings and Closings

A well-crafted chapter or book-length history starts and ends effectively. The first paragraph needs to grab the reader's attention. The ending paragraph of a chapter should pull the reader a tiny step into the material of the next chapter. Is there a story or episode you can use to attract the reader? Can you start out with a statement that makes the reader curious? Why not begin a chapter with an interesting question that makes the reader want to know the answer?

Just as with openings, good writers try to craft endings that make readers feel fulfilled. For family biographies, the death of one or more of the main characters can serve as an appropriate ending. Another good ending is an appropriate statement that summarizes or captures the essence of the lives discussed.

Draw some conclusions. Give the reader your final reflective thoughts about the person or family you wrote about. Make some assessments of the person's life course, or about his or her character or personality.

You could even conclude with a comparison between one and another or between siblings. One biography, for example, ended by contrasting an American man's impressive rise to wealth with his immigrant grandfather's swineherding beginnings in Sweden.

Finishing Touches for the Biographical History

When typing or word processing your final version of the history, several finishing touches are essential. They are:

Proofreading and Reviewing the Contents for Accuracy

You don't want the final manuscript to have errors, either content or typing/word processing. To find and get rid of both kinds of errors, you need to proofread the final manuscript carefully. You should also have at least one other person proofread it too. It's useful, and sometimes politically vital, for you to have one or more relatives who know something about the individuals you wrote about read your manuscript for historical accuracy. Proofreading is a chore, but it can save you from some terrible embarrassment and regrets after the manuscript is printed as a book and is circulating among your relatives.

Creating the Final Manuscript

The final manuscript, either typed or word-processed, should be neat, error-free, and nicely formatted on the pages. It should have footnotes or endnotes that document the sources from which you gathered the text's information. Endnotes can be at the end of each chapter or all together at the end of the book.

Don't Clutter the Final Narrative with Non-Narrative Distractions

Family history is not one of those really exciting subjects. So, you need to make your writing reader friendly.

One major mistake many family historians make is to clutter up their narration with charts, documents, and pictures. Some published books contain page after page of these "illustrative materials" set right in the middle of narration. Your guiding principle should be that you want the reader to read. Therefore, you don't want to interrupt the reader with long quotes, masses of pictures, detailed genealogy charts, or anything else.

There is one simple way to determine whether or not to include a picture, chart, document, or map. If it helps the reader to understand the text without breaking the sequence of the narrative, it's okay to use it. If it illustrates quickly, then use it. But if it is reference material that the reader needs to look at closely, put it in the appendix—not in the text.

Include Humor

Readers like any narrative that includes humor. So, you should watch for humorous events in your relatives' lives, and tell those in your history even if they are not historically important. The fact that funny things happened to your relatives is itself important to know.

Simple Charts

Any illustrative material you insert into the narrative needs to be simple. Complete genealogy charts have no place in the narration itself; they should be presented in the appendix section at the back of the history. Readers do need genealogy charts to help them understand who the people in the narration are, but charts within the text need to be very simple and basic. Just group names without dates or use only the year (not the day and month).

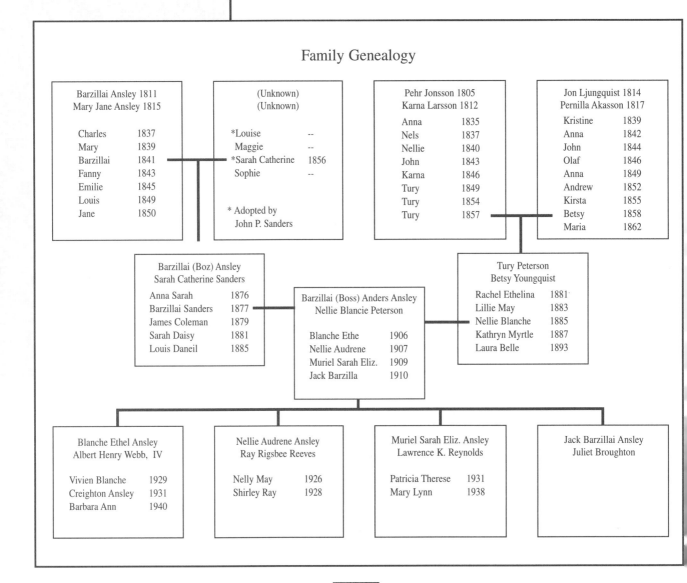

Family Genealogy

Barzillai Ansley 1811
Mary Jane Ansley 1815

Charles	1837
Mary	1839
Barzillai	1841
Fanny	1843
Emilie	1845
Louis	1849
Jane	1850

(Unknown)
(Unknown)

*Louise	--
Maggie	--
*Sarah Catherine	1856
Sophie	--

* Adopted by
John P. Sanders

Pehr Jonsson 1805
Karna Larsson 1812

Anna	1835
Nels	1837
Nellie	1840
John	1843
Karna	1846
Tury	1849
Tury	1854
Tury	1857

Jon Ljungquist 1814
Pernilla Akasson 1817

Kristine	1839
Anna	1842
John	1844
Olaf	1846
Anna	1849
Andrew	1852
Kirsta	1855
Betsy	1858
Maria	1862

Barzillai (Boz) Ansley
Sarah Catherine Sanders

Anna Sarah	1876
Barzillai Sanders	1877
James Coleman	1879
Sarah Daisy	1881
Louis Daneil	1885

Barzillai (Boss) Anders Ansley
Nellie Blancie Peterson

Blanche Ethe	1906
Nellie Audrene	1907
Muriel Sarah Eliz.	1909
Jack Barzilla	1910

Tury Peterson
Betsy Youngquist

Rachel Ethelina	1881
Lillie May	1883
Nellie Blanche	1885
Kathryn Myrtle	1887
Laura Belle	1893

Blanche Ethel Ansley
Albert Henry Webb, IV

Vivien Blanche	1929
Creighton Ansley	1931
Barbara Ann	1940

Nellie Audrene Ansley
Ray Rigsbee Reeves

| Nelly May | 1926 |
| Shirley Ray | 1928 |

Muriel Sarah Eliz. Ansley
Lawrence K. Reynolds

| Patricia Therese | 1931 |
| Mary Lynn | 1938 |

Jack Barzillai Ansley
Juliet Broughton

Simple Maps

The same principle regarding charts applies to maps. A map should be included in the text if it quickly helps the reader understand the narrative. Detailed maps should be placed in the appendix.

Rarely will a published map be just right for your history. It is also against copyright law to copy and use someone else's map without obtaining permission. So, what works best is to trace in outline form a map or part of a map that covers the geographic area you want to show. On it, insert a minimal number of cities, towns, or lines that let the reader know the general location, and then add your own dots to printouts of site names. In essence, tailor your map to show only what you want it to show.

Proper Front Matter and Back Matter Pages

If it is book-length, your history needs to have all the proper elements of a book: title page, preface, table of contents, chapters, appendix (if needed), bibliography, and index.

Title and Title Page

Writers face a dilemma when creating a title. On the one hand, they want a title that has some excitement and appeal to it, one that is catchy or creative. That impulse produces bold titles like *Oak Trees in the Wind*, *Heritage of Courage*, or something similar. On the other hand, librarians, book catalogers, and readers need to know from the title what the book is about. Consequently, you have only two reasonable solutions to the dilemma, and neither one produces very exciting titles. The simplest solution is a title that tells exactly what the book is about in direct and plain words, such as *The Family History of Juan and Rosa Gomez, 1906 to 1983*. The other solution is the blend of a bold or catchy title with a descriptive subtitle, such as *Heritage of Courage: The Life and Times of Louis Bernstein.*

The title page needs to include the name of the author, the book title, the publisher's name, and the place of publication. The back of the title page should include the date of publication, a copyright, and the name of the person or group holding the copyright. Published books also need to have an ISBN number obtained from the Library of Congress included on this page.

Preface

An author writes a preface in order to chat with readers about the history to follow on the next pages. A preface should be written in the first-person—"I wrote this...." Your preface gives you, the author, a chance to tell the reader about the project.

Include the who, what, where, when, and why information discussed earlier in this chapter. Also include acknowledgments and thank-yous—give credit to people who helped you with the project.

Explain in the preface any editorial methods you used in the history. For example, if you used an old document and corrected its spelling or added punctuation to it, inform the reader you did so.

Tell the reader also what you did not do. If certain relatives receive short shrift in your history, explain why—no living descendants, could not find any records, was unable to go to Ohio to research that group, or whatever. Mention searching for particular records that proved to be futile. Comment on problems you encountered. Advise your reader of gaps you know are there and that you hope to fill them in later.

Table of Contents

You should list the chapter or section titles along with the page numbers where they are located. This will serve as a reference to your reader, as well as an overview of the book.

Appendix

An appendix is placed in the back of the book or manuscript. It is material added to supplement or reinforce the text. This is where you should put detailed genealogy charts, certificates, detailed maps, blocks of quoted diary materials, copies of letters, and other reference materials.

Bibliography

Readers need a list of all the sources you consulted while researching for the biography. It should list published items, in alphabetical order according to author's last name, and unpublished materials by title or author. Families especially appreciate having a full list of records you used and where they can be found.

Index

Nonfiction books have indexes. Readers like indexes, especially for books containing family history. With an index, a reader can look up one of the relatives he or she favors and go to the page to read what you wrote about that person.

Publishing and Distributing

You write a family biography so that it will be read. You need to be sure, then, that it seems appealing and attractive to the readers in your family. Therefore, don't dress your beautiful baby in shabby or unattractive clothes—people do judge a book by its cover.

As books go, a family biography is not as appealing as fiction or books published by well-known publishing houses. Your book will compete with expensive, nicely printed books. At the least, it needs to look like a real book and not like a college master's thesis or dull business report. Give it as attractive a cover as you can afford. If possible, have a professional artist or designer help you design the final book.

Publishing or duplicating the history is a serious project in itself. It is not a quick and easy process to accomplish once the hard task of writing the narrative is finished. A lot of work is involved in publishing a manuscript. (See Chapter 8 for details on the publishing process.)

Contracting for a Family History to Be Written

Many book-length family histories and biographies have been published, given that so much hard work goes into researching and writing them. But how do they get written? A book-length history about a family is either a labor of love by a relative or committee of relatives, or was produced by a hired historian. Families deciding they want a book-length history need to have some idea of the costs required or at least how much work it will take by relatives donating their time and skills.

How much does it cost to hire someone to write a book-length history for a family? A hypothetical case provides a rough answer that can help families see what to expect. Let's say a family hires a historian at $10 per hour (which they can't do, because no historian will accept that small a salary) and they want a book of 10 chapters. Let's say they give the historian one week to produce each chapter (which is impossible because you can't do all of the research in just one week, let alone write a first draft and revise it to produce a final draft). And, let's say he or she works 40 hours

per week to produce each chapter. That comes to 40 hours times 10 weeks (1 week per chapter) or 400 hours at $10 per hour, or $4,000 for a 10-chapter book.

But $4,000 is not realistic. Actually, a family needs to expect to pay between $8,000 and $20,000 for a free-lance historian to produce a well-researched, well-written family history. Most historians doing this kind of work do it as a side project, not full-time, so such a project may take from two to five years to complete. Historians need to be paid as they go, rather than in a lump sum when finished.

Of course, the above costs are only for researching and writing the final manuscript—they do not include publishing costs (see Chapter 8 for publishing information).

Here are basic matters a family needs to consider when contracting with a historian to produce a family history:

1. Family initial decisions:
    A. What kind of history it wants: What people the history will cover; how many generations; what kind of final book they hope to produce; and how they plan to make it available to the family.
    B. How the project will be funded. Will one relative pay for it? Will funds need to be raised from the relatives before the project can start?
    C. Who will be the family's committee or contact person to work with the historian? (Committee must be small to be workable, no more than 3 people.
    D. What time frame is acceptable? What is essential?
2. The family must round up all files and information useful for the history and create lists of family contacts for the historian.
3. Hiring an historian:
    A. Locate an historian willing to do the project.
    B. Give him/her a prospectus about the history.
    C. Show him/her available family resources.
    D. Ask him/her for an estimate of costs and time.
4. Frame and sign a written agreement that spells out:
    A. Who the family contact person or committee is.

Need to Find a Writer?

Have you completed gathering your family history, but you now need to find a writer to help pull it all together? The National Writer's Union, through their national job bank service is one place to look. Published writers of non-fiction and fiction are members.

The National Writer's Union may be reached at:

National Writer's Union
113 University Place
New York, N.Y. 10003

Telephone: 212-254-0279
Fax: 212-254-0673
E-mail: nwu@nwu.org

B. Rate of pay for the historian, and what expenses will be covered (travel, photocopying, phoning, pictures, tapes, transcribing tapes, etc.

C. Decide on reporting proceedures. Monthly or bimonthly works best. Written reports only, or written and verbal? Some historians require that they be paid for in advance for each work period between reports; others are paid each time they report work done during that report period.

D. Projected time and expenses. Projects need to be kept open-ended, in case more research is needed or rich finds of information are discovered that need to be tapped.

E. Historian has the right to have his/her name on book as author.

F. Historian should be guaranteed right to tell the story accurately.

G. Family contact person or committee has the right to review the chapters and critique and proofread.

H. Historian agrees to give the family:
(1) final typescript/printout that is totally finished history; (2) all oral history tapes he or she generated for the project; (3) computer disks and backups, (4) file materials generated by the historian's research.

Part 3
SHARING YOUR FAMILY HISTORY

CHAPTER EIGHT

Publishing
a Family
History Book

It is important to share with other relatives what you discover about your family heritage. You can do this through videotapes, audiotapes, sets of family photographs, and by creating books and booklets that you self-publish.

What a difference fifty years makes! A half-century ago, before computers and photocopy machines, a person typed a life story. After all this hard typing work, how could the individual make copies of the material for other family members? He or she had two choices: type the typescript using carbon paper, making one or two hard-to-read copies; or, take the pages to a printer, be charged to have them typeset, and then pay huge sums to have it offset printed on a printing press.

Today, you can publish your own book or booklet fairly easily. Self-publishing is now made possible by easy access to personal computers, quick-copy centers and photocopy machines, and inexpensive binding services. You can print as many copies as you want or can afford. And, unlike even a decade ago, personal computers let you produce very attractive typefaces, page layouts, maps, charts, and good-quality copies of photographs.

Families and individuals are self-publishing history and genealogy books in record numbers. They are flooding libraries and providing relatives with family histories, genealogies, collections of letters, diaries, and autobiographies.

About 99 percent of published family histories and genealogies are designed for relatives, not for commercial sales in bookstores. As a rule, bookstores will not accept family histories because of their limited sales audience and sometimes because of their lower quality compared to printing press–produced books.

Publishing a book or booklet is a project all its own, independent of the writing or compiling effort. It is hard work, to be sure, but it is a task that is creative, exciting, and satisfying when completed.

To do the actual publishing—the photocopy printing and the binding—you first need to have a finished manuscript. How you prepare the final typescript depends on what kind of material it is—a narrative; a genealogy collection; an edition of documents, such as letters or a diary; or a biography. Refer to Chapter 7 to learn how to prepare a final manuscript for publication.

Editing Documents to Be Published

Let's say you have an autobiographical account from your grandfather. The simplest way to publish it is merely to photocopy all of the original pages and bind them, with a title printed or stamped on the cover.

But more should be done than that. At the very least, create a title page and a "Publisher's Preface" to follow it. In the preface, tell the reader in a paragraph or two who your grandfather was, when and where he lived, where his original life sketch is, and why you decided to publish it. Another helpful addition is a simple index—a name index is the minimum—following the life sketch pages.

It is vital that you write an introduction. Include in it a history of the documents themselves—how they originated, how they transferred from one generation to the next, and where they are now. Provide your readers with needed context information about places, people, and events mentioned in the document.

When Transcribing

Words underlined in the original should be typed in italics.

Before transcribing you might want to consult *A Guide to Documentary Editing* by Mary Jo Kline and published by John Hopkins University Press.

Transcribing to Make a Typescript

It would be much more useful to your readers, however, to present a typescript of your grandfather's autobiographical sketch. This can be the typescript alone, or it can be the typescript followed by a copy of the handwritten original.

Making a transcript from an original document involves more than simply typing. When you transcribe from handwritten material, you face interesting challenges about how to render in type what is handwritten. If the original is missing punctuation, do you add it? What about strange or incorrect spelling? How do you treat a nearly illegible word that could be one of two words? What about abbreviations?

You can choose from one of three editorial methods when publishing a transcribed version of a document: literal, expanded, or modernized. Your choice depends on your audience.

If you choose the *literal method*, you type the material exactly as it is in the original—without changing anything. When a word or number isn't clear, you can put a question mark in square brackets: [?]. You can help the reader decipher strange or incorrect spelling

Documentary Editing Samples: Literal, Expanded, and Modern

Literal: Exactly Like the Handwritten Original

I was born in Simpson Co Ky Aprile 8th 1808 my Father name was James Butler he was the 5th child of Wm. and Phebe Butler my grand mother was named Childres before her marriage My Grandfather Butler had 9 children Elizabeth whoo maried James McKonnel John William Thomas James Samuel Aaron Edmund & Fany whoo maried Joseph Plumer. My Mothers name was Charity Lowe before her marige she was the second child of Wm and Margaret Lowe.

Expanded: Edited for Minimum Punctuation and Paragraphs

I was born in Simpson Co Ky Aprile 8th 1808. My Father name was James Butler. He was the 5th child of Wm. and Phebe Butler. My grand mother was named Childres before her marriage. My Grandfather Butler had 9 children:

by putting the correct spelling in square brackets immediately following the difficult word. Scholars prefer the literal method due to its historical accuracy.

The *expanded method* lets you make sentences by capitalizing the first word and putting a period at the end of the phrase and allows you to spell out abbreviations. You may not, however, begin proper names with a capital letter if the original doesn't. Even the most serious scholars insert minimal punctuation to make a document read the way the writer meant it to be read, though. You should likewise feel free to add minimal punctuation and paragraphing.

If you use the *modern method*, you can modernize spelling, capitalization, and punctuation, but not the grammar. You may even break up overly long sentences and paragraphs. This method is best for the general audience.

No matter what changes you make, inform your readers in your preface about the type of editing you've done and in what ways it makes the typed version different from the original.

In addition to providing the reader with a good transcript, you can make the material even more valuable and sensible by providing annotations—comments you insert either in footnotes or in the text in square brackets [ ]. Annotations clarify names, places, events, or problems in the original document, for example, [torn], [illegible], [name erased]. If the document says that Sally did something but never explains who Sally is, you can tell the reader it was Sally [his daughter] or Sally [Lembke].

Some people not only create paragraphs in unparagraphed documents, they create sections or chapters, each with a heading or title. This not only helps the reader understand what the document contains, but it allows the document editor to create a table of contents listing those headings or chapter titles with the page number where each section begins.

You can also choose to shorten your grandfather's autobiographical account. Perhaps you want to delete repetitious information or censor something very offensive. If you do delete from the original, tell your readers in the preface that the book is a shortened, edited version. In the text itself, indicate with ellipsis points (. . .) where material is missing.

Among historians, a bible on the subject of transcribing is Mary-Jo Kline's *A Guide to Documentary Editing* (Baltimore, MD: Johns Hopkins University Press, 1987).

Preparing Genealogy Records for Publication

A published genealogy is a reference, not a book you sit down to read late at night in the living room chair. You face a minor dilemma when you decide to publish your genealogy data: How do you include all the details without confusing and confounding the reader with them?

Your goal is not to confuse the reader. So, you need to make as crystal clear as possible who the family group is that you are discussing in each section. Do that by using names and descriptions of relationships rather than numbers.

There are numbering systems professional genealogists use, the most common of which is the Register Plan or Register Form. It assigns numbers to each generation, as well as to each person in that generation. The starting number, 1, is assigned to the common ancestor, and his next descendants in order of birth receive the next numbers. To keep the generations straight, each person has a superscript generation number after his or her personal number.

The numbering system, while complex, works well for families of males in direct descent. It poses special problems for females who marry and take on new last names, however. If you intend genealogy experts to be your main audience, you should consider numbering. Several in-depth genealogy guidebooks explain the system. See, for example, Patricia Law Hatcher's *Producing a Quality Family History* (Salt Lake City, UT: Ancestry, 1996), pages 105–109.

The numbering system is too complex and confusing for standard family histories, though. Instead of numbering, you can devote separate chapters to each family cluster, and then employ descriptive phrases as titles of your sections. Let's say your grandfather's name was Abel Smith. To describe his second son's family, title that section "The Children of Robert and Loretta Jones Smith, Abel Smith's

(continued)

Elizabeth who maried James McKonnel, John, William, Thomas, James, Samuel, Aaron, Edmund, & Fany whoo maried Joseph Plumer.

My Mothers name was Charity Lowe before her marriage. She was the second child of Wm and Margaret Lowe.

Modernized: Edited for Punctuation, Paragraphs, and Spelling

I was born in Simpson County, Kentucky, April 8th 1808. My father's name was James Butler. He was the 5th child of William and Phoebe Butler. My grandmother was named Childress before her marriage. My Grandfather Butler had 9 children: Elizabeth, who married James McConnell, John, William, Thomas, James, Samuel, Aaron, Edmund, and Fanny, who married Joseph Plumber.

My mother's name was Charity Lowe before her marriage. She was the second child of William and Margaret Lowe.

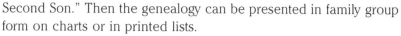

Keep the Book's Scope Reasonable

"So often ambitious researchers set out to do comprehensive genealogies, only to burn out in the process of trying to produce an overwhelming amount of research and writing. If you are compelled to do a book, give yourself a break and do a small book. If you survive the small one and are still game, then go after a telephone-directory size production" from Bill R. Linder's *How to Trace Your Family History*, published by Fawcett.

Second Son." Then the genealogy can be presented in family group form on charts or in printed lists.

Group your genealogy charts into distinct sections, and give each section a good title page that fully explains how the people on those charts relate to individuals already covered in the book. Also provide a biographical overview of the families listed genealogically in that section. In the overview, describe some life story details to make the people seem real and not merely names on a list.

Several store-bought genealogy record-keeping programs for word processors (see Chapter 2) contain book-generating programs. These prevent you from having to retype or re-enter genealogy data or having to proofread, and they provide a workable format for the book.

It is essential that any book of genealogy have a name index that has been carefully checked for accuracy. A female should be listed under all her names—maiden, first marriage, second marriage, etc. Each variation of a name's spelling (Durphy, Durfey, Durfee) should be listed separately and not combined into one standard spelling.

"How Much Does It Cost?"

People who want to publish a book ask that question first. It's a simple question, but it has no simple answer. It is like asking how much a house costs. Who can give a simple answer, other than "It depends"? Do you want the house to have two stories or one? Six bedrooms or two? A basement or attic? Just like the price of a home, your book's cost depends on a dozen or more variables.

Among matters you must decide before you can determine book costs are:

How will you print your manuscript? Will you photocopy it, print it on a word processor, or have it typeset?
What color, weight, and finish of paper will you use?
Do you want the book to be standard size, smaller than normal, or oversize? What size pages do you want?
What color ink do you want?

If you typeset it, what typefaces will you use?

Do you want footnotes, endnotes, or appendix materials printed in reduced-size type?

How big will margins be on your pages?

Based on the size of typeface, pages, and margins, how many printed pages will your text require?

Who will design the book's cover, maps, and artwork?

Will pictures be in one section or scattered throughout the book?

Will you use color pictures?

Do you want a designer to lay out the picture pages for you?

Will the book's cover be hardback, softback, or spiral-comb bound?

Will the binding be glued or handsewn?

Will the cover be one piece or a three-piece wraparound?

Will the cover be one color or more?

Will you use colored end sheets in the front and back of the book?

Will you include maps? How many? How many map pages?

Will you pay for proofreading?

Will the family do the indexing or will you hire an indexer?

How many copies will you print?

To figure out publishing costs, the family needs to talk to local quick-copy centers or book printers. You should obtain bids for the publishing job from three companies since prices vary greatly.

Before you can ask a printer to bid on your project, however, you need to know three vital facts about your manuscript:

1. *Exactly how many pages your manuscript is.* You should take the finished manuscript with you, including mock-ups of picture pages, and introductory pages, and appendices.

2. *Approximately how many books you want printed.* If you want to print under 200 copies, expect a book publisher to turn you down and send you to a quick-copy or photocopy center. To fire up a publisher's big presses for a run of less than 200 books would push your cost-per-book so high that you will not be interested. Most commercial printers prefer a run of at least 500 books.

Remember . . .

Most families who publish a book of genealogy print less than 500 copies.

3. *What kind of book features you like*—paper, print size and style, and bindings. How can you decide on these factors and then communicate your preferences to a printer? Here are two good suggestions:

   A. Spend about four hours in a large library. Visit the shelves that display published biographies and family histories. Thumb through these books, one at a time, and examine their printing and binding styles. Select two or three books that have the features you like the best in terms of:

   > paper color and texture
   > size, style, and color of printing
   > bindings and covers
   > design and layouts—how the title page, chapter
   >   headings, pictures, maps, charts, etc., are presented

   Borrow the books you like and take them with you to show to the publisher.

   B. Better yet, take your library books to a professional artist who does book designing. Discuss your project with him or her. For a fee, designers will show you several creative mock-ups for your book. They can even let you see various color combinations of paper and binding stock. Once you have decided on a design, the artist can discuss the book's specifications with the printer you select, in printers' language.

Budget Printing

The fewer copies of your book that you print, the lower your total cost is. However, your cost per book goes higher.

Photocopying your typescript will give you a readable unbound set of pages. You can arrange for the text on the page to be double-columned instead of the standard single, if you choose. You can add a copy-center cover of heavy paper stock, cardboard stock, flexible plastic, or even hardcover binding.

Let's say you have a 200-page typescript. You can photocopy one or more copies for $.07 per page, or $14 per volume. Add on a paper cover for $2.00, and you have one book or dozens "published" at the same per-book cost of around $16 to $18.

Word Processing

Using computers for manuscript preparation is terrific because changes are easily made. Word processors with letter-quality printers also provide excellent copy for reproduction (quick-print or photocopy). Some software programs allow you to "desktop publish" your manuscripts using word processors with high-quality printers that produce pages that are almost typeset-quality and are "camera ready." Camera-ready copy can be photocopied, and the copies look good enough to be bound, without any other in-between steps taken.

Design Considerations

Too many family history books on our library shelves look and feel cheap, and it's sad to see. They are sloppy typescripts instead of typeset or word processed with adjusted margins. Their covers are plain and in an ugly color. Their pictures are carelessly positioned and badly copied. Some family histories lack vital parts that all respectable books have, such as a table of contents and publishing data following the title page. When relatives buy or receive such poorly packaged books, they subconsciously decide not to read them.

Many families run out of energy and money once the manuscript is finished. They falter at one of the worst possible moments. Money and time should be budgeted from day one so that the manuscript, when complete, can be attractively dressed.

You write a history or biography to be read, so the book should be packaged to appeal to readers. Most commercial books in bookstores are well designed and attractive. People know by sight and touch which books are high quality and which are cheap. Therefore, give good attention to how your book will look, and find some way to spend more in order to make it as attractive as possible.

Warning

When making photocopies, use acid-free paper. Standard paper will discolor and become brittle within fifty years. Also, use a heavier, 60 lb. paper instead of the usual 20 lb. The 20 lb. paper is too thin to print on both sides of the page.

The layout should be appealing to the reader's eye. For example, small print across the entire width of a page is too hard for the normal eye to read comfortably. Use a larger typeface and normal margin widths, or prepare your final text in two columns. You can align your type on both sides (justify) or only on the left side as in this book.

No matter how you space the text on the page, if you plan to do double-sided copying, be sure that the binding edge on each page is 1/4-inch wider than the outside edge. That means the left margin of the front of the page will be indented 1/4-inch extra, and the text on its flip side will have that extra indentation from the right margin. That way, when you hold the page up to the light, the blocks of text on both sides of the page match up with one another.

The title page and the table of contents are always on the right-hand page—never on the left. In most professional books, chapters also start on the right page.

It is useful but not necessary to employ a designer to help you format and design the book. A designer can help you decide on such things as the size and style of typeface, the weight and color of your papers, the size of the margins, where to place page numbers, whether to use a short title or header at the top of each page, what kind of oversize type you should use for chapter titles, and how you position pictures on the page.

The cover design should be original and suitable for your family. Cover materials and colors should also be compatible with the color and texture of the pages inside. Maps should be drawn with lines and text that blend well with the printed pages. Color-matched end papers can be added to the front and back of the book. Title page and chapter beginning pages could have an ornament (artwork) that repeats throughout the book, giving it unity.

Photographs

Be generous with photographs. People usually look at photographs in books before they read anything. Black-and-white pictures copy

better than color ones. Photographs can be scattered throughout the text or put in a picture section in the middle or back of the book. If scattered, however, photos should be used to illustrate the narration, not detract from it. If readers are constantly interrupted by pictures, their train of thought gets broken, helping them lose interest in the narration.

Balance your selection of pictures to give equitable coverage to each family. Also, be sure you include short but adequate captions that identify each picture.

Printers can enlarge, reduce, and crop pictures, so your photographs can be made into assorted sizes. If you want the pictures in your book to be printed in color, expect to pay terrifically high costs for it.

Binding Options

Consider these four realities when deciding how to cover and bind your book:

1. The book must be able to stand in a bookcase in a row with other upright books.
2. Standing upright on the shelf, your book needs to have at least a short form of the title and the author's last name printed on the spine. No book on a shelf should show a blank spine.
3. The book's binding should be sturdy enough not to break apart or lose pages if the book is dropped or falls to the floor.
4. The cover needs to have a finish or coating such that normal skin oil on fingers won't discolor or smudge it.

These considerations weigh against spiral-comb-bound books because such books don't stand upright very well on a shelf and their bindings are fatter than the book itself. Therefore, spiral-comb-bound-books don't fit well with other books on a shelf. These considerations, too, argue against paperback bindings (which are glued on) and in favor of sewn bindings and hardback covers.

Three Publishing Rules-of-Thumb

No matter what you intend to publish, two commonsense principles need to be applied:

1. Make the final appearance and feel of the book—its cover, pages, and illustrations—attractive. You want people to read what you publish, so try to entice them to thumb through the book. If it looks like a cheap project, people will subconsciously decide the contents also are not very valuable.
2. Make the text easy to read. Make type big enough for the elderly to see, chapters or sections short enough to read, and headings throughout the chapters to break up the narration.
3. "Don't dress your beautiful new baby in ragged clothes."

The cover design should be in taste with the overall look of the book.

Printing or Publishing the Book

Once the design and printing specifications are chosen for your book, you can obtain three estimates for the printing and binding. Select the best bid. At that point, you know how much the total printing and binding will cost, so you can determine how much each book will cost to publish. Set a price for the book that covers its per-book cost, and add a little extra for your other expenses if you need to. You generally cannot charge enough to cover the costs of the time and labor expended to research and write your book. You will probably charge only for the printing and binding costs, with maybe a dollar or two added on. Due to their small production run, most family history books carry expensive prices, usually in the $20 to $40 range.

Printers charge half of the printing costs up-front and the other half upon delivery. They will box the books for you. You usually have to pick the boxed books up, though.

It is vital that you open the boxes and quality-check the books. Some books have pages that didn't copy or that smeared, crooked paper or type, missing pages, or covers misaligned. You need to locate those defects right away. Printers usually produce an extra 10 percent of books beyond the original order, knowing there could be mistakes in the printing run.

Plans must be made to ship books that are ordered. Box and container companies sell mailing boxes in bulk quantities, so each box is much cheaper than if you bought them in a local discount store. Books can be shipped at a special fourth-class book rate, which saves a fortune in mailing costs. Contact your local post office for details.

Between the time the printer finishes all of the books and the day when you sell the last copy, someone needs to store the inventory in a safe, dry place. Someone also needs to keep the account books—tracking the inventory, the money coming in with book orders, and the expenses for boxes and postage.

Distributing Copies of Your Book

You are publishing your book so that others can read about the family's history. But how do you make it available to them? Here is how other authors have done it:

1. Before the book comes off the press, send flyers to as many relatives as you can find, asking them to send money to you to reserve copies. You can use that pre-publication money to defray the first payment to the printer. Then you ship books to those relatives when the printing is done. As an incentive, you can offer a pre-publication price, one lower than the post-publication price.

2. Send flyers to your family members after the book is printed so that your flyer can display pictures of its pages.

3. Send follow-up flyers for the next two holiday seasons (if you have not sold out your inventory by then).

4. Take copies to family reunions and other gatherings, and show them off.

5. You or someone else in the family can host a special open house to honor and display the book, making it available to relatives and friends.

6. Send complimentary copies to any and all libraries in locations covered in the book. This can involve several dozen copies.

7. Ask local newspaper book review editors to do a review of your book.

8. Run advertisements offering your book for sale. Place these ads in local newspapers or in family history publications.

9. Be sure your publisher sends two copies to the Library of Congress as part of your copyright obligation.

10. A book of compiled genealogies needs to be made known to the world of genealogy researchers. Therefore, send review copies, or a four-paragraph write-up about the book, to major genealogical societies, libraries, and journals. For names and addresses, see Anita Cheek Milner's *Newspaper Genealogy Columns* (Bowie, MD: Heritage Books, 1984) and Mary K. Meyer's *Directory of Genealogical Societies in the U.S.A. and Canada* (Mt. Airy, MD: 1984).

For Further Information . . .

For discussions on nearly every aspect of publishing a family history book, see Patricia Law Hatcher's *Producing a Quality Family History* (Salt Lake City, UT: Ancestry, 1996).

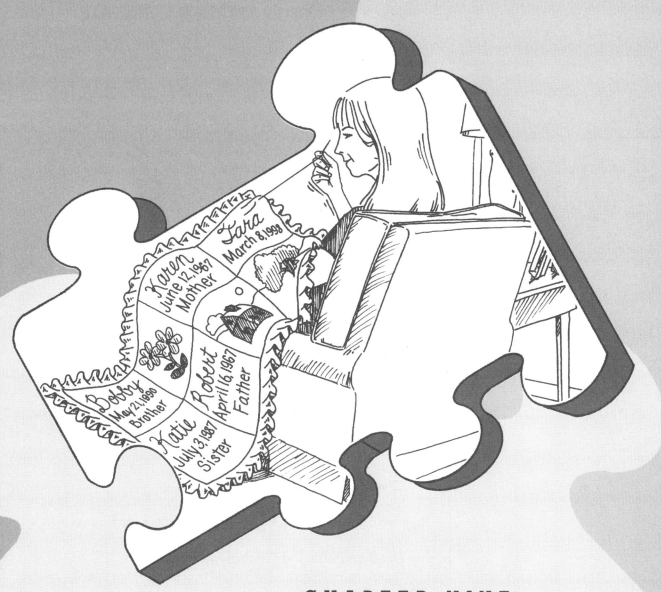

CHAPTER NINE

Fun Family
Heritage Activities

In prior chapters you read about a wide range of family history–related activities: researching genealogy, diary-keeping, writing your life story, researching and writing the history of a relative or family group, preserving family records, tape-recording oral histories, and taking pictures and videotaping. Each chapter suggested activities you could do in connection with those projects.

Here are even more family history–related projects you should know about and consider doing. Sharing the family heritage and involving even distant relatives in it can be not only useful but fun and memorable.

Sharing Genealogy Information

When you have collected parts of the family's genealogy, you can share them with relatives in several ways.

Give Charts to Others

Print out sets of genealogy charts and give them to each of your immediate family members and other relatives. Send them loose or in a 3-ring binder.

Give Computer Files to Others

Make copies of your computerized genealogy on disks and share them with family members who have compatible software programs.

Desktop Publish a Genealogy Booklet

Using your computer, create a small booklet about one branch of the family. Include genealogy charts, some photos, and some life sketches. (For a book-length project, see the discussion of book publishing in Chapter 8.)

Wall Displays

You can use the walls in your home to display family heritage visuals. Or, in reverse, you can draw on your family heritage to help you decorate the walls of your home.

Framed Genealogy Chart

Arrange for segments of your pedigree chart to be enlarged at a quick-copy center and even printed on parchment paper. Then, frame the chart and display it on a wall in the living or family room.

Framed Family History Chart

This is a great idea not only for your own home but as a special gift for a favorite relative who "has everything." This chart combines three elements: a very simple genealogy chart, a handful of outstanding photographs, and a few paragraphs of text. Using these three elements, you can create an attractive collage, have it copied or printed, and mount it in a handsome frame.

Family Photographs

Small photos can be enlarged, printed on sturdy parchment paper, put in frames, and displayed singly or in groups on an appropriate wall in the home. Photo retailers have digital-enhancement equipment that can copy the photograph and then restore and enhance it by removing stains and tears. Copy centers are able to make beautiful color copies of photographs, even enlarged ones. They can even produce a poster-size reproduction, if you want one that large.

Family History Sites Map

Using computer software that generates maps, or enlisting the help of an artist in the family, create a large map on which are shown the family's historic sites. This can be a map of the United States, Europe or another continent, or the world. Mount short explanations of each site by its name. Such maps give relatives a sense of the family in the larger perspective of nation and world.

Family Coats of Arms

See Chapter 3 to learn how to create or locate a family coat of arms.

Products for Children

Family heritage becomes important to a child much more easily if the child has heritage materials of his or her very own. Here are some ideas for children's heritage items.

Booklet of Genealogy Charts

This can be a collection of simplified pedigree or family group charts, or the same ones you use. Having a group chart of their own family, with them listed as a child, means they have a reference booklet to keep track of birthdays, wedding anniversaries, full names, and basic information about the births of everyone in their immediate family.

Coloring Book about the Family's Heritage

Have someone with some artistic ability draw outlines and scenes for a family coloring book. Include people, places, and objects important to the family's past. The drawings can even be renderings of favorite or interesting family photographs.

Diaries or Journals

Many diaries are begun because the person received a blank journal as a gift. Such a blank book entices a young person to write something. Consider giving a blank journal as a gift to your child, a niece, or a nephew.

Family Photos on T-shirts

Photos can be transferred onto clothing. Specialty T-shirt shops and even some quick-copy centers can help you make those transfers.

Family Song

Using some catchy and well-known song, have your child help you create a family song by writing verses about family members or happenings.

Memory Boxes

Give your small child a special box. Let him or her decorate it. In it, put school papers, pictures, vacation souvenirs—items that one

GREAT GRANDPA
GREAT GRANDMA
WAS A PREACHER
IN 1899

day will be in a scrapbook. Demonstrate the importance of saving items. They will enjoy having their own box of their own stuff.

Photo Albums

Children benefit from having their own cameras and collections of photos. Give them quality photo albums for holidays or birthdays so that they have a place to put the photos. Make copies of family photographs and give them to children so that they have their own copies.

Photographic History of Children's Physical Growth

Photograph your children, separately or together, in the same pose every year during their growing years. These photos add up to a remarkable documentation of their physical change and development, year by year.

Scrapbooks

Scrapbooks are discussed in detail in Chapter 3. Usually the parents are the keepers of scrapbook items relating to children. Then, at some point, a parent assembles a scrapbook as a gift for the child. Or, the parents involve an older child in making a scrapbook.

Taped Interviews of Children

Every year or so, have a chat with your child that you both know is being tape-recorded. Ask the child about his or her everyday doings—routine of getting up in the morning, meals, school, teachers, friends, what they like to spend money on, what they think about things going on in the town, hobbies, pets, etc.

Word Games

Adults can easily design simple word puzzles, such as word searches, scrambles, and even crossword puzzles that contain names of people, places, and events that are part of the family's heritage.

Child's Oral History:

Q: What do you do in the morning before you go to school?

A: I get up and I feel kind a tired. And then I go up and I watch cartoons and I get dressed and I eat breakfast, and I brush my teeth and I get a drink and I go to the bathroom, and I brush my hair, and then I go to the bus stop, and ride the bus to school.

Jeffrey W, age 5 (1974)

A Grandmother's birthday letter to her granddaughter

(January 16, 1914)
Dear Granddaughter

Got your mother's letter to day glad to hear you was well. Yes, I got your nice letter and how glad I was to get it. Yes, it is your birthday Monday. I hope you will have a nice party. I wish I could be there. Eat a little for me and have a good time.

It has been raining the last too days, is clearing up, so then I can get out again. I walked four blocks the other day to get some cards. I sent Elizabeth one, it is her birthday today. Did Paul get his card? Evan is having quite a time with ear and tooth ache.

Well Ruth it's nice down here. I spend lots of time watching the big breakers come up. It's a pretty site. I wish you was here. Picture shows every day.

Vacations to Family History Sites

Plan a vacation that will let you and your immediate family visit one or more sites important to your family's past. Visit the town where the immigrant ancestor first lived in America. See the battlefield where a great-great-grandfather fought during the Civil War. Go inside the old church your ancestor once worshipped in. Look at cemetery markers.

You should videotape the family sites you visit, if possible. At the very least, you and the children should take lots of pictures.

Prepare youngsters for the trip by learning enough about your heritage to share it with them in a well-informed way. Tuck fun into the sight-seeing by letting the children enjoy some activities—swimming, amusement parks, camping, boat rides, movies, etc. They need to have fun in addition to just "seeing old things."

Grandma's Family Treasure Chest

Children (and adults, too) love to see what's in old boxes of stuff. So, you can help young people appreciate their family heritage by having a special box with heritage items in it.

Put an old trunk or cedar chest to good use as a treasure box that contains important family objects. Trunks were the precursors of today's luggage, and some families have trunks that immigrant ancestors brought across the Atlantic or across the plains to the West. You can buy old trunks from antique dealers and cedar chests from specialty furniture stores. Or you can get both from people selling them through want-ads in the newspaper.

Put old family objects in the trunk or chest. These items can include Grandpa's baseball glove, an old family Bible, a shaving mug and brush, a locket, a woman's bonnet, a wedding dress, toys, money, stamps, a pocket watch, a lock of hair, eyeglasses, house keys, and other such items.

Family Photos on CD

Technology now makes it possible for us to have our photo albums scanned or digitized and entered into the computer. They then can be viewed on the computer screen or on the TV screen. Once in a

computer file, the photos can be enlarged, reduced, moved around from page to page, and have captions written beside them. And, you can share family photos via the Internet.

Computerized photo collections promise to become the photo albums of the future. Several genealogy software packages let you create digitized copies of your photographs. Check with a computer specialty store for the latest options regarding scanning and digitizing photographs.

Birthday "Yearbook"

This works well for children through about age 10. For a birthday—but not every birthday—create a small booklet by using colored paper folded in half. On the pages list some of the child's favorite things at that stage in his or her life such as a favorite breakfast cereal, TV program, friends, and clothes. Include a few pictures. Add a paragraph here and there that recalls a favorite happening in that child's life during the previous year. Include a current picture of each member of the family, the grandparents, the family pet, or the school. This becomes a yearbook-like folder designed for that particular year of the child's life.

Family Letters

A generation ago, some families kept in touch by sending around a "round robin" letter: one relative wrote something and sent it to someone else; they added their letter and sent both letters to another person who added something, etc. When the letter and the additions returned, the originator removed his or her letter, added a new one, and sent the pack on to the next person.

That "round robin" letter idea can still work. Recipients should be told to not keep the letter more than three days before sending it to the next person.

Because of photocopy machines, fast computer printers, and e-mail, people are sending copies of the same letter to many relatives at once. The relatives respond to the letter the same way.

Until e-mail came along, the telephone was used in place of letter writing in most families. But e-mail is a new alternative, incorporating

(continued)

Got the butter from home to day it was nice, glad to get it, Wish I had some of your mama's bread to eat with it. We have nice vegetables, they taste good. Had some dried apricot pie for dinner, it was good. Anything tastes good here.

Your Nette has gone to town this afternoon. When Joe comes from school I will send him to the Postoffice with this.

Tell me who you have to your party.

Don't worry about me, I am enjoying my self watching other people having a good time. It's so nice and warm in here all nite and I sleep so good.

I wanted to send you something for your birthday but it has been too stormy to get out to find something so please accept this little letter and card with best wishes.

From grandma.

writing plus quick sending and receiving. Its one big advantage is that you can "chat" to the person at your convenience, whether the other person is home or not.

Family Heritage Mural

Murals are large illustrations depicting a sequence of scenes related to each other. Someone with artistic ability could design, sketch, and then paint a mural depicting faces and places important to the family's history. It could include a birthplace, home, school, pet, etc. The potential images are endless. The mural, however, should not be too large to frame or to hang on a wall in the home.

Family Heritage Quilts

Quilts are almost synonymous with heritage. When anyone makes a quilt, it often becomes a family heirloom. However, quilters can create a quilt specifically designed to depict the family heritage.

Blocks from favorite-but-discarded clothing items

Some quilters have created memory-laden quilts by saving pieces of clothing worn by family members until they were discarded. These were favorite shirts, dresses, ties, and other clothing. A quilt need not be made totally from such materials, but it can include several blocks made from them.

Genealogy Baby Quilt

For a baby shower, make a baby quilt that has, among its squares, one square for each immediate family member's name and birthdate—the mother, the father, and each sibling. And, of course, one square should be stitched in after the baby is born that has the baby's name and birthdate.

Family Tree Quilt

Design a family tree showing the parents, grandparents, and back even further. Or, design the family's pedigree chart into a quilt.

Birthday Party Honoring an Ancestor

Host a birthday party in honor of a deceased ancestor, on that person's birthday or near it. Make decorations and food appropriate to the time period and the place where the ancestor lived. Make placemats that depict the ancestor or his or her hometown. Show off objects that once belonged to that person. Have someone read a short tribute to and about the ancestor.

Readers Theater

A readers theater involves three or more people taking turns reading aloud from a script. Each reader represents the person whose words are in the script. If you have letters, histories, or diary entries written in the first person, you can pull quotes from those, modify them to fit the presentation, and write a script. Some liberties can be taken with the history source materials, so you can invent some statements recited by readers. But the essence of the reading parts should be close to authentic history. This program can be performed by children or adults or both.

Future Museum Objects

Instead of throwing away no-longer-useful everyday objects, put some away for descendants fifty years from now. Store them in a box with instructions indicating that the items should be saved until a selected year.

Time Capsule

You will not live forever. Fifty years from now, you probably will have descendants, some of whom may never have known you. It would be fun for them to open up a time capsule created by you. It will also mean something to them that you cared enough to try to communicate with them long after you are gone. A time capsule should contain items from today intended to be interesting to someone opening it years from now.

In a sturdy metal box, such as an ammunition box you can buy at an army-navy surplus store, store items typical of the present year:

photos of family members, the house, the pet; coins and bills of various currencies; a store catalog; an issue of a current magazine; a map of your town; or a cassette tape or CD. Include predictions you and your family members write. Put in a note or letter to your future grandchildren or descendants. Add copies of life sketches of you and/or your relatives as well as some genealogy charts.

Family Service Project

Service projects can be designed to deepen your sense of family. Work projects, for example, can assist an older relative, thereby helping the family get better acquainted with that relative. Work parties can fix and clean up an old family home. Or, a cemetery where several relatives are buried might need some sprucing up.

Tape-recording older relatives to preserve their recollections is also a vital project. It not only records the history but also makes that relative feel important.

Cemeteries and Gravestones

It is rewarding and often exciting to find and visit a gravestone marking the resting place of one of your deceased ancestors. It becomes more meaningful the older the gravestone is and the higher up the family tree it goes.

Four activities relating to family gravestones are:

1. to find and visit it
2. to write down all the information carved or written on the headstone
3. to photograph the headstone
4. to make a gravestone rubbing

Types of Cemeteries

Since Colonial times, the main American custom for disposing of the dead has been to bury them. Burial used to be either a church affair or a private matter. Up to and during the Revolutionary War era, there were essentially two kinds of graveyards—church and family.

In time, communities set up cemeteries at taxpayers' expense. Most towns and cities now have public cemeteries. Some of these are literally memorial parks, nicely landscaped and containing impressive markers for famous local citizens buried there.

Private companies, too, have created cemeteries as commercial ventures. Probably the best known is the Forest Lawn Cemetery in Los Angeles, where many celebrities are buried.

To honor soldiers killed in America's wars and prominent government officials, the federal government has created national cemeteries. Located next to Washington, D.C., Arlington is the best-known federal cemetery. Millions of visitors have stopped there to see, among other memorials, the Tomb of the Unknown Soldier and President John F. Kennedy's grave.

Church, public, government, and commercial cemeteries have survived the centuries rather well. Family cemeteries in rural isolation have fared poorly. When families sold the land to nonrelatives, the new owners or their descendants felt no interest in keeping up the little cemeteries. So, grass and weeds and trees took them over or grazing cows and horses knocked headstones over or broke them.

It is not enough for gravestones to stay standing or to survive over the years. They also must stay readable. No matter where gravestones are located, they must weather well and survive plant, insect, animal, and human damage if they are to be legible.

Finding and Visiting Cemeteries

To locate a burial site, you need to know the town where your ancestor died, or at least the probable county. Many counties have compiled lists of cemeteries within their boundaries, where they are located, and often the known names of people buried in each. These lists include not only public and church cemeteries, but also family cemeteries on private property.

From America's earliest days, cemeteries have had sextons who have kept official records regarding who was buried where, fees paid, and the next of kin who authorized and paid for each burial. Most sexton records of burials are alphabetized, so you can look for a particular name to see if that person was buried there.

Headstone Symbols

On headstones dating from the 1600s, 1700s, and early 1800s are found symbols representing life and death realities:

An eye	The eye of God
Arrow	Mankind being directed by God
Skeleton	Mortality
Hourglass	Swiftness of time
Willows	Sorrow or mourning
Reaper	Death
Hand pointing upward	Way to heaven and just reward
Trumpet	Judgment Day
Crown	Crown of righteousness
Angel	Flight of the soul into Eternity
Books	The Bible
Dove	The Holy Spirit
Grapevines	Christ as the True Vine
Wreaths	Victory in death

Headstone Inscriptions and Messages

A number of headstones from those earlier centuries contained poetry and was serious or matter-of-fact about the cause of death:

Behold and see as you
pass by
As you are now, so once
was I;
As I am now, so you
will be—
Prepare for Death and
follow me.

Reading and Copying a Headstone Inscription

The lettering and design on most headstones is not easy to read by the naked eye, let alone through a camera lens. It helps to clean off the headstone and enhance the lettering—but do so in ways that do not hurt the stone or the lettering. If you use detergents, chemicals, or stiff brushes to remove the dirt or moss, you will cause damage. Instead, gently rub off the headstone with a soft toothbrush or vegetable brush.

Another way to create some contrast of light and dark between the lettering and the stone itself is to wipe the stone's face with a damp sponge or cloth. That will darken the stone but leave the indented letters and design dry and legible.

When writing down the headstone's inscription, be careful to copy the lettering exactly as you find it. Use a slash mark—/—to indicate the end of a line of text. If you cannot decipher a letter or number, copy down what you do see and then write a question mark in square brackets [?] next to it. Be extremely careful when recording numbers, especially on very old headstones. A 7 can look like a 1, an 8 like a 0, a 3 like a 2, a 5 like a 3, a 6 like a 10, and a 4 like a 1.

Photographing Headstones

The carved or etched lettering and design show up best when partly filled by shadows. So, photograph when the sunlight is on the face of the stone making shadows in the indentations. Or, photograph from a side or top angle using a flash, or even a hand-held light, that will make slight shadows. With most of the inexpensive personal cameras, you cannot get closer than four feet from the object or your picture will be out of focus.

Making Gravestone Rubbings

A gravestone rubbing is fun to make and nice to show to family members or frame and display on a wall.

You must, however, respect the cemetery's policy about grave rubbings. Some cemeteries do not permit them. Others require that you obtain permission. It is illegal to do gravestone rubbings in Massachusetts, for example, without permission from town and/or cemetery officials.

To make a rubbing you need sketch-pad paper that is fairly heavy but still flexible enough that you can feel the face of the stone through it with your fingers. Or, at a fabric store you can buy medium-weight pellon, a white fabric that is used to line sports jackets. A light pellon will shred when you rub on it, and the heavy grade is too stiff for the headstone's indentations to show up.

Take a sheet of the paper or pellon that is big enough to cover a headstone inscription, about three to four feet long and about two feet wide. Attach the paper or pellon sheet to the headstone with masking tape, securing all four sides. Be sure the paper or pellon is pulled very tight across the face of the stone, is wrinkle-free, and is taped down securely.

You also need a rubbing crayon. Do not use children's crayons. They are too soft, smear easily, and drop crayon shreds down onto the base of the headstone. Do not use pencils, charcoal, or colored chalk for the same reason. Your best rubbing medium is a colored wax cake sold by art and graphic supply stores. It is shaped somewhat like a hockey puck and comes in standard brown and black. Sometimes it is called a lumber-marking crayon, used to mark boards in lumberyards.

With cloth or paper firmly attached, rub gently and lightly with a flat side of the crayon over and over, using small circular motions in the same direction. The crayon color will show where the stone's surface is and will not show where the indented letters and design are. The indentations will remain white. Gently color the area well and completely, making it as dark as you prefer.

Carefully remove the masking tape from the headstone and from the pellon or paper. Blow off (don't wipe!) any crayon dust that fell on the base of the grave marker. Roll up the rubbing and put it in a cardboard mailing tube. Do not leave it in your car, where the sun's heat will melt the rubbing's wax.

Tag the rubbing's bottom corner with a small card or ink notation telling the location of the gravestone: city, cemetery name, and plot in the cemetery.

Family Organizations

Setting up a family organization or association is the best way to make family reunions, newsletters, books, and information-sharing possible. Suggest the idea, find out who is interested, call them together for an informal meeting, elect someone to be the president, and then authorize the president to recruit people to serve as the beginning officers. To be a legal organization you must select a board of directors, draw up by-laws, and file incorporation papers with the secretary of state's office in the state where the organization is being established.

For help in setting up a family organization, see Joan Hummel's *Starting and Running a Nonprofit Organization 2nd ed.* (Minneapolis: University of Minnesota Press, MI, 1996.) and Christine Rose's *Family Associations: Organization and Management* (Rose Family Association, San Jose, CA, 1994.)

Officers

A president and secretary/treasurer are the minimum needed to begin a family organization. It's an effective move to form a council of members to serve as the board of directors, with at least one councilperson representing each main branch of the family.

List of Family Members

A main activity for the new officers is to contact relatives. Their goal at this stage is to obtain names and addresses of as many family members as possible.

Family Newsletter

The main vehicle for reaching the entire family is some kind of newsletter. It can be printed up and sent off once or twice a year, or more often. The president or a council member can be the editor, or someone else can be asked to be the editor. The newsletter should share information about family members past and present; announce upcoming family events; report news about births, weddings, deaths, and accomplishments of living relatives; and recount reunions or other family events after they occur.

Memberships and Money

In order to have funds to work with, the officers need to raise money. All relatives should be asked to join and to support the family organization by paying a modest annual dues. This fee would entitle them to the newsletter and to be kept informed about family projects and history.

Tax-Exempt Status

You need to register your family organization with the Internal Revenue Service as a tax-exempt, nonprofit organization established for research and educational purposes. That means paperwork, account books, and filing annual tax forms. However, it allows you to receive and expend money independent of sales and income-tax considerations.

Products to Provide

Your family organization should produce history materials and items that can benefit the relatives and bring income into the family organization. Your main concern is to be able to afford to produce these family history materials. To make them available, you need to sell these items at a price that covers printing and mailing, and perhaps a little extra for the family fund. Here are some ways to produce sellable family history items:

Edit, print nicely, photocopy, and bind an ancestor's life story, diary, or set of letters.

Reprint a family history long ago out of print.

Package a full set of a relatives' oral history interviews.

Make copies of oral history tapes.

Produce a multimedia presentation of some part of the family's history, and of the family reunions.

Gather a set of family photographs in a binder.

At a family gathering, sell a donated family heirloom for the highest bid above minimum.

Arrange for a family history tour. Make a videotape of the tour and distribute copies to relatives for a reasonable price, making a small profit off of each copy.

Bulk-Rate Mailing Permit

If you will be sending out more than 200 items at once regarding your family organization, several times a year, you can save money by obtaining a bulk mail permit from the post office. Using a bulk rate saves a lot of money per mailing.

Family Organization Activities

Depending on leadership, budget, and vision, a family organization can do a number of worthwhile things, such as:

- Publish a family newsletter
- Sponsor family reunions
- Provide genealogy and family history information to the membership
- Sponsor a family history tour
- Establish a college scholarship fund
- Hire professional genealogists to further the family's genealogy research
- Preserve, repair, or restore a family site
- Establish a wedding fund, to give a meaningful check to newlyweds in the family as a gift
- Raise money to help family members in need
- Spruce up a cemetery or gravestones of deceased relatives

Family Reunions

A family reunion serves two great purposes: It puts relatives in contact with each other, helping to build family awareness and relationships, and it lets family members share genealogy and family history information with one another. The best reunions are those planned well in advance and that involve as many relatives as possible.

Organizing and Planning

Plan at least a year or two in advance, if possible. Create a reunion committee. They and you can contact relatives to recruit those willing to work on the reunion. Establish a reunion executive committee and have them select the following officers:

1. Chairperson to coordinate with other officers and subcommittees, make sure planning moves ahead, and call and conduct planning meetings as needed
2. Treasurer to collect, account for, and issue funds
3. Secretary to develop and maintain accurate member and mailing lists and to mail letters, newsletters, invitations, and registration materials
4. Program and Activities Chairperson to create a subcommittee to select and carry out activities at the reunion
5. Family Historian to be responsible for photographing the reunion; providing family history materials for use at the reunion; calling for and collecting updated genealogy and family information from reunion attendees; and tape-recording interviews of older relatives attending the reunion

Your executive committee rounds up addresses of relatives to create an address/phone list. Send these relatives a copy of your list of relatives and ask them to send you names and addresses not included on it. Mention in your cover letter that a family reunion is being planned. Add to your master list all the new names sent in.

The program chairperson and executive committee decide what they want the main reunion activities to be. Based on these activities, pick a place for the reunion. Find out when the place is available, and pick a date for the reunion. Recruit people to serve on the reunion program and activities subcommittee, and include at least

one representative from each branch of the family on it. Assign one person from the subcommittee to take charge of the following reunion activities:

A. lodging
B. food
C. events
D. transportation
E. communication

Mail announcements to relatives on the list. Suggest they pay a small registration fee per family to help defray costs. Ask them to pay in advance by mail if possible, or at the reunion.

Possible Sites

A reunion involving a small circle of relatives can be held in one of the larger homes of one of the relatives. The most common reunion for a large family group is one held outdoors at a park or picnic pavilion. A church or community center or organization's hall can also be rented for the occasion.

A very meaningful reunion can occur on a site that is linked to the family's past—the town or a family farm where an ancestor lived, the city where an ancestor was born, a church or school that an ancestor attended, etc.

Whatever site is selected, it should be close to activities that individual families can enjoy before or after the reunion, such as an ocean beach, a swimming pool, an amusement park, hiking and biking trails, horseback riding, or important historic sites or renowned buildings and gardens.

Be sure to arrange for tables, chairs, and garbage cans at the reunion. You also must remember a microphone/speaker system, electricity if needed, water, and adequate restroom facilities at the site you choose.

Date and Time

Plan on a daylong reunion, or at least most of a day. If family members are coming from a long distance, a two- or three-day reunion should be planned.

(continued)

- Design and install historical markers honoring a relative or family site
- Create a central family library or records center that contains a copy of all genealogy, biographical, and documentary materials relating to the family

Reunion Themes

You can build a reunion around a special occasion or theme, such as a fiftieth wedding anniversary, or the eightieth birthday of a dear relative in the family.

Hold the reunion at a time when it is most convenient for the greatest number of relatives to attend. For many families, that means a time when school is out. Seasonal weather is a big factor, not only if the reunion is held outdoors, but also for those driving long distances.

When you have the date picked, reserve the place for the reunion well in advance. Some sites are so popular that they must be scheduled more than a year ahead of time.

Reunions with a Theme

You can pick a theme for your reunion around which to build the decorations, food, program, games, and attire. For example, put on a Laff-Olympics reunion and give menu items names from Olympic events: pole-vault pie, javelin juice, marathon meatballs, and shotput spaghetti. Hold fun, simple games and give ribbons to the winners.

The games can be geared toward the elderly for one competition, teenagers for another, and little children for another. Observers often have as much fun as participants. Advertising for this reunion could feature a drawing of the family's grandmother or grandfather dressed in a Greek robe, holding an Olympic torch, and crowned with a laurel wreath.

Your imagination can create themes based on well-known stories, movies, cartoon characters, nursery rhymes, songs, historic events, or types of people.

Invitation and Registration Form

Make this invitation exciting and attractive, not just plain black print on white paper. Even the envelope and stamp should not be plain.

Insert an enthusiastic welcome to attend in the first paragraph. Provide exact details regarding where the reunion is being held, including a map showing how to get there; date; time; dress; what kind of weather to expect; and a schedule of events. Inform them what they should bring in terms of food, genealogy charts, photographs, etc.

In the letter accompanying it, include a registration form they can send in. The form should provide a place for their name, address, and phone number; number in party; how much money they are sending for the registration fee; name to whom to make their checks payable; and the address where you want the registration form mailed.

Let people know about area attractions worth seeing near the reunion site. Include attraction brochures, available from tourism offices and chambers of commerce.

Follow-Up Letters

A second and even a third letter to those who did not respond can bring good results and more registrations.

Photography

The historian on your executive committee should arrange for the reunion to be photographed and/or videotaped.

Souvenirs and Money-Making Items

Why not design a T-shirt for the reunion? Or a baseball-type hat? Or a cup or mug? You can contact souvenir companies who specialize in designing souvenirs for businesses and conventions for wholesale, quantity prices. You can even create a cookbook containing favorite family recipes or have a special quilt made for the reunion and auction it off.

Videotape the Reunion

Edit it into a film that you can sell to the family. This lets those who could not attend see the people at the reunion and the day's activities. If sold above cost, it can generate funds to help pay for the reunion or other family projects.

Name Tags

Have blank name tags ready for attendees. Color-code the tags so that each branch of the family has a particular color name tag. Writing should be large enough for others to see at a slight distance and so that the names are visible in photographs taken. Pre-print

Reunion Game Ideas

- Gunnysack race
- 3-legged race
- Crab walk
- Egg-on-spoon-between-teeth relay race
- Balloon darts
- Balloon basketball
- Balloon shot putting
- Whiffle-ball bat javelin toss
- Blindfolded babystep race

names on tags, or have attendees write their own name, city, and state where they live.

Decorations

Decorations make a reunion seem festive. Balloons work well, as do crepe paper ribbons, flowers, banners, signs, enlarged photographs, and posters. You can even order imprinted napkins from a wedding-supply store.

Displays

Set up table displays for each branch of the family. Mount large pedigree and family group charts along walls.

Welcoming and Introductions

Select an enthusiastic person with a strong and likable voice to conduct the reunion. He or she should welcome the attendees, introduce special guests, and announce the events of the day. It is vital that you have a sound system good enough for everyone to hear the speaker clearly. Introduce attendees according to descendant groups by having them stand up together as you announce each group in turn.

Meals

The meal is the central activity around which the rest of the reunion is built. A bad reunion with good food is only half-successful; a good reunion with bad food is likewise only half-successful. Food makes a big difference in the enjoyment and overall attitude of reunion attendees.

Your reunion committee needs to decide what kind of meal to provide. They have sseveral options:

1. Everybody brings their own picnic lunch or supper.
2. Everybody brings their own picnic lunch or supper, but the reunion committee provides the drinks, or the drinks and desserts.

3. Food assignments are given to each family, some to bring a salad sufficient to serve a particular number, others to bring desserts or chips. In addition, each family could be asked to bring its own meat to barbecue.
4. You can have the meal catered. Contact a local restaurant, catering service, or a church or service organization for catering. Find out menu possibilities and prices, and then decide what you want them to serve.
5. You can schedule the meal at a large restaurant or cafeteria in the area. Most attendees will prefer a buffet meal over a served one. Buffets please more tastes, including those of children, than meals on a menu do.

Getting Acquainted

Announce recent weddings, births, deaths, honors, and such. Have those being fussed over stand and be recognized.

Give prizes to the oldest person, the youngest person, the family with the most children, the person with the most grandchildren, and the people who traveled the farthest to come to the reunion.

Reunion Activities

If you pick a site that is part of the family's heritage, that will determine some of the activities for the day. If the site is in a town where an ancestor lived, you can arrange for a tour of the town, a local history expert to speak to the group, a visit to a cemetery where relatives are buried, or a meeting in the old church your ancestor attended.

Let the town newspaper and historical society know you are coming. Arrange for a town official to come to the reunion and officially welcome the family to the town.

Activities need to be planned to appeal to children, adults, and older folks. Here are some possibilities:

Business meeting
A special presentation about an ancestor

Show-and-tell

Have two or three relatives bring some old family objects, heirlooms, or photographs to show and explain to attendees.

Family song

Ahead of time, find someone to write a fun and peppy family song. Create words and verses to a well-known song. Introduce the song to the group, pass out copies of the words, and have everybody sing along.

A reading

Have someone read from an old diary, autobiography, or letters.

A readers theater presentation (see discussion earlier in the chapter)

An explanation by an older relative about what took place near the site of the reunion (if held at a site important in the family's past)

Family history quiz, on paper

Sports tournament immediately before or after the reunion meal and program

Family softball game

Hayride

Volleyball

Wacky obstacle course

Water balloon toss

Treasure hunt

Talent show

Shadow puppet show

Riddles contest

A video about a family site, graves and headstones, or old photographs of places an ancestor lived

A wedding video produced for a relative who married during the previous few months

Square or round dancing

Slide show

A visit to a nearby family site or other attraction

Special Needs: Children, Teens, the Elderly

Reunions should feature activities designed for all age groups. Children are easy to please. The reunion can provide many games and activities that children can do while the others watch, or the children's activities can be separate from the rest of the reunion. A playground at the reunion site is a good idea.

Teenagers often come reluctantly and intend to be disinterested, so you need to plan well to involve them. (If they have cute cousins, half the problem is solved!) A well-planned hunt with clever clues to figure out can work well. So do sports, relay races, and card games.

Elderly people need to be provided with comfortable seats where they can see and hear well and are not in the sun. They need fewer activities and more opportunities to talk and visit with people. They can be interviewed and audio- or video-taped. As part of the program, they can be asked to tell family stories. They can be put up front with the microphone for a press conference–like session wherein the audience asks them questions about themselves and the old days. They can demonstrate an old-time craft or skill or sing an old favorite song the young generation has never heard.

Subsequent Reunions

A first reunion usually succeeds because it is something new and generates some curiosity and excitement. Subsequent reunions need to be held in new places and involve different activities than the ones before. Otherwise, the enthusiasm for attending the reunions will sag.

Many families fix a regular date each year, such as the third Saturday in June, for holding the annual reunion. Others fix a schedule for reunions to be held every three or five years.

For variations, families have planned reunions to be in different settings or to feature different adventures each time: an ocean beach, camping in the mountains, boating and houseboating, riding a steam railroad, a salmon or fish bake, a major league baseball game, an amusement park, or a cultural event.

For more ideas about family reunions, contact *Reunions* magazine at P.O. Box 1127, Milwaukee, WI, 53211-0727, (414) 263-4567. Their

Family Museum Items

To help young people, a youth organization put together an "instant museum." Each member brought the oldest objects they could find that belonged to their grandparents or ancestors before that. Among items the youths brought from home were:

1880s family bible
woman's nose-pinching eye glasses
silver cased pocket watch and chain
straight-edge razor, shaving mug,
   shaving brush
78 rpm record
45 rpm record with big hole in middle
oil painting
wall telephone with crank
ceramic head doll with real hair
1908 .22 rifle
1930s cathedral radio
World War I army uniform
trundle sewing machine
1940s Underwriter manual typewriter
camera with lens on end of bellows
lead toy soldier
Jackstraws game
bag of marbles
woman's hairbrush
gold lavalier (necklace)
Radio Boys on the Mexican Border
   book
blacksmith's hammer
ice tongs
china saucer and cup
braided hair necklace
old buttons collection

Web site is www.execpc.com/~reunions. A comprehensive checklist for reunion planners to learn from is Phyllis A. Hackleman's *Reunion Planner* (Baltimore, MD: Genealogical Publishing Company for Clearfield Company, 1993). Two excellent guidebooks published by Reunion Research in San Francisco, California, are Barbara Brown and Tom Ninkovich's *Family Reunion Handbook* (1992) and Adrienne E. Anderson's *Fun & Games for Family Gatherings, with a Focus on Reunions* (1996). Also helpful is a small book jam-packed with activity ideas: Shelley Loewer & Melody Cahoon's *Fun Family Reunions in 8 Easy Steps!* (Saskatoon, Saskatchewan, Canada: Lion Den Publishing, 1993).

Erecting Historical Markers or Plaques

While you are driving, you sometimes see historical markers along the highway. When you pass a building you might see a plaque containing history information about that building. Most markers are erected by state and county historical societies or by patriotic societies and civic groups. But families, too, can put up markers.

Often, these are cemetery gravestones. Many burial sites of our ancestors are marked by deteriorating old headstones or no marker at all. Families can gain a sense of family unity and pride when they pull together to fashion and install a new headstone honoring that ancestor.

In addition to gravestones, you can erect markers honoring a place or a person of importance to your family. This is most easily done when the site is on land owned by one of the relatives.

Stone markers with a bronze plaque attached were once the favorite type erected. But vandalism has made those markers fall from favor. Currently, the popular marker is one made of anodized aluminum, usually a dark brown or black, with gold or silver lettering and designs on it. Many are built like music stands, with the rectangle of text sloping toward the viewer. Others are perpendicular to the ground. Design, manufacturing, and installation costs can run about $2,000 for anodized aluminum historic site markers.

A Full-Life Story:
Topics and Questions

From cradle to grave, human lives pass through a vast array of experiences. Many people who have never written down their life stories claim, "Oh, I have nothing to talk about." The following extensive list of topics and questions is designed with such people in mind, to help them ponder hundreds of facts about their lives and find some memories they feel are worth recording (Chapter 6). This set of memory stimulators also serves well those making up questions to ask during tape-recorded oral history interviews (Chapter 5). And, the list should help those writing another person's history to deal with some life elements that otherwise might be forgotten (Chapter 7).

Your Family Heritages

Briefly tell about your grandparents and the ancestors before them. Who are the immigrant ancestors? When did they come to America, and why? What family stories survive about individual relatives? Were any involved in famous events? Are there family patterns relating to locations, work, social class, or genetic characteristics? What about family traditions, celebrations, heirlooms, and properties?

Communities You Have Lived in

Describe each community you have lived in or near. Tell about each community's geographic features, climate, economic activities, size, age, and the types of people living there. What are some of the community landmarks? Who were some of the leading families? What did you like or dislike about the place? Why did you move, if you did?

Neighborhoods

Tell about neighborhoods you have lived in. What part of town were they in? What difference did that make? Why did or didn't you enjoy living there? Mention favorite neighbors and any unusual features of the neighborhood, such as the corner store, train tracks, alleys, apartments, industries, creeks, or trees. How did the neighborhood change while you were there? How convenient were shopping areas, schools, parks, play areas, main roads, or workplaces to you? What has happened to the neighborhood since you lived there?

Homes and Residences

Discuss each house or apartment you lived in: where located? how old? main features? what were rooms like? how crowded? nice? shabby? what did you like and dislike about each? Mention remodelings or additions. Tell why you moved and what effect moving had on the family. What were your reactions to new residences and locations during your childhood, youth, and adult years? What modes of transportation did you commonly use at each home?

If raised on a farm or ranch, tell about fields, orchards, equipment, animals, and crops that were part of the homestead; its proximity to water, roads, and towns; the labor situation; telephone systems; and problems nature caused you.

Parents

Tell about your parents' physical characteristics and personalities. Was either previously married? How were your parents alike and how were they different? What were each one's talents, hobbies, interests, or skills? How did they adjust to each other's peculiarities? Was their marriage a happy one? Tell about their involvements in religious, civic, social, or trade activities. What personality quirks, disabilities, or health problems did your parents have while you were growing up?

Was there a constant family unit of the same two parents? If not, what effect did the loss of a parent have on your family? On you? If they divorced, what caused it and how was it handled? What change did remarriage bring, if applicable?

What was each parent's respective role in the family regarding disciplining children, managing finances, decision making, and religious training? What were the main contributions they each or together made to your life? What were the negative effects?

Father

Tell about your father's work or career. Did he earn the family's basic income? How did his work affect his being a husband and father? Did any children learn some of his skills?

Comment on what you remember about his role in the home. Was he happy as a husband and father? Was he boss in the family? Cite examples from your experiences with him to show what kind of father he was to you. Mention memorable experiences you had with him or family stories about him.

What were his talents, interests, hobbies, and skills? How was he similar and different from his brothers, sisters, or parents?

Mother

What was your mother's role in the family? Was she primarily a housewife? If so, how did she like it? What domestic skills did she have? How well did her pregnancies and childbirths go? Did she work outside the home or have paid employment within the home? What jobs or careers did she have?

Was she happy as a wife and mother? Cite examples from your experiences to show what kind of mother she was. Mention memorable experiences you had with her and family stories about her. What were her talents, interests, hobbies, and skills? Compare her to her parents and to her siblings.

Brothers and Sisters

Name, characterize, and describe each sibling. Give a sketch of each of their lives while they were in the same home with you. Comment on memorable experiences you had with each. Which ones did you grow up close to? Why? Tell about things you did with each or all of them. How did they compare with you and with each other in terms of personalities, talents, physical looks, and interests? Tell about adopted children, foster children, or other children living in your parents' home. Were those born first or last or in the middle treated any differently than the others?

Other Relatives

Name, describe, and tell about your grandparents, uncles, and aunts. Who among them were important to you as you grew up? Relate favorite family stories about each one. Mention something about where they lived, their occupations, and their children. Did you have any favorite cousins? Cite memorable experiences with them. Were you close with any nieces and nephews?

Parents' Family as a Unit

What were your family's tastes in books, magazines, reading, art, radio, TV, music, musical instruments, and out-of-home entertainment? What did your family do together for recreation? Tell about family pets. What were some memorable family vacations or outings? How did your family celebrate religious and civic holidays, birthdays, Halloween, Thanksgiving, Valentine's Day, 4th of July, Mother's Day, Father's Day, weddings, funerals, graduations, reunions, and the birth of babies?

What were family rules, standards, and expectations for the children? Was there affection in the home? Was home life a satisfying experience for you? How well did your home training and experiences prepare you for life?

Family's Health

Tell about allergies of particular members, including yourself, and any physical disabilities, accidents, major surgery, or serious illnesses (physical or mental). What do you remember about doctors, house calls, operations, hospitals, shots, medicine, vitamins children had to take, dental care, braces, or eyeglasses?

Pre-School Years

What were the circumstances of your family when you were born (where you lived, your father's occupation, how many children, any birth complications)? Earliest memories of home, father, mother, brothers, and sisters? Babysitters? Pre-school? What family stories are told about you as an infant, toddler, and child?

My Brother

My brother Harry was born when I was five. Up to then I'd had no problem that couldn't be fixed, but he arrived and wouldn't go way. . . My own birth had come after four girls, one of whom died just before I was born, and as a cousin put it, "If you'd been another Christ child, there couldn't have been more rejoicing." . . . I was, in fact, treated like something pretty special and I came to take my 'specialness' for granted . . . everything went swimmingly until that second boy appeared. . . . Papa wasted no time transferring his attention to the newcomer. From Wyatt Cooper's *Families: A Memoir and a Celebration*, published by Harper and Rowe.

Childhood Play and Friends

Tell about your closest friends: names, what you liked about them, and things you did together. What types of outdoor play did you enjoy? What about indoor play? Toys? Games? Dolls? Model building? Relate stories about getting into mischief. How did you learn to ride a bike, swim, play baseball, skate, ski, surf, do computer or arcade games, sew, cook, or camp? What groups did you belong to, like Cub Scouts, Little League, Brownies, gangs, and interest clubs? What were your childhood hobbies?

Beliefs as a Child

What were the religious preferences of your parents? What influence did your father have upon your religious beliefs? Mother? Other relatives? What religious teachings in the home do you remember? Tell about practices like prayers, special diets or fasts, and religious reading materials.

What church or faith did you belong to? How devoted were you? Comment on Sunday Schools, summer camps, and children's organizations you belonged to. What were your religious meetings like? Tell about memorable religious ceremonies, lessons, readings, leaders, or friends. What were your own beliefs about right and wrong and about God?

What were your parents' beliefs about politics, social issues, current affairs, patriotism, education, and race relations? Tell about issue groups they belonged to.

Grade and Intermediate School

What schools did you attend, and when? Public or private? Mentally walk through rooms, halls, cafeteria, and playfields and note what experiences pop into mind. What teachers influenced you for good or ill? Describe memorable classes and learning experiences. Tell about school rules, report cards, field trips, nurses, singing, assemblies, and travel to and from school.

What serious, fun, humorous, or embarrassing experiences come readily to mind?

What characteristics did you develop as a young student that influenced your later schooling? What were your family's attitudes about schooling? What were yours? Did you and your parents feel you received a good elementary education?

Your Physical Development Between Grade School and Age 18

Discuss generally how your own body grew and changed during these years in terms of height, weight, growth spurts, onset of puberty, body build, and conditions of eyes and teeth. What effects did your physical features and abilities have on things like acceptance by adults or by peers, sports abilities, musical talents, jobs, buying clothes, and choices of friends of the same or opposite sex?

High School

Describe your high school(s) in terms of buildings, classrooms, types of students, location in the community, and reputation. What classes did you take and why? Which did you like best? What teachers particularly influenced you, in either a good or bad way? What were highlights of your high school experience? What did you like best? Least? What humorous, tragic, or embarrassing things do you easily remember?

How well did you fit in with the other students in terms of your abilities, social class, interests, or race? Who were your friends grade by grade? Were you involved in school assemblies, athletics, musical groups, special events, pep rallies, or dances? What fads were "in" while you were in high school: dances, clothing, music, hair styles, expressions, jokes, heroes, or heroines? What current events were of particular concern to students? How did your own personal standards fit in or conflict with your peers' attitudes regarding honesty, dating, morals, smoking, drinking, dancing, or drugs?

How well did you do academically? What were your main problems? Any honors or awards? Describe your graduation and activities connected with it.

Remembering Play

"Some boys taught me to play football. This was fine sport. You thought up a new strategy for every play and whispered it to the others. You went out for a pass, fooling everyone. Best, you got to throw yourself mightily at someone's running legs. Either you brought him down or you hit the ground flat out on your chin., . . . Your fate, and your team's score, depended on your concentration and courage. Nothing girls did could compare with that. From Annie Dillard's *An American Childhood*, published by Harper and Row.

Teenage Friendships

Tell about schoolmates and nonschoolmates who were your best friends. What were some of the favorite or usual activities you did together? Hangouts? Eating places? Music? Concerts? Sporting events? What transportation did you or they have? Mention humorous, serious, or tragic experiences together. Were you part of a clique or the "in" group at school? What has become of those friends?

Teenage Activities

What high school extracurricular activities were you involved in? Tell about highlights, experiences, important coaches, instructors, coworkers, honors, and awards. What about nonschool groups you belonged to? What was your involvement with them? What were the best experiences or unforgettable personalities? Did you go to retreats or conferences? On outings or trips?

How did you learn to drive? What cars did you drive? What are your main memories of driving and of cars? Accidents? Tickets? Trips?

What free-time activities did you enjoy the most as a teenager? How did you finance your teen years and buy things you needed, such as clothes, cosmetics, and sports equipment? How did you pay for dates? Did you have part-time jobs that taught you skills or attitudes that were helpful later in life?

Teenager and Family

What was your role in your home? What was your relationship with your parents? How did you gain independence relating to time, money, privacy, and belongings? How central were brothers and sisters in your life then? How did you feel about your house, family, parents' work, and social class when you were with your friends? What were major family developments then? Were you close to any particular uncles, aunts, grandparents, or cousins?

Teenage Beliefs

How did your religious beliefs change from your childhood to teen years? Tell about meetings you attended, members and leaders of your group, special Sunday School classes or activity programs, positions or responsibilities you were given, reading you did, and special events. What religious questions or problems did you experience, or what beliefs did you reject?

Tell about your own conversion or about your converting others. How were your convictions challenged by friends or family? Were you more or less religious than your family members? Can you summarize your beliefs about God and religion by age eighteen and your standards of right and wrong?

What new values or beliefs became important to you? What were your feelings about politics, social issues, drugs, new lifestyles, and military service? What values of your parents' generation did you question or reject?

Boy-Girl Matters

By 11 or 12 we were all expected to have boyfriends, or at least to want to have them. Blaine's pool was a proper place to find them. . . Being shoved under water was recognized as a sign that a boy had noticed you. From Susan Allen Toth's *Blooming: A Small-town Girlhood*, published by Ballantine Books.

Boy-Girl Relationships

Did your interest in the opposite sex develop early, at the average time, or late? How did you learn the "facts of life"? Discuss your first date and earliest dating experiences. What were your parents' feelings about your dating? What rules did they set for you? What did you do, and where did you go on dates? Tell about serious romances or going steady. (Any customs regarding rings, pins, sweaters?) Which romantic interests benefitted you most, or mutually helped each of you? What became of your former girlfriends or boyfriends?

If you did not date much, how did you feel about it? Did you try to change it? Were your dating experiences generally happy ones? How did your dating experiences help prepare you for marriage later, if applicable?

Post–High School/Young Adult Years

Why did or didn't you serve in the military? If you did serve, in which branch? Why that one and not another? Comment on highlights of your military experiences, including basic training,

specializations, where you were stationed, your pay and benefits, what you liked and disliked, friends, and leaders. How did your time away affect your relationship with family, friends, and sweethearts? Did you have any combat experience, special assignments, or missions? Tell about them.

Describe missionary or humanitarian work (Peace Corps, Vista, volunteer work) you performed. Mention work companions, leaders, programs you implemented, details of your normal work, highlight experiences, and main problems.

What technical, professional, or academic schools did you attend? Why? Where? When? Did you have any problems qualifying for admission? Tell about the community the school was in. If you changed schools or dropped out, why?

Where did you live, who were your roommates, and what was your transportation? Mention your taste in clothes, hair styles, cosmetics, and leisure activities. How did you finance your schooling?

What courses did you take? Which were most worthwhile? Comment on influential teachers, courses, books, and learning experiences. Did you earn any honors or awards? How beneficial was this schooling?

Were you involved in extracurricular clubs, teams, or fraternities or sororities? How did you spend semester breaks, vacations, and summers? How did schooling help you later in jobs or in the home?

Describe your involvement in and feelings and beliefs about social issues, politics, and religion. Did your beliefs and values change during these years? Tell about influential books, teachers, classes, ideas, or friends.

Who were your best friends of both sexes? What activities did you do with them? Tell about roommates. Did you drop out of school or work to do any traveling? What were your interests, hobbies, talents, and hangouts? How did you use your leisure time?

What about dating and romantic interests? Mention attachments that were important to you, engagements, and your feelings then about marriage. How easy or hard was it to get dates? How did your dating activities compare with your high school dating?

Courtship and Marriage

How did you and your spouse meet? What did you like about each other? What common interests did you share? How did your relationship turn from casual to courtship? Tell about the proposal, the engagement, rings, parties and showers, saving money, planning the wedding details, the announcements, decorations, and reactions of parents. Did you have any problems deciding where, when, and how to get married, and by whom? Tell about the ceremony itself and your own feelings at the time. Where did you honeymoon?

As newlyweds, where did you first set up house? How did you furnish and supply it? How did you finance the first few years? What happened to friendships with single people after you were married? What marital adjustments were required? What was your relationship with in-laws? How did your spouse get along with your parents?

Marriage Relationship

Assess the "health" of your marriage during the child rearing years. What was good? What deepened and strengthened the relationship? What hurt or weakened it? How did you handle problems of finances, sex, health, divergent interests, changing personalities, career competition, declining physical appearances, wife working, husband's night shifts, extended separations, in-laws, philosophies of child rearing, and major crises or tragedies which beset the family? Were problems caused by differences in religion, race, class, education, or age? After being married for a fair length of time, how were you and your spouse alike? How different? What did you like best about your spouse?

Child Rearing

If childless, discuss your feelings about it. Did you want children? If not, why not? If so, what efforts did you make to become a parent?

If you had children, what were your thoughts about having them? Tell about the birth of each child and how names were selected.

What financial, housing, and emotional adjustments did each new child require you and your spouse to make? Were babies breastfed? How did your other children react to new babies? Were any of the children handicapped? If so, how did you help them?

Tell about your children as each grew up. What was your basic child rearing philosophy relating to manners, chores, discipline, and money? What were each child's characteristics and personality traits? Mention special memories, humorous episodes, achievements, problems, and favorite family stories told about each child. How were your children alike, and how were they different? When the children became teenagers, how did that affect you and the family unit? Comment on teenage drivers, parties held at home, and experiences during their teen years. How did stepchildren and natural children get along together?

As your children grew older, at what stage did you feel most fulfilled and useful as a parent? Least? Do you feel you were a successful parent? Was yours a happy and affectionate home for the children?

Tell how each child "left the nest," and your feeling about it. How do you feel about each child's course in life since he or she left home? About each one's spouse? What has been your relationship with your grown children?

How did parenthood affect your life as a private person in terms of time, money, privacy, hobbies, talents, and career? What impact did having children have on your marriage?

Work and Careers

Tell about full-time jobs you have had: how you landed the job: what work the job entailed; your promotions and firings; the job's pay and benefits; coworkers, supervisors, bosses, customers, and competitors; and car pools. What did you like best and least about each job? Describe memorable experiences and stories connected with your work. If self-employed, tell about your business or operation, its building(s), lands, equipment, crops or animals, employees, finance and tax structure, how you produced and marketed goods or services, and what the main problems were that hindered your profit making.

What were turning points in your firm's history? Why did you leave or change jobs? Or why did you stay so long with the same job? What contributions were you able to make to your company or in your field of specialty?

Did you have special training or additional education? What business, trade, and professional organizations or unions did you join? Tell about them. How did your work help or hinder your development as a person? Your family's well-being? How did you balance time spent at work and time spent at home?

Finances

Tell something about your financial affairs as an adult: earnings, raises, benefits, typical monthly budgets, major expenditures, standard of living, buying of homes and cars, financing children's schooling or lessons, major financial commitments, your savings and investments, insurance, and retirement programs. Which family members helped with the household earnings? Who managed the money? What were financial turning points or key decisions? What would you do over if you had the chance?

Home and Domestic Matters

What experience did you have in domestic skills before marriage? Full- or part-time, what were your main skills in managing the home? Tell stories to illustrate how you handled such household jobs as meals (planning, shopping, cooking), care of clothes, care of children, cleaning, and home maintenance.

Did you have a regular routine for things like laundry, housecleaning, and shopping? Over the years what things helped you to be more effective (classes, books, other homemakers, improved housing, better appliances, simpler food products, better fabrics and cleaning aids, help from children and spouses)?

How did you feel about each house you lived in: its space, conveniences, and appliances? Tell about chauffeuring children and doing volunteer work for groups your children belonged to. Tell about unique family tastes in foods. What memorable meals or parties did you host?

Why Did You Write Your Life Story?

To entertain the descendants of the Joseph King family, to help others remember their own growing years.
　　　　　Mary King Timothy

To inform my children, grandchildren, brothers, and sisters of my life work.
　　　　　Orson W. Israelsen

Chiefly for my family and friends. . . Life has been good.
　　　　　Andrew Karl Larson

I have regretted many times that my parents and my grandfathers and grandmothers did not leave a more complete record of their lives.
　　　　　Wayne B. Hales

What was most rewarding about your domestic efforts? Most frustrating? Were you appreciated by your spouse and children?

The Unmarried Adult

Explain your feelings about being single. How did that affect your relationship with your parents, married brothers and sisters, married men and women at work or in organizations you belonged to, and your choice of career and subsequent advancement in it? Did being single affect your religious activity, attending cultural events, spending holidays, and finding male and female friends? What were advantages of being single? Disadvantages? Did you try to adopt or raise any children?

Divorce

Tell something about what caused the divorce, how you and your spouse reacted to it, how you worked it out, and what the settlement was. How did it affect the children? Your own self-image? What damage and what good came of it? Were any religious problems caused by it?

In the long run, was it a wise decision? What did it change in terms of your own financial position, former friendships, and your housing arrangements? What about dating and social life following the divorce? If a homemaker, did you have to go to work? How were the children cared for if you worked outside the home?

Death of Spouse

When and how did your spouse die? How did you deal with it? How did other family members accept it? What readjustments were required in terms of housing, finances, and social life? How did you manage the household and care for the children? Was it possible for you to be both mother and father to your children? What things strengthened you during the death and adjustment period? What was hardest? How well did the will or estate settlement provide for you and your family? Tell about subsequent dating and relationships with other couples and former friends and family of your spouse.

Remarriage

How soon after the divorce or death of your spouse did you think about remarriage? How did you meet your new spouse? What ways were there for you to meet new, eligible companions? Was there a stigma attached to being divorced or widowed?

What characteristics did you like most in your new companion? How did your children, and the children of your new spouse, react to the new marriage? (Refer to the "Marriage Relationship" topic above and apply the questions to your new marriage.)

Physical Health

Comment on your general physical condition and health from about age eighteen to the present. Note major changes (height, weight, eyesight, hearing, teeth, joints) and problems (diseases, accidents, handicaps, operations, diet). What about exercise? If female, what long-range effects did the bearing of children have on your body? How did menopause affect you?

Relationship with Relatives

During your adult years, what was your relationship with your parents and your spouse's parents in their retirement years? How did you help them financially? How did you decide which children would help them or house them? How often did you visit or have contact with the parents? How did you react to the death of your father? Mother? If one parent remarried, how did this change your relationship with that parent? If a parent lived in your house, how did your spouse and children adjust to it?

After being an adult and family person yourself, how do you judge how well your parents did as human beings, as parents, and as providers? Which of their beliefs and values do you still accept, and which do you reject?

In middle age, what has been your relationship with your brothers and sisters and their families, with nieces and nephews, or with uncles and aunts? Have you helped, financially or otherwise, any of these relatives?

(continued)

My children, for several years, have been asking me to write a story of my life. Since I am now 84 years of age, if I am ever going to do it, I must start now. I have decided to make an effort before I get any older.

Jesse A. Udall

In this biography, I have tried to express my own philosophy of life in my own words, reinforced by the words of others, and I hope that in what is written here those who come after me may see a picture of their own lives lived at their best.

Sterling Sill

The Livermore Kiss: A Memory Test

In my life story I wrote about an experience during my high school days that I called "Livermore Kiss." I remembered that after a football game which my high school team won, a junior class cheerleader gave me, the student body president, a congratulatory kiss. That made me want to date other girls than the one I was going with. This was a nice story in my memory.

But, my memory had some details, such as the kiss, correct, but it garbled some of the other facts. I found that out because one day I checked my high school yearbook and looked up the game and the girl. The yearbooks showed that I remembered the girl and had her

Personal Beliefs

What have been your feelings about religion as a college student, in the military, and as a mature adult? How have your beliefs changed during your lifetime? Comment on major religious problems, doubts, or disbeliefs you have had. How active have you been in organized religion? Tell about local congregations you have belonged to, leaders and members, preaching meetings, lessons and study classes, and social groups. What positions have you held, and what did each require of you?

What has been most rewarding about your religious activity? Most bothersome? What special spiritual experiences have you had? What effects have your beliefs and religious standards had on your career, earnings, and use of leisure time? Has religion benefitted your marriage? Has it helped during trials and tragedies? Has religion affected the way you have reared your children? Tell about their religious training, commitments, and activities.

How did you feel about important political issues over the years? What presidents have you liked? Why? What are your views on government spending, taxes, free enterprise, unions, social welfare programs, unemployment, and farm subsidies? How did you feel about America's involvement in the World Wars, Korea, and Vietnam? How do you feel about the effectiveness of schools and colleges? About the lifestyles of upcoming generations?

Interests, Activities, and Service

Comment on your adult hobbies, favorite recreational activities, athletics or exercise programs, talents, groups you belong to, typical weekends, types of vacations, and tastes in things like TV, radio, music, cultural events, movies, and sports. How have family members shared in these interests? What equipment did you buy to support these interests (recreational vehicles, fishing and hunting gear, tools, sewing machine, musical instruments, paints)? What classes or lessons did you take? Mention highlight experiences and special friends related to these activities. What hobbies or activities would you have engaged in if you had had more time or money or if your spouse had let you?

Tell about volunteer service or charitable work you participated in. What service organizations or auxiliaries did you join? Tell about meaningful projects you helped with. How did you financially help people in need?

Friendships

Of all the people you meet and work with during a lifetime, only a few become really close friends to you. These usually include a few fellow workers, employers, employees, classmates, neighbors, and people met at various activities and through organizations you belonged to. Comment on longtime family friends and close personal friends and some of the memorable things you have done together. How have you kept in touch with each other?

Current Events

Comment on how you and your family have been affected by such events as the Great Depression, the flu epidemic, wars, natural disasters, growth or decline of towns, campus unrest, new inventions, changes in standards of morality, civil rights programs, federal aid programs, fads and fashions, crime, drugs, job obsolescence, housing shortages, medical techniques, zoning laws, and climatic changes.

Experiences as a Grandparent

Discuss your feelings about each of your children and their families. What has been your relationship with your grandchildren? What do you do and talk about with them when you get together? What influence do you exert upon the way each grandchild is being raised? Have you enjoyed being a grandparent? How do you feel about each grandchild's development and character as a human being?

If you are not and *will not* be a grandparent, how has this "end of the family line" made you feel?

(continued)

name right. But, I discovered that the football game was in fact a basketball game. And Jill was not a cheerleader but was a junior class officer.

So, twenty years after the fact, my memory kept sharp the heart of the experience but confused some of the supporting details.

Retirement Years

Tell why you retired and your feelings about it. Comment on others' attitudes toward retirees. What changed about your life and that of your spouse with retirement? What adjustments in roles did you and your spouse have when one or both of you left careers and returned home full-time?

Discuss your situation regarding housing, finances, standard of living, leisure activities, and physical health. What have been your main worries and concerns? Your main pleasures? What new interests have you developed? What keeps you motivated?

Reflections about Life

Discuss your life beliefs, standards, values, religious convictions, feelings about your family's progress, and judgments about how the nation and society have changed for better or worse. Evaluate what have been the most important ideas you have accepted, and the best things you have enjoyed. What have been the values of your life? Did you do as well as your parents? As well as your brothers and sisters? What achievements bring you satisfaction? What would you do differently if you had a chance?

If you had to honestly characterize yourself in one paragraph, what would you say? Similarly, how would you characterize your spouse? How have each of you changed in character and personality over the years?

What are your feeling about death and dying? What suggestions would you offer to the upcoming generations about living successfully, finding happiness, raising children, practicing religion, helping society, and choosing careers?

APPENDIX TWO

Libraries and
Organizations

Major Genealogy Libraries and Centers

Library of Congress
Local History and Genealogy
  Section
Thomas Jefferson Building
1st-2nd Streets, N.W.
Washington, D.C. 20540
(202) 707-5537

Library of Congress
Genealogy Reading Room
James Madison Memorial
  Building
Washington, D.C. 20540
(202) 707-2726

Library, Daughters of the
  American Revolution
1776 D Street, N.W.
Washington, D.C. 20006
(202) 879-3229

National Genealogical Society
  Library
4527 17th Street, N.
Arlington, VA 22207
(703) 525-0050

New England Historic
  Genealogical Society
101 Newbury Street
Boston, MA 02116
(617) 536-5740

New York City Public Library
Local History and Genealogy
  Division
Fifth Avenue and 42nd Street
New York, NY 10018
(212) 930-0828

New York Genealogical and
  Biographical Society
122 East 58th Street
New York, NY 10022
(212) 755-8532

Western Reserve Historical
  Society
10825 East Boulevard
Cleveland, OH 44106
(216) 721-5722

Newberry Library
60 West Walton Street
Chicago, IL 60610
(312) 943-9090

Burton Collection
Detroit Public Library
5201 Woodward Avenue
Detroit, MI 48202
(313) 833-1000

Allen County–Fort Wayne Public
  Library
900 Webster Street
Fort Wayne, IN 46801
(219) 424-7241

State Historical Society of
Wisconsin
816 State Street
Madison, WI 53706
(608) 264-6400

Dallas Public Library
1515 Young Street
Dallas, TX 75201
(214) 670-1400

LDS Family History Library
35 North West Temple Street
Salt Lake City, UT 84150
(801) 240-2331

Los Angeles Public Library
630 West 5th Street
Los Angeles, CA 90071
(213) 228-7000

Sutro Library
Branch of California State Library
480 Winston Drive
San Francisco, CA 94132
(415) 731-4477

Selected Genealogical Societies

Afro-American Historical and
Genealogical Society
P.O. Box 73086
Washington, D.C. 20056
(202) 234-5350

American-French Genealogical
Society
P.O. Box 2113
Pawtucket, RI 02861

Association of Jewish
Genealogical Societies
1485 Teaneck Road
Teaneck, NJ 07666

Daughters of the
American Revolution
1776 D Street, N.W.
Washington, D.C. 20006
(202) 879-3229

German Genealogical Society of
America
2125 Wright Avenue, C-9
La Verne, CA 91750

Hispanic Genealogical Society
P.O. Box 1792
Houston, TX 77251

Irish Genealogical Society
P.O. Box 16585
St. Paul, MN 55116

Jewish Genealogical Society, Inc.
P.O. Box 6398
New York, NY 10128
(212) 330-8257

National Genealogical Society
4527 17th Street, N.
Arlington, VA 22207
(703) 525-0050
www.genealogy.org/NGS

New England Historic
  Genealogical Society
101 Newbury Street
Boston, MA 02116
(617) 536-5740
www.nehgs.org

Polish Genealogical Society of
  America
984 North Milwaukee Avenue
Chicago, IL 60622

Scandinavian-American
  Genealogical Society
P.O. Box 16069
St. Paul, MN 55116

National Archives and Regional Branches

(For more detailed information, consult the National Archives' home-page via the Internet at http://www.nara.gov.)

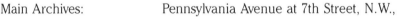

Main Archives:	Pennsylvania Avenue at 7th Street, N.W., Washington, D.C. 20408 (202) 501-5400
Main Archives II:	8601 Adelphi Road, College Park, MD 20740 (301) 713-7250
New England Region:	380 Trapelo Road, Waltham, MA 02154 (617) 647-8100
Berkshires Region:	100 Dan Fox Drive, Pittsfield, MA 01201 (413) 445-6885, ext. 26
Northeast Region (and Puerto Rico):	201 Varick Street, New York, NY 10014 (212) 337-1300

NATIONAL ARCHIVES

Mid-Atlantic Region:	9th & Market Streets, Room 1350, Philadelphia, PA 19107 (215) 597-3000
Southeast Region:	1557 St. Joseph Avenue East Point, GA 30344 (404) 763-7477
Great Lakes Region:	7358 South Poulaski Road Chicago, IL 60629 (312) 581-7816
Central Plains Region:	2312 East Bannister Road Kansas City, MO 64131 (816) 926-6272
Southwest Region:	501 West Felix Street, P.O. Box 6216 Fort Worth, TX 76115 (817) 334-5525
Rocky Mountain Region:	Building 48, Denver Federal Center P.O. Box 25307 Denver, CO 80225 (303) 236-0817
Pacific Southwest Region:	24000 Avila Road, Los Angeles, 92656 or P.O. Box 6719, Laguna Niguel, CA 92607 (714) 643-4241
Pacific Sierra Region (and Hawaii):	1000 Commodore Drive San Bruno, CA 94066 (415) 876-9009
Pacific Northwest Region:	6125 Sand Point Way, N.E. Seattle, WA 98115 (206) 526-6507
Alaska Region:	654 West Third Avenue Anchorage, AK 99501 (907) 271-2441

Canadian National Archives

The Canadian Historical Association, National Library of Canada, and Public Archives of Canada are all located at:

395 Wellington Street, Ottawa, Canada K1A ON4, (613) 995-5138

Civil War Pension File

Information and Materials found in Pvt. Jackson Hartley's Civil War Pension File, National Archives, Washington D.C.:

Physical Description:	5' 7" tall, light complexion, black eyes, dark hair
Occupation:	Shoemaker
Unit:	Company G, 148th Pennsylvania Infantry Volunteers
Enlisted:	Aug. 11, 1862, 3-year term
Mustered out:	June 1, 1865
Service:	List of engagements with Army of the Potomac

Disability:

To obtain a pension, he had to prove he was disabled by the war. To prove that he had to have friends from before the war and after the way send letters describing his health and working abilities. His file contains many letters from his associates that describe in detail their contact and experiences with him:

Ervin Foreman, boyhood friend
Martha Jane Dibble, neighbor and sister-in-law
Robert Freeman, neighbor
Charles D. Swalley, brother-in-law
Mahama Hoover, sister-in-law

State Historical Societies and Libraries

Each state has an official state history library. Often it is also home to the state's historical society. However, in some cases the historical society is in a separate place. Using the addresses below, direct inquiries to

_____ State Historical Library
(NAME OF STATE)

Alabama	624 Washington Avenue, Montgomery, AL 36130
Alaska	State Office Building, P.O. Box G, Juneau, AK 99811
Arizona	949 East 2nd Street, Tucson, AZ 85719
Arkansas	One Capitol Mall, Little Rock, AR 72201
California	914 Capitol Mall, Library-Courts Building, P.O. Box 942837, Sacramento, CA 94237
Colorado	1300 Broadway, Denver, CO 80203
Connecticut	One Elizabeth Street, Hartford, CT 06105; also, 231 Capitol Avenue, Hartford, CT 06106
Delaware	505 Market Street Mall, Wilmington, DE 19801
Florida	R.A. Gray Building, Tallahassee, FL 32399
Georgia	330 Capitol Avenue S.E., Atlanta, GA 30334
Hawaii	560 Kawaiahoa Street, Honolulu, HI 96813
Idaho	450 North 4th Street, and 325 West State Street, Boise, ID 83702
Illinois	Old State Capitol, 501 South 2nd, Springfield, IL 62701
Indiana	140 North Senate Avenue, Indianapolis, IN 46204 also, 315 West Ohio Street, Indianapolis, IN 46202
Iowa	Historical Building, 600 East Locust Street, Des Moines, IA 50319; also, 402 Iowa Avenue, Iowa City, IA 52240
Kansas	Memorial Building, 120 West 10th Street, Topeka, KS 66612
Kentucky	300 West Broadway, P.O. Box H, Frankfort, KY 40602
Louisiana	3851 Essen Lane, P.O. Box 94125, Baton Rouge, LA 70804; also, 760 Riverside Mall, P.O. Box 131, Baton Rouge LA 70821

Maine	LMA Building, State House Station 64, Augusta, ME 04333
Maryland	350 Rowe Boulevard, Annapolis, MD 21401; also 201 West Monument Street, Baltimore MD 21201
Massachusetts	State House, Beacon Hill, Boston, MA 02133; also 1154 Boylston Street, Boston, MA 02215
Michigan	717 West Allegan Avenue, P.O. Box 30007, Lansing, MI 48909
Minnesota	345 Kellogg Boulevard. W., St. Paul, MN 55102
Mississippi	100 South State Street, P.O. Box 571, Jackson, MS 39205
Missouri	2002 Missouri Boulevard, P.O. Box 387, Jefferson City, MO 65102; also University Library Building, 1020 Lowrey Street, Columbia, MO 65201
Montana	225 North Roberts Street, and 1515 East 6th Avenue., Helena, MT 59620
Nebraska	1500 R Street, P.O. Box 82554, Lincoln, NE 68501
Nevada	100 Stewart Street, Carson City, NV 89710; also, 1650 North Virginia Street, Reno, NV 89503
New Hampshire	30 Park Street, Concord, NH 03301
New Jersey	185 West State Street, CN520, Trenton, NJ 08625; also, 230 Broadway, Newark, NJ 07104
New Mexico	325 Don Gaspar, Santa Fe, NM 87503
New York	Empire State Plaza, Albany, NY 12230
North Carolina	109 East Jones Street, Raleigh, NC 27611
North Dakota	Liberty Memorial Building, 604 East Boulevard Avenue, Bismarck, ND 58505; also, North Dakota Heritage Center, 612 East Boulevard Avenue, Bismarck, ND 58505

Ohio	State Office Building, 65 South Front Street, Columbus, OH 43266; also, 19872 Velma Avenue, Columbus, OH 43211; also, Campus Martius Museum Library, 601 2nd Street, Marietta, OH 45750
Oklahoma	Historical Building, 2100 North Lincoln Boulevard, Oklahoma City, OK 73105
Oregon	250 Winter Street, N.E., Salem, OR 97310
Pennsylvania	Walnut Street and Commonwealth Avenue, P.O. Box 1601, Harrisburg, PA 17105; also, 1300 Locust Street, Philadelphia, PA 19107
Rhode Island	State House, 82 Smith Street, Providence, RI 02903; also 121 Hope Street, Providence, RI 02906
South Carolina	1500 Senate Street, Columbia, SC 29201; also, Capitol Station, P.O. Box 11669, Columbia, SC 29211
South Dakota	State Library Building, 800 Governors Drive, Pierre, SD 57501
Tennessee	State Library Building, 403 7th Avenue, N., Nashville, TN 37243
Texas	1200 Brazos Street, P.O. Box 12927, Capitol Station, Austin, TX 78711
Utah	300 Rio Grande, Salt Lake City, UT 84115
Vermont	Pavilion Building, 109 State Street, Montpelier, VT 05609
Virginia	12th and Capitol Streets, Richmond, VA 23219; also, 428 North Boulevard, P.O. Box 7311, Richmond, VA 23221
Washington	Capitol Campus, P.O. Box 42460, Olympia, WA 98504
West Virginia	Cultural Center, State Capitol Complex, Charleston, WV 25305
Wisconsin	816 State Street, Madison, WI 53706
Wyoming	Supreme Court–Library Building, Cheyenne, WY 82002

Sailing Ships: Information and Visuals

Essex-Peabody Institute
132 Essex Street
Salem, MA 01970
(508) 744-3390

The Mariners Museum
Museum Drive
Newport News, VA 23606
(757) 595-0368

Overland Trail Travelers, Companies, and Histories

Oregon-California Trails Association
524 South Osage Street
P.O. Box 1019
Independence MO 64051
(816) 252-2276

Standard State Abbreviations

Alabama	AL	Idaho	ID
Alaska	AK	Illinois	IL
Arizona	AZ	Indiana	IN
Arkansas	AR	Iowa	IA
California	CA	Kansas	KS
Colorado	CO	Kentucky	KY
Connecticut	CT	Louisiana	LA
Delaware	DE	Maine	ME
District of	DC	Maryland	MD
Columbia		Massachusetts	MA
Florida	FL	Michigan	MI
Georgia	GA	Minnesota	MN
Hawaii	HI	Mississippi	MS

Missouri	MO		Puerto Rico	PR
Montana	MT		Rhode Island	RI
Nebraska	NE		South Carolina	SC
Nevada	NV		South Dakota	SD
New Hampshire	NH		Tennessee	TN
New Jersey	NJ		Texas	TX
New Mexico	NM		Utah	UT
New York	NY		Vermont	VT
North Carolina	NC		Virginia	VA
North Dakota	ND		Washington	WA
Ohio	OH		West Virginia	WV
Oklahoma	OK		Wisconsin	WI
Oregon	OR		Wyoming	WY
Pennsylvania	PA			

Some Standard Foreign Country Abbreviations

Australia	AUT		Holland	HOL
Austria	AUS		Ireland	IRE
Bavaria	BAV		Japan	JPN
Belgium	BEL		Laos	LAO
Brazil	BRA		Mexico	MEX
British West Indies	BWI		Netherlands	NTH
Cambodia	CAM		New Zealand	NZD
Cuba	CUB		Philippines	PHL
Denmark	DEN		Prussia	PRS
Egypt	EGP		Scotland	SCT
England	ENG		Spain	SPN
France	FRA		Sweden	SWD
Germany	GER		Switzerland	SWT
Great Britain	GBR		Uruguay	URA
Greece	GRE		Wales	WLS

APPENDIX THREE
Preservation Resources

Further Reading on Preservation

Ilene Chandler Miller, *Preserving Family Keepsakes* (Yorba Linda, CA: Shumway Family History Services, 1995).

Barbara Sagraves, *A Preservation Guide: Saving the Past and the Present for the Future* (Salt Lake City, UT: Ancestry, 1995).

Craig A. Tuttle, *An Ounce of Preservation: A Guide to the Care of Papers and Photographs* (Danvers, MA: Rainbow Books, 1995).

Nancy Davis, *Handle with Care: Preserving Your Heirlooms* (Rochester, NY: Rochester Museum and Science Center, 1991).

Archival-Quality Supply Businesses

Archival Products, Inc., Des Moines, IA, (800) 526-5640

Clearsnap, Anacortes, WA, archival-quality ink pads for rubber stamps, (360) 293-6634

Close to My Heart Scrapbook and Photo Album Company, Dublin, PA, (215) 249-3032

Conservation Materials Ltd., Sparks, NV, (702) 331-0582

Crafty Cutters, Pasao Robles, CA, hundreds of die-cut shapes and number and letter sets, archival-quality, (805) 467-2375

C. R. Gibson Company, Norwalk, CT 06856, markets Random Mount clear, self-stick, archival-grade photo protectors

Design Originals, Ft. Worth, TX, photo memory albums and scrapbook materials, (800) 877-7820

D. J. Inkers, Sandy, UT, cut-and-copy books, rubber stamps, CD-ROM packages (Stickerdoodles, Paperdoodles), (800) 325-4890

EK Success, Carlstadt, NJ, manufacturer of ZIG Memory System (range of quality markers made for scrapbooks and memory books, variety of tips, pure pigment ink that is acid-free, lightfast, waterproof, nonbleeding, fade-proof), (800) 524-1349

Ellison Craft and Design, Irvine CA, *Memories in Minutes*, a full-color idea book, includes 3-D designs, (888) 972-7238

Family Treasures, photo and paper craft supplies that make creative edges for background sheets used behind items being mounted in albums, catalog, (800) 413-2645

Frances Meyer, Inc., markets decorative scrapbook kits, at local craft and scrapbook stores

Gaylord Brothers, Inc., Syracuse, NY, (800) 448-6160

Hiller, Salt Lake City, UT, bookbinding, scrapbooks, photo albums, (801) 521-2411

Hollinger Corporation, Fredericksburg, VA, (800) 634-0491

Inspire Graphics, "Scrapbook Snips" (computer clip-art program), (800) 250-3988

Keeping Memories Alive, Spanish Fork, UT, (800) 419-4949

Krafter Kaddie, Bridgeport, CA, wooden covers and materials for designing covers—stencil, appliqué, paint, wood-burn, stain, iron-on transfers, (888) 552-3343

Light Impressions, Rochester, NY, free catalog, (800) 828-6216

Memories by Design, Layton, UT, complete scrapbook supplies, free catalog, (888) 727-2788 or (801) 775-9380

Micro Dynamics produces "Family Base," a program for publishing photo albums on CDs, (888) 327-6472

Our Favorite Things, Okemos, MI, scrapbooks, rubber stamps, creative paper

Pebbles in My Pocket, scrapbooking and stationery supplies, (800) 438-8153

Print File, Inc., Schenectady, NY, (518) 374-2334, markets Print File binders and preserver's pages for storing slides, prints, and negatives

Provo Craft, Electronic Clip Art on CDs, hundreds of images, (800) 563-8679

Restoration Source, Salt Lake City, UT, preservation instructions and materials, (901) 278-7880

Sakyura of America, Hayward, CA, has a line of pigma ink products, permanent ink that has acid-free characteristics, writing instruments for stenciling, printing, coloring, calligraphing, and sketching.

Stickopotamus, Inc., Carlstadt, NJ, acid-free stickers, vivid stickers with many designs, (800) 524-1349

The C-Thru Ruler Company, Bloomfield. CT, templates and edgers for laying-out, cropping, and decorating photographs, (860) 243-0303

The Paper Patch markets quality printed background papers, available from scrapbook suppliers and by phoning (800) 397-2737

The Paper Rabbit, Montrose and Valencia, CA, creative scrapbooking supplies

The Photo Safe, Eldersburg, MD, full line of photo albums and scrapbook supplies, (410) 549-5211

The Scrapbook Company, for catalog call (888) 750-6844

University Products, Holyoke, MA, (800) 628-1912

Pedigree Chart

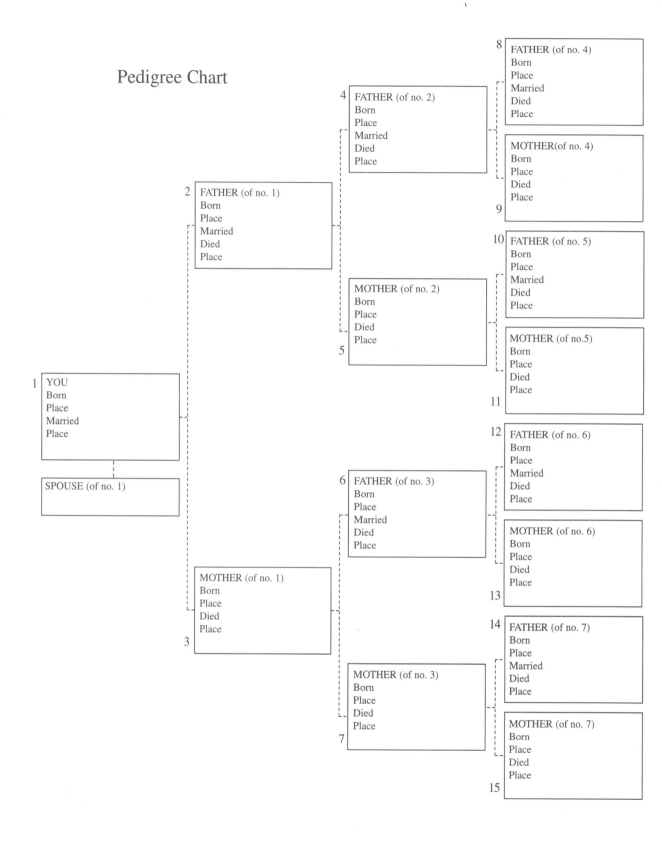

1 | YOU
Born
Place
Married
Place

SPOUSE (of no. 1)

2 | FATHER (of no. 1)
Born
Place
Married
Died
Place

3 | MOTHER (of no. 1)
Born
Place
Died
Place

4 | FATHER (of no. 2)
Born
Place
Married
Died
Place

5 | MOTHER (of no. 2)
Born
Place
Died
Place

6 | FATHER (of no. 3)
Born
Place
Married
Died
Place

7 | MOTHER (of no. 3)
Born
Place
Died
Place

8 | FATHER (of no. 4)
Born
Place
Married
Died
Place

9 | MOTHER(of no. 4)
Born
Place
Died
Place

10 | FATHER (of no. 5)
Born
Place
Married
Died
Place

11 | MOTHER (of no.5)
Born
Place
Died
Place

12 | FATHER (of no. 6)
Born
Place
Married
Died
Place

13 | MOTHER (of no. 6)
Born
Place
Died
Place

14 | FATHER (of no. 7)
Born
Place
Married
Died
Place

15 | MOTHER (of no. 7)
Born
Place
Died
Place

Pedigree Chart

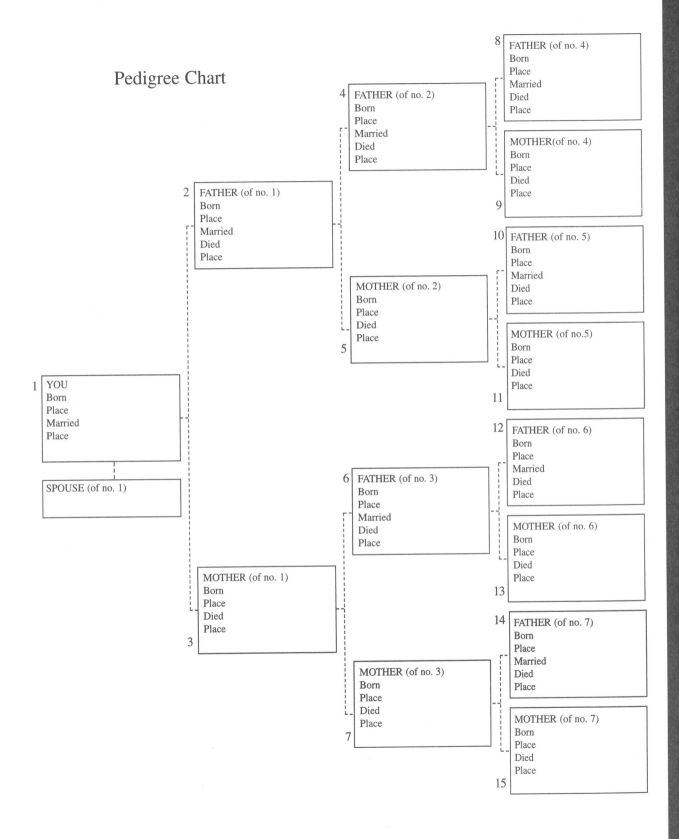

Pedigree Chart

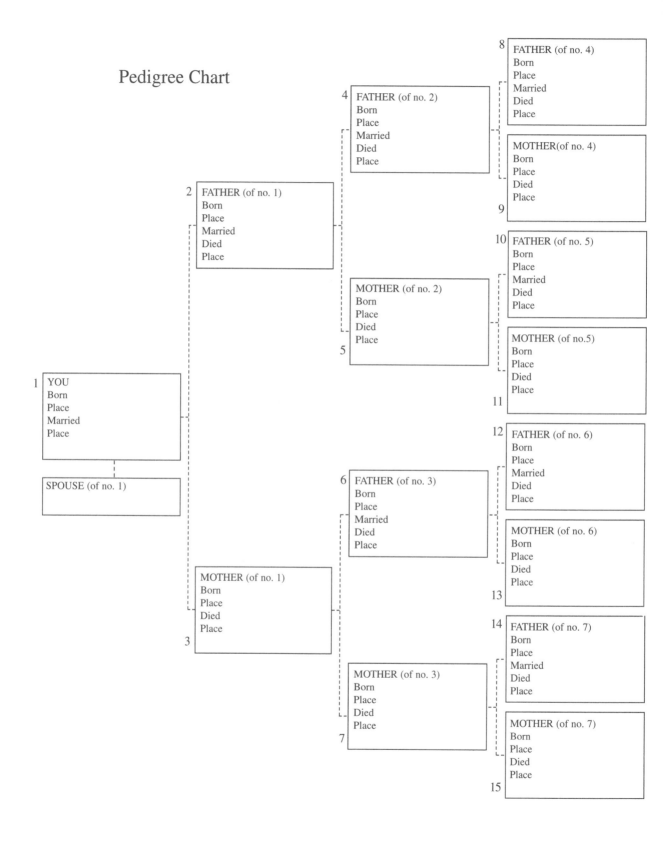

1 | YOU
Born
Place
Married
Place

SPOUSE (of no. 1)

2 | FATHER (of no. 1)
Born
Place
Married
Died
Place

3 | MOTHER (of no. 1)
Born
Place
Died
Place

4 | FATHER (of no. 2)
Born
Place
Married
Died
Place

MOTHER (of no. 2)
Born
Place
Died
Place
5

6 | FATHER (of no. 3)
Born
Place
Married
Died
Place

MOTHER (of no. 3)
Born
Place
Died
Place
7

8 | FATHER (of no. 4)
Born
Place
Married
Died
Place

MOTHER (of no. 4)
Born
Place
Died
Place
9

10 | FATHER (of no. 5)
Born
Place
Married
Died
Place

MOTHER (of no.5)
Born
Place
Died
Place
11

12 | FATHER (of no. 6)
Born
Place
Married
Died
Place

MOTHER (of no. 6)
Born
Place
Died
Place
13

14 | FATHER (of no. 7)
Born
Place
Married
Died
Place

MOTHER (of no. 7)
Born
Place
Died
Place
15

Pedigree Chart

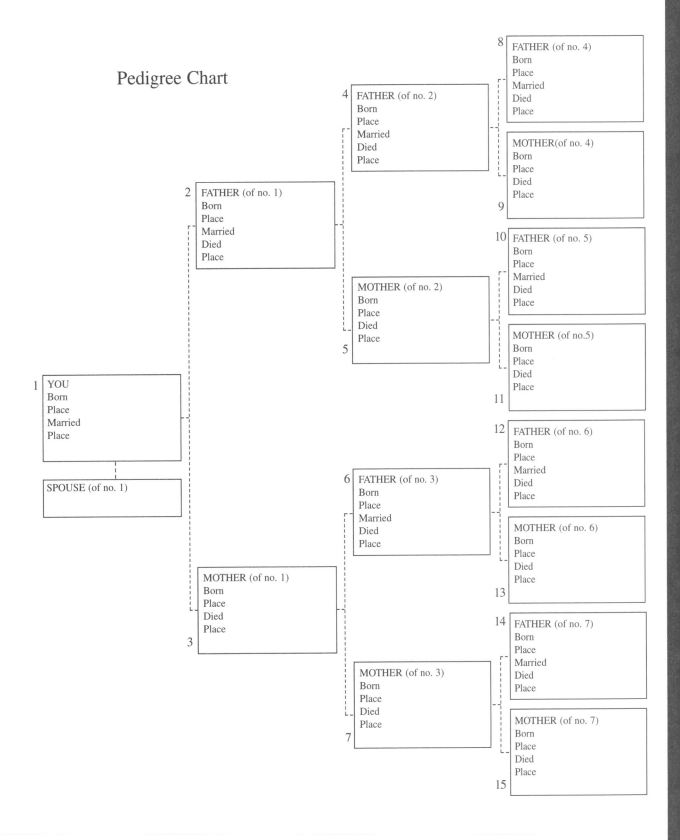

1 YOU
Born
Place
Married
Place

SPOUSE (of no. 1)

2 FATHER (of no. 1)
Born
Place
Married
Died
Place

3 MOTHER (of no. 1)
Born
Place
Died
Place

4 FATHER (of no. 2)
Born
Place
Married
Died
Place

5 MOTHER (of no. 2)
Born
Place
Died
Place

6 FATHER (of no. 3)
Born
Place
Married
Died
Place

7 MOTHER (of no. 3)
Born
Place
Died
Place

8 FATHER (of no. 4)
Born
Place
Married
Died
Place

9 MOTHER(of no. 4)
Born
Place
Died
Place

10 FATHER (of no. 5)
Born
Place
Married
Died
Place

11 MOTHER (of no.5)
Born
Place
Died
Place

12 FATHER (of no. 6)
Born
Place
Married
Died
Place

13 MOTHER (of no. 6)
Born
Place
Died
Place

14 FATHER (of no. 7)
Born
Place
Married
Died
Place

15 MOTHER (of no. 7)
Born
Place
Died
Place

Pedigree Chart

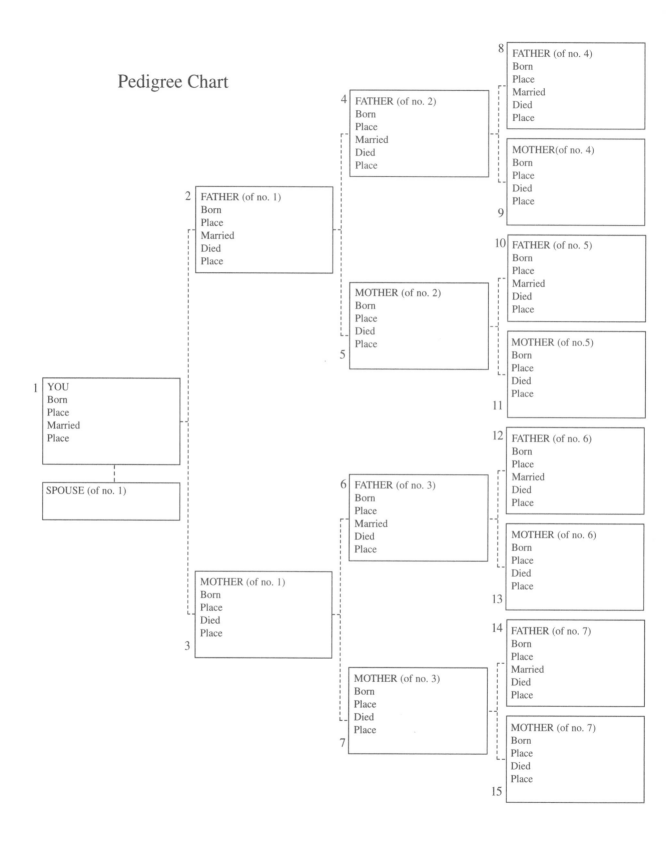

8 FATHER (of no. 4)
Born
Place
Married
Died
Place

4 FATHER (of no. 2)
Born
Place
Married
Died
Place

MOTHER(of no. 4)
Born
Place
Died
Place
9

2 FATHER (of no. 1)
Born
Place
Married
Died
Place

10 FATHER (of no. 5)
Born
Place
Married
Died
Place

MOTHER (of no. 2)
Born
Place
Died
Place
5

MOTHER (of no.5)
Born
Place
Died
Place
11

1 YOU
Born
Place
Married
Place

12 FATHER (of no. 6)
Born
Place
Married
Died
Place

SPOUSE (of no. 1)

6 FATHER (of no. 3)
Born
Place
Married
Died
Place

MOTHER (of no. 6)
Born
Place
Died
Place
13

MOTHER (of no. 1)
Born
Place
Died
Place
3

14 FATHER (of no. 7)
Born
Place
Married
Died
Place

MOTHER (of no. 3)
Born
Place
Died
Place
7

MOTHER (of no. 7)
Born
Place
Died
Place
15

Family Group Record

Husband's name

Born		Place
Chr.		Place
Mar.		Place
Died		Place
Bur.		Place

Father	Mother

Husband's other wives

Wife's name

Born		Place
Chr.		Place
Died		Place

Bur.

Father	Mother

Wife's other husbands

Children

#	Sex	Name		Spouse	
1	Sex	Name		Spouse	
		B/Chr	Place	Mar.	Place
		Died	Place	Bur	Place
2	Sex	Name		Spouse	
		B/Chr	Place	Mar.	Place
		Died	Place	Bur	Place
3	Sex	Name		Spouse	
		B/Chr	Place	Mar.	Place
		Died	Place	Bur	Place
4	Sex	Name		Spouse	
		B/Chr	Place	Mar.	Place
		Died	Place	Bur	Place
5	Sex	Name		Spouse	
		B/Chr	Place	Mar.	Place
		Died	Place	Bur	Place
6	Sex	Name		Spouse	
		B/Chr	Place	Mar.	Place
		Died	Place	Bur	Place
7	Sex	Name		Spouse	
		B/Chr	Place	Mar.	Place
		Died	Place	Bur	Place
8	Sex	Name		Spouse	
		B/Chr	Place	Mar.	Place
		Died	Place	Bur	Place

Other Marriages

Family Group Record

Husband's name

Born	Place
Chr.	Place
Mar.	Place
Died	Place
Bur.	Place

Father	Mother

Husband's other wives

Wife's name

Born	Place
Chr.	Place
Died	Place
Bur.	

Father	Mother

Wife's other husbands

Children

1	Sex	Name		Spouse	
		B/Chr	Place	Mar.	Place
		Died	Place	Bur	Place
2	Sex	Name		Spouse	
		B/Chr	Place	Mar.	Place
		Died	Place	Bur	Place
3	Sex	Name		Spouse	
		B/Chr	Place	Mar.	Place
		Died	Place	Bur	Place
4	Sex	Name		Spouse	
		B/Chr	Place	Mar.	Place
		Died	Place	Bur	Place
5	Sex	Name		Spouse	
		B/Chr	Place	Mar.	Place
		Died	Place	Bur	Place
6	Sex	Name		Spouse	
		B/Chr	Place	Mar.	Place
		Died	Place	Bur	Place
7	Sex	Name		Spouse	
		B/Chr	Place	Mar.	Place
		Died	Place	Bur	Place
8	Sex	Name		Spouse	
		B/Chr	Place	Mar.	Place
		Died	Place	Bur	Place

Other Marriages

Family Group Record

Husband's name

Born	Place	
Chr.	Place	
Mar.	Place	
Died	Place	
Bur.	Place	

Father		Mother
Husband's other wives		

Wife's name

Born	Place	
Chr.	Place	
Died	Place	
Bur.		

Father		Mother
Wife's other husbands		

Children

1 Sex	Name		Spouse	
	B/Chr	Place	Mar.	Place
	Died	Place	Bur	Place
2 Sex	Name		Spouse	
	B/Chr	Place	Mar.	Place
	Died	Place	Bur	Place
3 Sex	Name		Spouse	
	B/Chr	Place	Mar.	Place
	Died	Place	Bur	Place
4 Sex	Name		Spouse	
	B/Chr	Place	Mar.	Place
	Died	Place	Bur	Place
5 Sex	Name		Spouse	
	B/Chr	Place	Mar.	Place
	Died	Place	Bur	Place
6 Sex	Name		Spouse	
	B/Chr	Place	Mar.	Place
	Died	Place	Bur	Place
7 Sex	Name		Spouse	
	B/Chr	Place	Mar.	Place
	Died	Place	Bur	Place
8 Sex	Name		Spouse	
	B/Chr	Place	Mar.	Place
	Died	Place	Bur	Place

Other Marriages

Family Group Record

Husband's name

Born	Place	
Chr.	Place	
Mar.	Place	
Died	Place	
Bur.	Place	

Father	Mother

Husband's other wives

Wife's name

Born	Place	
Chr.	Place	
Died	Place	
Bur.		

Father	Mother

Wife's other husbands

Children

	Sex	Name		Spouse	
1		Name		Spouse	
		B/Chr	Place	Mar.	Place
		Died	Place	Bur	Place
2		Name		Spouse	
		B/Chr	Place	Mar.	Place
		Died	Place	Bur	Place
3		Name		Spouse	
		B/Chr	Place	Mar.	Place
		Died	Place	Bur	Place
4		Name		Spouse	
		B/Chr	Place	Mar.	Place
		Died	Place	Bur	Place
5		Name		Spouse	
		B/Chr	Place	Mar.	Place
		Died	Place	Bur	Place
6		Name		Spouse	
		B/Chr	Place	Mar.	Place
		Died	Place	Bur	Place
7		Name		Spouse	
		B/Chr	Place	Mar.	Place
		Died	Place	Bur	Place
8		Name		Spouse	
		B/Chr	Place	Mar.	Place
		Died	Place	Bur	Place

Other Marriages

Family Group Record

Husband's name

Born	Place
Chr.	Place
Mar.	Place
Died	Place
Bur.	Place

Father	Mother

Husband's other wives

Wife's name

Born	Place
Chr.	Place
Died	Place
Bur.	

Father	Mother

Wife's other husbands

Children

1 Sex	Name		Spouse		
	B/Chr	Place	Mar.	Place	
	Died	Place	Bur	Place	
2 Sex	Name		Spouse		
	B/Chr	Place	Mar.	Place	
	Died	Place	Bur	Place	
3 Sex	Name		Spouse		
	B/Chr	Place	Mar.	Place	
	Died	Place	Bur	Place	
4 Sex	Name		Spouse		
	B/Chr	Place	Mar.	Place	
	Died	Place	Bur	Place	
5 Sex	Name		Spouse		
	B/Chr	Place	Mar.	Place	
	Died	Place	Bur	Place	
6 Sex	Name		Spouse		
	B/Chr	Place	Mar.	Place	
	Died	Place	Bur	Place	
7 Sex	Name		Spouse		
	B/Chr	Place	Mar.	Place	
	Died	Place	Bur	Place	
8 Sex	Name		Spouse		
	B/Chr	Place	Mar.	Place	
	Died	Place	Bur	Place	

Other Marriages

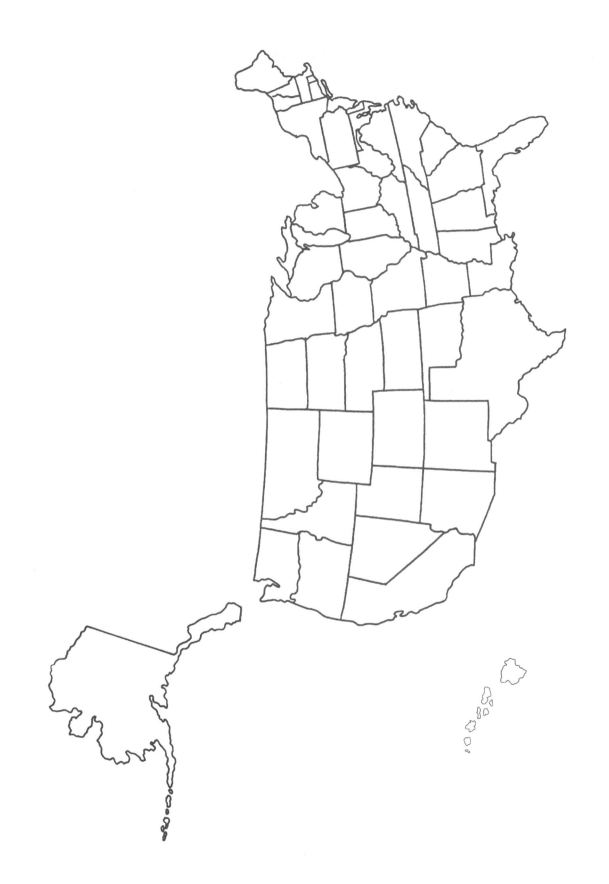

Index